Home Game

Home Game

A Ball Can Change the World
The Official Story of the Homeless World Cup

MEL YOUNG and PETER BARR

Luath Press Limited
EDINBURGH
www.luath.co.uk

First published 2017

ISBN: 978-1-912147-19-9

The paper used in this book is recyclable. It is made from low chlorine pulps produced in a low energy, low emission manner from renewable forests.

Printed and bound by CPI Antony Rowe, Chippenham

Typeset in 11 point Sabon by Lapiz

For the players

Contents

Homelessness does not respect any national borders. It can happen to anyone, anywhere at any time. It can happen to me and to you. Home Game

We all love football and we all hate homelessness – it's a no brainer.
Irvine Welsh – Novelist and Ambassador for the Homeless World Cup

We have to unite against homelessness as we did when we fought apartheid.
Archbishop Desmond Tutu, speaking at the Homeless World Cup in Cape Town (2006)

I have seen how the Homeless World Cup really does inspire homeless people to change the direction of their lives.
Colin Farrell – Actor and Ambassador for the Homeless World Cup

Sport and football are very important, and that is why I decided to be an Ambassador for the Homeless World Cup. At first I was a bit sceptical, but I've seen the social impact, and I also see the impact in the eyes of the players. C'est magnifique!
Emmanuel Petit – Footballer and Ambassador for the Homeless World Cup

Football and the Homeless World Cup have the power to fire up a person to excel as a human being, to change their lives for the better. It is fantastic that football brings this opportunity to their lives.
Eric Cantona – Footballer and Ambassador for the Homeless World Cup

For seven days in July, George Square in the heart of the city will be the most inspiring place on the planet.
HRH The Duke of Cambridge, in a message to participants before the Homeless World Cup in Glasgow (2016)

The Homeless World Cup opened the door to success and gave me a once-in-a-lifetime opportunity to make a change in my life and be part of something positive.
Lukes Mjoka – Represented South Africa at the Homeless World Cup in Rio (2010) and coached the team in Paris (2011).

I realised that soccer was my freedom. After Rio, I had a new purpose in life. I saw how people loved the game and also the impact of the Homeless World Cup. That's why I love the game, and think it's the most powerful sport in the world.
Lisa Wrightsman – Represented the USA at the Homeless World Cup in Rio (2010) and now coaches the USA women's team.

I am pleased to know that present at the conference are the founders of the Homeless World Cup and other foundations that, through sport, offer the most disadvantaged a possibility of integral human development.
Pope Francis – speaking at a conference about sports and faith in the Vatican (October 2015)

Introduction

This is not the story of the Homeless World Cup goal by goal or year to year but the story behind it – and the stories of the million homeless people who have been involved since 2003. It's also the story as seen through my own eyes and shared with my friend Peter Barr, who has been part of the adventure from the start, as co-author of *Home Game* and also a fan of the Homeless World Cup.

The Homeless World Cup simply would not have happened without the conscientious efforts of the staff who made it possible. We have always had a tiny team in the international headquarters and they have worked all the hours under the sun to make the Homeless World Cup what it is today.

There are also hundreds of volunteers who support our national partners in more than 70 countries across the world, every day of the year. They are brilliant individuals determined to help homeless and excluded people change their lives through football. Some even fund-raise for the privilege of coming to the annual event where they usually work at least 16 hours every day.

The corporations, football authorities and the people behind the bids to host the annual tournament also deserve huge praise. Many of them have stuck their necks out to support the Homeless World Cup. They have played a really important part in our history.

And of course, this would never have happened without the courage and determination of the homeless people who have changed their lives completely, sometimes against all the odds. They are the real heroes – every single one of them.

There are so many people to thank, but it would be impossible to mention every single individual by name. You know who you are. So, please accept this as a personal thank you. This book is for you.

Mel Young

I

Hold Your Breath Time

Q: Will all the teams arrive on time?
A: It's taken us ten years to get here...

FRIDAY, 5 OCTOBER 2012: I hold my breath. Just one more day. The tenth Homeless World Cup will kick off tomorrow in Mexico City, and everything's ready for action – including three new stadiums for thousands of spectators which appeared overnight in the heart of the main city square.

The transformation of the plaza is almost complete. But this is not the first time that the Zocalo has seen dramatic change – it used to be the centre of the universe until it was destroyed by the Conquistadores. And now it is the venue for the Homeless World Cup.

The location may be different (last year it was Paris and the year before Rio) but every year I hold my breath right till the very last minute. Something unexpected always happens, but there's nothing more I can do now except think about how far we've come since the tournament started in 2003, and how much more we'll need to do to reach our goal – a world where homelessness has been eradicated altogether and the Homeless World Cup no longer needs to exist.

Every year is also very different. Every tournament takes on a life of its own and has a momentum of its own.

The scale of the event is also growing all the time, not just in terms of numbers but its international impact. Street-soccer teams from more than 50 countries are converging on the Zocalo – our home for the rest of the week. The 500 players selected to play for their countries will represent thousands of others who also played in tournaments during the year – about a million people since the organisation was founded just over a decade ago. And everyone who makes it here tomorrow will be part of a sporting event that will not only transform the lives of the players but also change the way that homeless people are perceived.

Some players will be nervous as they sit looking down on the world tens of thousands of feet in the air, wondering what Mexico City will be like and hoping they will go back at the end of the week with the trophy. Most of them have never even flown before or owned a passport. Some have never even had identity papers. Most of them have never spent the night in a hotel before, and some of them have never even slept in a bed with a mattress, a pillow and sheets. But all of them are gearing up to represent their country and heading for the most important week of their lives. In 24 hours, these homeless men and women – once excluded and invisible – will be treated like heroes by thousands of fans crowding into the square.

* * * * *

Lisa Wrightsman will be flying here tonight from California with the rest of her team. Lisa is a coach now but she also knows exactly what it's like to be a player, and was part of the first women's USA team two years ago in Rio de Janeiro, when the games were played on Copacabana. She was one of the stars of the tournament then, and returned a year later as one of the coaches in Paris. Lisa also knows exactly what it's like to be homeless, struggling to get free from drugs. Today she is running a programme for excluded women in Sacramento, using soccer to help them to transform their lives, just as she has also turned her own life around. She loves the game of soccer and has always dreamed of playing for her country. She is also in love with the Homeless World Cup and excited to see what will happen this year.

Coming in the opposite direction, 25-year-old Lukes Mjoka hopes that this week in Mexico City will be another stepping stone in his eventful life. Like Lisa, he made his début in Rio, playing for South Africa. And like Lisa, he's also a coach now. His dream is to go back to Rio, where Pupo the manager of the Brazil team has offered him work as a coach. It's a long way from the township in Cape Town when Lukes was a six-year-old boy being squeezed in through broken car windows to steal whatever he could get his six-year-old hands on. It's also a long way from running his neighbourhood drug-dealing 'business'. Now part of the coaching staff helping South Africa manager Cliffy (Clifford Martinus), Lukes will have to persuade him and Pupo that he is now ready to take on the challenge of moving across the Atlantic to Rio.

Arkady Tyurin used to be homeless, like Lukes. He is flying in from Russia, thinking this year will probably be his farewell to the Homeless World Cup. He has been involved since 2003 when the tournament started, so this is the tenth year he's managed the team. Maybe it is time for someone else to take over. Was the highlight when Russia won the trophy in Cape Town in 2006? Perhaps. But the challenge continued. In Melbourne in 2008, the team reached the final again, this time losing 5-4 to Afghanistan. This year, it's another group of players, with their individual battles and their individual hopes and desires.

'Will I see you next year in Poland?' I ask. And the look in his eyes says that Arkady is already starting to have second thoughts...

Melbourne was the first year Hary Milas got involved with the Homeless World Cup. Like most Australians, he loves sport and also loves the underdog, and as a referee he gets the opportunity not only to make sure the players respect all the rules of the game but also make new friends and meet up with dozens of old friends. He's also confident that nobody will hate his decisions so much that they stab him – something which happened a few years ago in Australia, long before he started refereeing at the Homeless World Cup. For Hary, the annual event is about a lot more than just soccer. It's all about people transforming their lives – not just the homeless players but Hary himself and all the other people who volunteer year after year.

Like Hary Milas, Alex Chan from Hong Kong is not one of the excluded, but his life has also been deeply affected by getting involved in the Homeless World Cup. Because Hong Kong is now part of China, there are no 'homeless' people in the eyes of the authorities, but Alex knows there are excluded people in the city, including many heroin addicts, and he has done something about it – his company sponsors the team. It's a long way from Hong Kong to Mexico City, but Alex hopes that one day Hong Kong will also play host to the Homeless World Cup.

Harald Schmied knows a lot better than most what the Homeless World Cup is about. He's not involved in day-to-day activities now and this year he is covering the tournament for Austrian TV, but Harald was one of the founders of the organisation and is proud of the progress made over the years since his home town Graz in Austria played host to the inaugural event in 2003. It's grown from 18 teams to well over 60 teams this year, and partners in 70 countries. Every year is different but the 'crazy idea' still has the same impact on Harald and everyone else.

Also flying to Mexico City tonight are human rights campaigner Boby Duval from Haiti, Bongsu Hasibuan from Indonesia, Becca Mushrow (one of the youngest players in the tournament), Mauva Hunte-Bowlby (one of the oldest) and Aaron Ranieri (returning for the first time to the land where he was born) from England; Bill and Debbi Shaw from Michigan who are coming to support their adopted homeland, the Philippines; another 'exile' who has fallen in love with the people of Asia, Paraic Grogan, an Irish-man now based in Australia, sitting near two of his star players, Chan 'Ton' Sophondara and midfielder Phiyou Sin from Cambodia; Ireland coach Mick Pender, who has been to every tournament since Graz in 2003, and hopes that his credit card will not be called into service this year; and US-based volunteer Chandrima Chatterjee, who confesses she's fallen in love with the Homeless World Cup.

Boby is an activist who spent 17 months in prison in the mid-1970s as a 'guest' of Baby Doc Duvalier, the country's much-hated dictator. Amnesty International and US President Jimmy Carter secured his release in 1977 and, 18 years later, Boby created Fondation L'Athletique D'Haiti, an organ-isation which provides soccer training, free school and free meals for thou-sands of children and 'at-risk youths', and is now a partner of the Homeless World Cup. In 2007, Boby was named CNN Hero of the Year for his work, but this year he is just pleased that his players have made it to Mexico City – Haiti has been battered by disasters in the previous couple of years and it wasn't until the last minute that they managed to raise enough money to fly here. Two years ago, thousands of people made homeless by the devastating earthquake set up camp on the soccer field used by L'Athletique D'Haiti. Now Boby has a dream to build a brand-new stadium in Haiti which will rise like a phoenix from the rubble of Cité Soleil.

There are three million homeless people in Indonesia, and Bongsu was one of them for over 15 years until he started playing soccer with Rumah Cemara, the Homeless World Cup's Indonesian partner, an organisation which helps people living with HIV/AIDS and people who are trying to stop taking drugs – intravenous drug use is the major cause of the killer disease in his country. Bongsu doesn't know it yet but later this week the team will be wearing black armbands and he will dedicate his 'goal of the tournament', a superb overhead bicycle kick, in memory of a friend and former team mate who is about to lose his fight for life. Bongsu also doesn't know that next year he will coach the team – and one more of his dreams will come true.

This is the first year that England have entered a women's team at the Homeless World Cup and 52-year-old Mauva is the 'rock' at the heart of the team. She lost her home and spent two years 'sofa surfing' in London – one of the many 'invisible homeless' in so many countries. After 'accidentally' getting involved in the soccer, she loves it and hopes her five children and two grandchildren will be watching 'live' this week, via the website set up by the Homeless World Cup. Her team mate, Becca, also has her family root-ing for her back home in England, and like Mauva and the other England players she'll be keeping a diary to document what happens and set out her personal goals. One of the challenges for everyone is 'learning about defeat' but as the plane arrives in Mexico City, defeat is a long way from everyone's minds – especially Aaron Ranieri's, making an emotional return to the land of his birth for the first time since he took off from the very same airport at five years of age.

Bill and Debbi Shaw also have connections with two different countries, dividing their time between the Philippines and Michigan. The husband-and-wife team co-founded the Urban Opportunities for Change Foundation in Manila, which publishes the street paper *Jeepney* and has organised Team Philippines since Melbourne in 2008. The local managers now run the organisation but Bill and Debbi still support the team whenever they can. They first went to the Philippines in 2002 intending to stay for a year. Ten years later, they are heading for Mexico City to cheer on their adopted land and catch up with their Homeless World Cup family. Faith plays a big part in what motivates Bill, but he also believes that his idealism comes from his childhood and his parents' views on civil liberty and resistance.

This is the fifth time Cambodia boss Paraic Grogan and coach Jimmy Campbell have come to the Homeless World Cup, and the first time for Chan 'Ton' Sophondara and the rest of the players. After a 30-hour flight from Phnom Penh via Paris, 'the smallest player with the biggest heart' is destined to capture the hearts of the fans, like every other player from Cambodia before him. Ton is also lucky because two of the squad haven't made it to Mexico City – there were not enough funds to pay for their tickets but Paraic has promised them places in next year's team heading for Poland. It is a bitter blow for everyone but midfielder Phiyou Sin, sitting near Ton, can't contain his excitement. Like his hero, Portuguese superstar Christiano Ronaldo, he will play for his country tomorrow and hopefully help his team score a few goals.

Paraic is excited for the players around him, none of whom have flown before or been beyond the borders of Cambodia. He is also nervous – will Mexico City be safe, will his players get lost, will they cope with the crowds? Will the current team produce another coach like Ton's brother Rithy, who played in Milan in 2009 and will cheer on the players from thousands of miles away, with fellow coach Sam Yi, who made his appearance in Melbourne the previous year? Paraic also puts his thoughts into perspective – Cambodia was not a safe place to go until only a few years ago, when he went there as a visitor the first time, for a taste of adventure. Surely nothing would faze these courageous young players who come from such a beautiful yet traumatised country, recovering from years of war and genocide? But if one of the players gets lost in the city, with no phone or passport...

For Chandrima, this is Homeless World Cup Number Three. Last year, she was forced to cancel Paris at the very last minute, because of a family emergency, but her experience in Rio de Janeiro and Milan was something she'll never forget. With a degree in Biology and a Masters in Public Health, you may think that Chandrima would pursue a very different career, but she is beginning to live for the Homeless World Cup and hopes to get more involved in the future, working for Street Soccer USA.

Chandrima wants homeless people to have a sense of belonging. She also wants to help give the players their voice, so they can tell their story in their own words, and 'help make their experience at the Homeless World Cup as great as it possibly can be', so they go back at the end of the week with a feeling of accomplishment and lessons to pass on to others.

*****

The excitement is building. One by one, the flights start arriving in Mexico City. Then something goes wrong.

Asamoah Martin and the Ghana team are stuck in the airport in Dacca. The airline staff have told him that he and his players need visas for Germany because they will be changing flights in Frankfurt, to catch their connection to Mexico City. The airline staff are wrong about needing the visas, but nobody knows yet. Martin is advised to stay right where he is, at the desk, but time is running out. The flight leaves in 25 minutes.

Not everyone who wants to be in Mexico City will make it for this year's event. Some teams haven't managed to raise enough money to pay for their tickets, despite everyone's efforts. Some countries have decided to focus on next year or – like Zimbabwe – are faced with what seem insurmountable problems. They will have to follow the event from a distance, watching 'live' via the website, if they manage to find a computer and get themselves online. Our partner in Zimbabwe, Youth Achievement Sports for Development (YASD), took part in the Homeless World Cup in 2008, winning by a record score of 20 to nil over Belgium in one of their games, but this year they will not be able to join us. YASD coordinator Petros Chatiza and his colleague Filbert Neumann are still coping with the fallout from 2005, when three million people were made homeless overnight, when shanty towns were suddenly demolished by the government in Operation Clean Up.

At the same time as Petros and Filbert, David Duke will be watching the tournament online, in his Edinburgh office, wishing he could be there with coach Ally Dawson and the rest of the Scotland team. Once a player him-self, appearing in the second Homeless World Cup in Gothenburg, Sweden, in 2004, David is now CEO of Street Soccer Scotland. The organisation has made a huge impact in Scotland and this year has attracted record sponsor-ship as well as the support of fellow Scot Sir Alex Ferguson, the manager of Manchester United, but David had to make a hard decision a few days ago. There wasn't enough cash for him to fly out with the rest of the team, and because he had been to the tournament several times in the past, both as player and coach, it was time for some new blood. David also has other pri-orities, running the nationwide programme for hundreds of people – some of whom will play for Scotland next year.

As David composes an email to one of his sponsors, Biswajit Nandi (aged 16) and Surajit Bhattacharya (17) are kicking a ball around on a dusty patch of wasteland on the edge of Sonagachi, the largest red-light district in Kolkata and one of the largest in Asia. This is where Biswajit and Surajit grew up and also where their mothers are still busy working today, selling their bodies for a few hundred rupees. For both boys, the Homeless World Cup is a dream. They have heard all about it from friends who have played for Slum Soccer, the Indian organisation which has sent a team to the Home-less World Cup since 2007. This year, Team India has had financial prob-lems, however, and will not be going to Mexico City. Maybe next year in Poland? Maybe Biswajit and Surajit will be stars of the team?

For Patrick Gasser of UEFA at a conference in Sarajevo, there is only a short time to go till he flies out to Mexico City, returning to the country where he studied Spanish 30 years ago. The meeting in the capital of Bosnia has focused on 'football and social responsibility', and the lessons UEFA has learned from supporting the Homeless World Cup has been one of the topics discussed. Now Patrick wants to go and see the power of soccer in action.

Sitting in her office in Amsterdam, Maria Bobenrieth wishes that she could be with us. Now Executive Director of *Women Win* (an organisation which promotes the cause of sport to empower young women), Maria used to be the Global Director of Community Investments at Nike, and is still a big fan of the Homeless World Cup. Nike has been a key sponsor since the first event in Graz in 2003, not just providing funds but also practical help, including volunteers and merchandise. For the Nike people who become part of the team for the week, it is more than just another major sporting event where the company's logo is seen by the crowds – it has become an opportunity for something much more personal. And for Maria, it is one of her great passions in life.

Meanwhile, in Mexico City, Daniel Copto is busy preparing his Mexico players, including women's captain Mayra Vazquez and her team-mate Ana Aguirre. Daniel also has a dream – to build a rehabilitation centre in Mexico City for the addicts who live on the streets of the city, sniffing solvents until they get high and have damaged their brains. Many current treatment centres use outdated and sometimes very cruel methods, and Daniel would like to create a safe place where the addicts are treated as real human beings, and take part in his soccer-based activities. The project has steadily grown through the years and today almost 30,000 people come along every week to play soccer, in various locations nationwide. Thirty-thousand seems like lots of people, but Daniel is also concerned about the future of the hundreds of thousands of 'invisible' people who officially do not exist, and the addicts and victims of violence who live on the streets. Tonight, however, he is focusing all his attention on Mayra and Ana and the rest of the players, because tomorrow they will represent their country in front of their passionate fans. Can the 'home' team triumph in the Homeless World Cup? The pressure is mounting.

Everyone behind the scenes in Mexico City is also getting ready for action. The local organisers have reserved most of the nearby hotel rooms for the hundreds of players, volunteers and officials arriving tonight. The media centre is already buzzing with dozens of journalists searching for stories. But they won't need to wait very long. Every single player has a story to tell and the soccer will be full of human drama – and goals – from beginning to end.

* * * * *

The excitement is building but another player who will not be in Mexico City is 18-year-old Loredan Bulgariu. Loredan was one of the players selected for the Romania Homeless World Cup team, but on July the 17th, three months before the tournament kicked off, he was stabbed to death in Timisoara.

'My heart broke when I heard the news,' says Romania coach Mihai Rusos, when I meet him in Mexico City. 'Loredan was one of our most talented players. He was very proud to wear the Number Ten shirt and was very excited about representing his country in Mexico City.'

Loredan's death was yet another example of the dangers faced by homeless people all around the world. Sadly, it's a fact of life that homeless people are often the victims of violence. While so many people are infatuated with celebrities and luxury lifestyles, there are millions of lives being ruined by poverty and homelessness, and also lives being lost.

As the action starts and everyone cheers on the players, the Romania team will be playing their hearts out for Loredan, keeping his spirit alive. And Mihai knows more Loredans are living in the streets who will play for Romania next year – and the year after that.

* * * * *

In between interviews – with Agence France Presse and the BBC – I sit down in my room to draft my speech for tomorrow. This will be the tenth Homeless World Cup, a milestone in our history, and this year's tournament will be much more spectacular than ever before, so maybe I should say something special to mark the occasion?

I have an idea – to talk about 'dreams'. The dream that we can put an end to homelessness. The dream that every player has of getting a job and a place to call 'home'. Not just the dream of winning the Homeless World Cup but of winning the future. For some excluded people, any future at all is a dream.

I will work on it later. Every year, I talk about similar issues, but I know that whatever I say, it will be for the people who matter – the players. And for them, every word will be new.

Every year, journalists ask me what tournament I liked the most, and I honestly tell them that one event can't be compared with another. Some are bigger and louder than others. Some are better organised and some are more spontaneous and full of surprises. But for the players, this will be their only tournament. They are only allowed to play one year, so others can follow them later. Some players may come back as coaches, but we never lose sight of the fact every tournament may be the only chance some people get to experience what it's about.

Our local partners tell me they have found a translator called Andrea who will join me tomorrow at the opening ceremony to repeat my words in Spanish. We will need to rehearse. So I'd better get finished as soon as I can. Ten minutes should do it? Andrea wasn't aware till this evening that she would be standing in front of the crowds in the stadium, speaking 'live' on national TV, but if she is nervous, I don't really notice. And she probably won't notice I'm nervous, too.

I never feel nervous because of the crowds or the cameras, but every time I speak, I am conscious it could make a difference to somebody's life. You never know who may be paying attention and noting your words, whether it's a billionaire or someone who doesn't have one single cent to his name.

Later this week, I am giving a talk about the Homeless World Cup to a group of business people in Mexico City. What I say there will be different from my speech tomorrow morning, and the challenge is always to make it seem fresh, even though I've almost learned the words off by heart:

> The story of the Homeless World Cup is a story of how homeless people have transformed their lives through the power of soccer. But first the bad news. According to the United Nations, there are 100 million homeless people in the world. Millions more are living in extreme poverty, unable to access even basic commodities like drinking water. Meanwhile, the global economic system means the rich are getting richer while the poor are getting poorer, and the gap between them widens every day.

Every word may be engraved on my mind but the message is just as important today as it was when the Homeless World Cup first began, almost ten years ago.

> There is homelessness in every single country in the world. In the USA, the richest of them all, over three million people now live on the streets, including entire families. In every major US city, you see homeless people – and wherever you go, it's the same sorry sight.

It's hard for us to really comprehend such huge numbers – or know what to do. But I believe to make a difference we have to do something, no matter how small. If every single one of us did something constructive, together we *could* change the world.

* * * * *

Sometimes, small ideas grow much more than anyone ever imagines. The Homeless World Cup started as a very simple idea, dreamed up in Cape Town in 2001, over a couple of beers. Most people thought we were crazy and said it would never become a reality, but two years later, in July 2003, the first Homeless World Cup took place in Graz in Austria, with 18 nations taking part. And when the teams marched through the streets at the start of the week-long event, it was a very moving moment for me and the rest of the crowd, and the players proudly holding their national flags.

A lot of what we did in Graz is still the same today. We always try to play in the centre of cities, typically in the main square. Street soccer is a simple game to organise – you just need a ball – but we want to make it an exciting event for the crowd, so we erect small courts surrounded on all sides by stands, like a miniature stadium. And when the players enter at the opening parade, people cheer the same as at the Olympics.

Every year, three major changes take place in the people involved. First, the players stand there in their national colours, singing their national anthem with genuine pride. The way some of them have been treated, you could excuse them for ignoring or resenting the anthem, but most of them just sing their hearts out. They're fantastic ambassadors for their countries, and they almost grow taller in front of your eyes. Homeless people usually have low self-esteem and confidence and tend to look downwards, but when they stand there, hands on heart, they're suddenly transformed and look around the stadium – no longer stooped but standing straight and looking up, beaming with pride.

The second change is even more remarkable, in some ways – it's the crowd who are watching and cheering them on. Normally, they tend to avoid homeless people, or even think they're sick or dangerous. They won't let their children go near them. Yet, during every tournament, the children queue for autographs and treat homeless players as stars.

So what happens? Why do people change their attitudes all of a sudden?

All we do is change the environment. The day before, the homeless man or woman is hanging around in the street. People walk past and ignore them. The next day, they are standing in a stadium, and everyone's cheering. They are just the same people, both inside and outside. All we do is change the background and the way people see them, and a big change takes place. The stereotype is destroyed – and solutions begin to emerge.

The third change is the media. In Graz that first year, film crews and journalists turned up from countries all over the world – even from countries which were not taking part. On the day of the Final, there were hundreds of photographers and television cameras ringed around the pitch. There were thousands of stories in newspapers and on the web. And all the coverage was positive. Not 90 per cent or 99 per cent but 100 per cent positive.

Before then, most coverage of homeless people tended to be negative: 'Homeless people are upsetting the tourists, so get them off the streets. Homeless people are thieves who are up to no good. Homeless people are a drain on the economy.'

But in Graz, it was totally different. And every year since...

After Graz, we did some research and discovered that 80 per cent of the players involved had changed their lives completely. They had found jobs and homes, gone into further education, become football coaches, and so on. The results were so impressive, I couldn't believe it. I had worked with homeless people for several years and the statistics seemed too high to me – too good to be true. So, we checked and checked again and they kept coming back just the same. The idea was working. So we decided to hold the event every year.

In 2004, in Gothenburg, Sweden, 26 countries took part in the second event. In 2005, my home city, Edinburgh, hosted the tournament, after the event in New York had been cancelled at the very last minute due to visa complications, and 32 countries took part. It was a challenging experience for everyone involved, but we had great support from many local organisations, who provided everything we needed at very short notice, and the sun shone for seven days straight – which for Scotland is almost unheard of. In 2006, we went to Cape Town and 48 countries joined in, including many new African teams. We jumped up a level in Cape Town that year. The President of South Africa stood on the balcony – the exact same spot where Nelson Mandela had made his famous speech after his release from prison – and saluted the homeless players as they marched past at the opening parade. There were 100,000 people in the square that day. Later that week, Archbishop Desmond Tutu came to visit, on his birthday. He was scheduled to speak on the pitch for a couple of minutes but stayed for much longer, talking to the players and kicking a ball around just like a kid in the playground.

In 2007, Copenhagen hosted 48 countries, and something truly remarkable happened – my own country Scotland won the Homeless World Cup. In 2008, the event moved to Melbourne, where Zambia won the first Women's Homeless World Cup. The men's final was a classic between Russia and Afghanistan. The square was packed to overflowing. Afghanistan were leading with 30 seconds to go and Russia had a chance to equalise but missed an open goal and Afghanistan won – and the whole place went crazy. In his speech, the Afghanistan manager said there had been darkness in his country for the past 30 years and that this was the first time a light had come on – a moment I'll always remember.

In 2009, we held the event in Milan and more big-name celebrities like Formula One World Champion Lewis Hamilton and Italian soccer legend Marco Materazzi came along to show their support to the players. In 2010, the Homeless World Cup moved to Rio de Janeiro, where the games were played on Copacabana and – surprise, surprise – Brazil won both the men's and women's tournaments.

In 2011, the event was held in Paris in the shadow of the Eiffel Tower on the banks of the Seine – another iconic location. Scotland won the trophy for the second time, beating Mexico in a dramatic finale, while Kenya won the women's event.

Now, here we are in Mexico City – in the centre of one of the world's greatest cities. We will see players changing in front of our eyes as thousands of people applaud them. We will see changes all around us.

But the Homeless World Cup is about a lot more than this wonderful annual event. The important work is done on the ground every week of the year when our national partners in more than 70 countries work with homeless people on the streets of their cities and get them involved, playing soccer. Some countries also organise their own national championships, to select the players they will send to the Homeless World Cup.

The annual event is a celebration of all the hard work which goes on all year round. It is our chance to tell the world about our real aims – to create change and to put an end to homelessness wherever it exists, through the power of sport.

Homeless players are only allowed to play once at the annual event – which is a stepping stone for them towards a new and better life. It's not the end but the beginning of a life-changing process. Many players later return as volunteers and coaches. Others have become community leaders and now run their national programmes.

All of them prove that we can create change. But we all know we need to do more.

* * * * *

Homelessness is bad for everyone. Ask anybody anywhere – rich or poor, old or young – if they think homelessness can ever be a good thing. I ask this question all the time and no-one has ever said yes. So, why do we allow it to continue?

Human beings are ingenious – we can send people to the moon, wipe out killer diseases, invent the Internet and speak to anyone around the world whenever we want – to exchange a few words or make billions of dollars. But if we are so clever, why do we have homelessness?

> If we work together, we can put an end to homelessness now. And it's simple – all you need is a ball. A ball can change the world and this week in Mexico City, we'll prove it to you and the rest of the world...

So that's the easy part. I know how I will end my speech on Thursday at the Embassy, but what will I say tomorrow at the opening? The tenth Homeless World Cup is a special occasion for me and the rest of the organisation but for every single player who stands there tomorrow, it's the first time they have taken part in such an event. It's probably the first time they have ever represented their country, and the first time for a long while that anyone has treated them with any respect. But no matter what I say, it's the players who matter. It's their dreams that count most. And the world needs to wake up and do something now to make homelessness something that only exists in the past.

*****

Martin and the Ghana team are still stuck in the airport.

This is not the first time a team has been stuck at the very last minute with nowhere to go – or the first time that visas or identity papers have caused complications. In 2004, the Cameroon team were ready to fly out to Sweden. Every player had a passport but the immigration authorities were concerned they would 'disappear' during the tournament, and refused the team entry. The Cameroon project was recognised by numerous international organisations, and the Austrian authorities confirmed our exemplary record in Graz, but nothing we said seemed to work. Perhaps we were naive about official procedures, but the end result was that one of our teams didn't make it. At the media conference before the Gothenburg tournament opened, the journalists were keen to hear the details of the 'incident', but I felt that it should not be the dominant theme – there were 26 other teams eager for kick-off and their arrival was a cause for celebration.

Cameroon, however, were not forgotten. Before we presented the trophy at the end of the Final, I asked the crowd and all of the players to send out a cheer that would 'carry through the night sky and be heard by all the players left behind in Cameroon.' It was an act of solidarity that echoes in my memory even today, and later on the players signed a shirt and other souvenirs of Gothenburg which they sent to the Cameroon players to tell them how much they were missed. Homeless people know what it is like to be excluded. They all have some experience of being outsiders.

There have also been many near-misses. In 2009, the Cambodia team almost missed the event in Milan with a few hours to go because they didn't have the proper visas to pass through the airport in Bangkok, in neighbouring Thailand, despite the fact that no-one with a ticket to Europe was likely to try to abscond while in transit. Two years ago, I also held my breath, when it looked as if Uganda wouldn't make it to Rio. Last year, Haiti were two days late getting to Paris because their airline wouldn't let them board their flight, claiming that four of the women did not look like the photos on their passports. The airline eventually did let them on but when the team arrived, the tournament had already started. This was not the best way to prepare for competition, but the women stepped straight off the plane to make their début in the tournament – and win a load of respect.

*****

World travel can be challenging for anyone these days, but for homeless people it can be impossible. Many of them have no identity papers and can't even prove who they are – no birth certificate or even public record of their birth. As they try to survive day to day, the idea of applying for a passport never enters their mind. But if they want to play in the Homeless World Cup, in a faraway country, they need passports and visas, like everyone else.

Our national partners work hard with the players to get all the documents needed. This is often an extremely slow and complicated process. In some South American countries, for example, many homeless people were born on the street. They may have no idea when or where they were born – or even how old they are – and name themselves after the street where they live.

Once they get the basic papers needed, however, they are issued with identity papers, and this means they can also get a passport and a visa. Instead of being one of the 'invisible people' they can come to the Homeless World Cup and play in front of thousands of spectators in the stadium, and millions more who watch the games 'live' in countries all over the world.

*****

There are millions of invisible people all over the world – non-persons or people who do not exist. A survey in London once asked people what they had seen in the street as they walked to their work in the morning. They mentioned cars, advertisements and window displays in the shops but not the homeless person sleeping in the doorway on a bed made from pieces of cardboard. They could not see the homeless people living in the streets, right in front of their faces. And that is just the surface of the problem.

Invisible people live their lives according to a different set of rules from the rest of society. They are forced to create an alternative reality in order to survive. A different set of values. No identity – never mind passports.

In Russia, for example, it is easy to find yourself outside the system. During Soviet times, the regime created a system which meant that everyone had to have an internal passport called a Propiska. It was illegal to go anywhere without it, and you had to get official permission whenever you wanted to move – that was how the Soviets controlled the population.

The problem is that if you didn't have a Propiska, you were 'outside the system'. You couldn't own a house, you couldn't work and you couldn't get married or travel. So, you became a 'non-person' and you found an alternative way to survive. You existed but you were not part of society. You were excluded, and you soon became invisible.

When the Soviet system collapsed, the Propiska system was still in force. And overnight, many people also found themselves homeless. In the mid-1990s, I met an ex-soldier who had just become homeless. Like many Russian people, he was forced to do military service, and was sent to fight in Afghanistan. One year later, he went home to St Petersburg, and was told that his Propiska would be sent to him there.

He waited and waited, but his papers still did not arrive, so he made some enquiries and was told that the authorities had no idea where his papers were. And to complicate matters, he could not get a new Propiska because he did not have any identity papers to prove who he was. So, how could he get new identity papers? 'You need a Propiska!' the authorities told him.

So this young man who had been forced to risk his life for his country had ended up homeless and could not be a member of society because he had no way to prove who he was. Things are better now in Russia, but there are still too many homeless people – in Russia and everywhere else in the world.

* * * * *

Still no news from Ghana. Will they make it on time for the kick-off tomorrow? It's just like the Uganda team two years ago, and nobody wants to go through all that heartache again, when no matter what we tried to do to fix the situation, as soon as one door opened, another door closed.

The Homeless World Cup gives homeless people a voice so that their stories can be heard and shared and valued just like any other human being. But in 2010, we had only a few hours to fix things or the Uganda team would miss their flight to Rio – and their voices would never be heard. That year, Uganda was one of 12 teams coming to play in the women's event, and for me they were a special group of people. They had been living in a refugee camp set up during the Ugandan civil war, and what they had endured was unimaginable. They had been repeatedly raped, forced to marry soldiers whom they hated, and then have their children, while others had their own children forcibly taken away. Some had been forced to be sex slaves.

They had all endured unspeakable horror before they found protection in the camp, but because the civil war had officially ended, the women were effectively homeless.

Even though their spirits had been crushed, the women began to re-build their lives, starting with football. One day, they started kicking a ball around and formed a small community which revolved around football – a sport which brought the women close together and allowed them to develop self-esteem. When we found out what they were doing, we offered our support, and their organisation, Girls Kick It, became our partner in Uganda (we have only one partner per country). Playing in the Homeless World Cup became one of their primary targets, and a team was selected for Rio. The only problem then was how to pay for air fares, but we managed to raise enough money and sorted out visas and passports.

The women had never been on a plane before so they had to be taught about what to expect – how to put on their seatbelts and so on. Because they came from rural areas, they also had to learn about life in the city – how to cross roads, operate a shower and use strange-looking toilets. And finally the women were ready to go.

*****

Before every tournament, phones never seem to stop ringing. Then just before the teams arrive, everything seems to go quiet. It's a wonderful feeling. All the months it takes to organise the annual event now begin to pay off as the players fly in from countries all over the globe. But there's always a feeling that something is bound to go wrong, and that year all attention turned to Uganda, as the team were told right at the very last minute they didn't have the proper visas. The team were booked to fly from Kampala to Nairobi to Johannesburg and then on to Rio, but one of the officials insisted they needed a visa to change flight in Johannesburg for Rio. And nothing would change his opinion. 'No transit visa, no go!' was his mantra.

We called him up and tried to persuade him, but he simply repeated again and again, 'Doesn't matter! Need a transit visa!' Even though the team had visas to enter Brazil, and return tickets, he said it would take a week to issue transit visas, even if we paid for them immediately. 'These people will be representing their country, and they need to get to Rio on the next plane, or they'll miss it.' 'Doesn't matter! Need a transit visa!'

We know we're getting nowhere so we hit the phones and call up all the embassies and everyone else we can think of, including the airlines, in the countries involved. But no-one can help us.

Here is this courageous group of women who have fought back after going through those terrible atrocities and now they're being blocked by one official. All those months of hard work wasted. All those dreams shattered. I want to scream but know we need to keep the players calm and talk our way out of the problem.

Then we get an idea...

The Uganda team are travelling to Rio with South African Airways, and we know their chief in Australia – he helped us with similar problems in 2008. So I send him an e-mail, even though he'll probably still be asleep and won't be at work until nine in the morning, and the plane is due to take off from Nairobi hours before then.

The hours go by. Still no reply. Then he suddenly calls me, I quickly explain what has happened, and he springs into action at once.

With just a few minutes to go, we get through on a very crackly phone line to speak to the team and explain very quickly what's going to happen: 'Go to the check-in desk and airline staff will then escort you through immigration and onto the plane with your tickets to Rio. And hurry!'

Before I go to sleep that night, I don't know if they're going to make it or not, but the next day, I notice that someone has left me a message – Anna Phillips, an American who'd worked with the team in Uganda, had also been trying to fix things the previous night. 'Good news! They're on the plane!' she says, and suddenly I notice there are tears in my eyes. It feels like justice has been done. I also know how much it will mean to the players – and it isn't long until I see it written all over their faces in Rio.

*****

The Homeless World Cup always opens with a colourful – and very moving – parade through the streets of the city. There is always a carnival atmosphere, and in Rio it seemed extra special that year as the teams lined up on Copacabana.

Then I saw them – their beautiful smiles. The women from Uganda had finally made it to Rio and now they were dancing to the beat of the carnival drums.

All the teams were ready to get on with the soccer – that is what brought everyone together – but part of me could not help thinking what they had achieved was even greater than winning the World Cup itself.

Uganda played well in the competition but more importantly they went back inspired and put even more energy into Girls Kick It. Some of them became registered coaches and set up their own social enterprise – a chicken farm employing several women and earning the cooperative some regular income. They were leaders and ambassadors for 'the art of what is possible'. And despite all the obstacles placed in their path, with a little help from people far away from Uganda, the invisible were 'visible' again.

*****

The Ugandan women's story may have had a happy ending, but two years later as we're waiting in Mexico City to hear what has happened to Ghana, we are holding our breath once again...

Zakia Moulaoui, a member of staff who looks after the teams and their travel arrangements, sends me a message. Martin and his players are stuck at the airport, and the airline still insists they need a visa for Frankfurt, even if they never go outside the transit area. It's the same nightmare over again, but every time it happens, it feels even worse. Zakia is feeling the pressure but she'll never give up. She has handled situations like this in the past and is not surprised by anything that happens. She says she will contact the airline and everyone else who can help. She also keeps talking to Martin, to make sure he stays in the airport. I ask her to tell me as soon as she has any news – good or bad.

*****

As the evening continues, I go out to the plaza to soak up the atmosphere, and bump into lots of old friends who have flown into Mexico City that evening. Everyone is smiling and delighted that so many teams have made it this year. I shake hands with dozens of people and carry on smiling, but still in the back of my mind, I am thinking of Martin and Ghana, and all the other teams who won't be here tomorrow, even though they will be here in spirit.

The Ghana team has been part of the Homeless World Cup family since 2005 and made its début in the tournament in Cape Town the following year, when I first learned what motivates Martin and what makes his organisation such a powerful voice for so many people in Ghana.

Martin is director of the Gimat Volunteer Network, a social enterprise that helps deprived communities, using the power of sport. It supports street boys, orphans, school drop-outs and the disabled by giving them the chance to develop their talents and get free access to education. Gimat has also set

up a Football Academy to train the children and provide them with school-
ing, as well as food, clothing and somewhere to live.

According to Martin, the major problem for the young Ghanaians is a
lack of education which drives them onto the streets and into the arms of the
crime gangs. Unemployment, homelessness and poverty are then the result –
a vicious circle which the young men find hard to escape.

What Gimat does is get the men involved in playing football, then
provides the opportunity to study so they're better equipped to apply for
a job. Many have got into trouble with drugs and alcohol, but Martin
uses the power of football to build a new future. 'The Homeless World
Cup was a life-changing experience for me and the players,' he told me.
'Lots of guys transformed their lives after getting involved – guys like
Richard who was in the team in Rio, then trained as a teacher, and now
has a job in a school. He is also a qualified referee for the Ghana Football
Association.'

Many other players went back to Ghana and turned round their lives
after playing in the Homeless World Cup, and one player even went to
Argentina to join a professional team. 'Without the Homeless World Cup,
these guys would not have got the opportunity to travel,' said Martin, 'and
would never have seen what life is like in other countries.'

Playing in the Homeless World Cup also helped the players because
without a job or bank account, they would never be given a passport.

Martin later sent me a message: 'I urge the government and all politicians to support the Homeless World Cup and to open their hearts and their
minds to help anyone who has the opportunity to play. The Homeless World
Cup changes people's lives and I believe it will continue to change people's
lives, and help to put an end to poverty.'

*****

As I sit in the stands looking over the vivid-green field where the players will
show off their skills in the morning in front of thousands of supporters, I
see many people I've not seen since last year – and some I have not seen for
many years. I want to talk to everyone but it's time to go back up and finish
my speech for tomorrow.

As I go up to the reception desk, I meet a young reporter called Fernando, who says he wants to ask me a couple of questions. I remember I
spoke to him early this morning in the media centre and promised to give
him an interview during the week, but I didn't expect he would still be here,
just after midnight, armed with an oversized brown-leather notebook which

is charred at the corners and looks as if it's witnessed several wars. 'I am writing a feature,' he tells me. 'I would like to tell the story of the Homeless World Cup.' 'Me too!' I say. 'I'll see you tomorrow, Fernando.' 'Yes, *mañana*!' says Fernando, as he disappears into the night.

* * * * *

Then at 2.00am, Zakia calls me. There will be no happy ending for the Ghana team this year. But for hundreds of others, tomorrow can't come soon enough. Tomorrow will be their day – maybe even the day of their lives.

2

One Homeless Person is One Too Many

Q: What can we do about homelessness?
A: If we can land a human being on the moon...

SATURDAY, 6 OCTOBER 2012: I walk into the Zocalo soon after dawn for my interview with Al Jazeera's local reporter, a Brazilian journalist called Clara Russo. It's relatively quiet now, for Mexico City. Construction of the stadiums has finished, and the flags are gently waving in the early morning breeze. The traffic which circles the plaza is not very heavy so early on Saturday morning, and as I look around, it's easy to imagine what this place was like when the Aztecs were here. And in a few hours, it will echo to the roar of the crowds as the action kicks off in the Homeless World Cup.

There is time to take in my surroundings in peace – the spectacular plaza as big as several soccer fields, framed by the spectacular cathedral and the National Palace, opposite the colonnaded arches of the shops and hotels. Then I walk past the Madero, the fashionable avenue lined with boutiques leading into the square where the players' parade will emerge about four hours from now, to reclaim the streets of the city. The Homeless World Cup will begin with the opening speeches, the fireworks, the music and dancing, broadcast 'live' on Mexican TV and via the Internet, to millions of people worldwide. The emotions will be running high as kick-off approaches. And the players will experience something they have only ever dreamed of before – the applause from the stands as the first goals are scored, and homeless people win the hearts of soccer fans in Mexico and all around the world.

* * * * *

Doing interviews so early in the morning is a good way to kick off the day. And after I have finished with the crew from *Al Jazeera* and their colleagues from *El Globo*, who are meeting me half-an hour later, I'll be more free to focus on other things scheduled for later – meeting guests and old friends from around the world, and making my opening speech.

At the first Homeless World Cup in Graz in 2003, we were much less prepared for the media 'circus', despite the fact that most of us were journalists ourselves. When I walked into the room on the opening day with my friend Harald Schmied (co-founder of the Homeless World Cup) for our very first press conference, we didn't know what to expect. This could be the first and last Homeless World Cup. Maybe no-one would turn up to watch it. Maybe the media would simply ignore it, despite all our efforts to generate interest. Maybe the crowds would be hostile or laugh at the standard of soccer, and develop an even more negative image of what homeless people are like. And worst of all, maybe the players would be disappointed, and go away feeling more alienated than ever before.

Ten years ago, the media were also very different when it came to reporting on homelessness issues – they were nearly always negative in those days. The transformation in their attitudes since then is truly amazing, and journalists – in most countries – now have a totally different perspective. 'We organise the tournament but you have the power to change things,' I say to many journalists, remembering that I was once one of them, too – aware that every conversation could make a huge difference in somebody's life, including what I say to *Al Jazeera* this morning.

* * * * *

As the sun rises over the plaza, I meet Clara inside the stadium, ready for action, and we wait for the cathedral bells to stop ringing out through the city before we begin. Clara asks how it all started – and why. I talk about how playing soccer changes people, making them fitter and playing as part of a team, and how the tournament has grown so dramatically over the years, with three street soccer stadiums now occupying the centre of Mexico City, and one million people involved since the organisation was founded a decade ago. 'How big is the organisation?' asks Clara, looking round at the thousands of seats in the stadium as if they somehow represent the number of people who work for us.

I think about the office back in Edinburgh, but even though the number of people at HQ has fallen, because of a cut in our funding since Paris, the international network has continued to grow, and become more self-sustaining – as we always intended. So instead of describing the size of the organisation, I focus on what really matters: 'We're a pioneering organisation which manages to operate with very few resources, and we've proved that we *can* change the world – with a ball.'

'How can other people help – including our viewers?'

'Homelessness is a problem which should not and need not exist. And the solution is for everyone to make the decision today to do something about it – today.'

We talk some more, over the sound of the bells from the nearby cathedral, and standing on the bright green field, it doesn't seem a year since we were playing in Paris, or two years since Rio. One multi-coloured stadium begins to seem like every other stadium in every other city we have staged the event, and the experience for many of the players will also be the same as it has always been. The difference is that this is the chance of a lifetime for all of the players.

For Clara, it's a wrap. I see the *El Globo* crew patiently waiting at the side of the field. It's time for the next conversation...

＊＊＊＊＊

Every year, when the players march into the stadium, waving their flags, I am filled with emotion. And so is everybody else I see around me in the stadium, as well as the crowds who are lining the streets.

When we see the teams lined up in their national colours, we should always remember they are wearing those shiny new shirts with the official recognition of their national soccer associations. It's an honour to play for your country and the players are not only proud but aware what it means. When they pull on their shirts, they take responsibility for everything they do.

Some players have not been to cities before – never mind a huge metropolis like Mexico City – and that includes some of the Mexico players themselves, most of whom have never even been to the capital city before. One day the teams are waiting in the airport, feeling nervous because they've never flown before or been abroad, and the next day they are meeting other players from countries all over the world and surrounded by thousands of cheering spectators. One day, they are spat on by people who think they are worthless, and the next day they're treated as heroes.

＊＊＊＊＊

When I give my speech, and Andrea repeats my words in Spanish, I notice every player is staring straight at me as I stand on the field. I realise that even if I've given the same speech before, it's the first time the players have heard it, and it means more to them than to anyone else. I tell them that I have a dream that homelessness will one day be eliminated everywhere, that every single player will return as a winner. And as I speak, I remember the hundreds of thousands of players who have taken part over the years, and the impact they continue to have in their homelands as coaches and mentors – in fact, I see some of them standing a few feet away with the new generation of players.

When the fireworks are over, I wander around in the Zocalo, shaking hands with what seems like thousands of people. Later, I am told that almost 30,000 people watched the games in the three different stadiums during the day – more spectators than ever before.

Film crews, reporters and photographers follow me everywhere, asking the same questions journalists ask every year, but I try hard to answer them all as if this is the first time I have ever heard the question – describing when the tournament started and why. Among the journalists, I also recognise a lot of faces – people who've been following the tournament for years. They know how the whole event started and why, but every year, their personal perspective is different, and every year, something new happens. Every year, there are hundreds of stories. Every year, the action never stops.

* * * * *

'Homelessness is a complex and increasing global problem. The causes are diverse, including poverty, a lack of affordable housing, refugees fleeing from war, floods and famine, health and mental illness problems, joblessness, domestic violence, substance abuse and addiction, and family break-ups.'

I am sitting in a corner of the media centre, talking to a small group of journalists, including Fiona Crawford, who comes to the Homeless World Cup every year, and my new friend, Fernando, who knew nothing about it until just a few days ago, but is keen to tell the story to the Mexican people. Fernando knows a lot about the poverty and homelessness in Mexico City (it is hard to avoid), but is not so aware of the scale of the problem in the rest of the world, including the USA, Mexico's neighbour. 'According to UN statistics,' I tell him, 'there are 100 million homeless people all around the world.'

Fernando writes the figures down and underlines what he has written in his brown-leather notebook, which looks so big it probably contains every word he has written since starting his job.

Even though the figures are important, we should never become too obsessed with the numbers. I have always said that homeless people are not statistics. They are all individuals, like you and like me. That is why the Homeless World Cup always tries to present homeless people as people, but sometimes there is no other way to express it. The statistics are simply a fact.

'Homelessness also affects every country, from the poorest – like Cambodia and Haiti – to some of the richest,' I tell the reporters, who all start to quiz me, the same as Fernando.

Q: The richest? So, you mean the USA?

A: Yes! In the richest, most powerful nation on Earth, three million people are reported to be living on the streets. These are frightening figures but we have to tackle the issue without getting stuck on statistics. One homeless person is one homeless person too many.

Q: Is homelessness the same in every country?

A: Homelessness looks different in different countries due to different economies, political systems and climates, as well as different cultural values. For example, some people in Africa think that you cannot be homeless if you have a roof over your head. A recovering addict in a homeless shelter in Europe may seem 'better off' than a refugee fleeing from a war zone in the midst of a famine, but the look of homeless people is the same throughout the world. The isolation, exclusion and hopelessness are universal. Once you fall out of the system and onto the streets, it is very difficult to get back into regular society. Homeless people everywhere tend to have low self-esteem and self-respect. They quickly lose their confidence.

Q: How do players qualify as homeless?

A: There are many different ways of defining 'homelessness' but I believe it simply means those people who don't have anywhere they can call home – 'the poorest of the poor' in any country, whoever is excluded, marginalised or alienated from mainstream society. Homelessness is like another planet.

* * * * *

Definitions can be a barrier to understanding. Paul Gregory, the Canada manager, told me in Gothenburg:

> The problem is that everyone is put into silos – mental health and addiction, and so on. Then we invent new terminology and even homeless people start saying things like, 'I can't do this because I'm in the addiction silo', or 'I can't do this because I'm in the illiterate silo'. We've created a system where everyone believes in their own label and they won't move on as a result.

As Paul himself said, the reality is different: 'Not everything is black and white. The football in Gothenburg proved that – a group of people who weren't being dissected or classified. That's why it was so liberating.'

* * * * *

Sometimes, when I sit and watch the soccer, like today in the centre of Mexico City, I forget just like everyone else that these are homeless people playing for their country. Maybe just a few weeks before, they were homeless and hopeless, and now they're being cheered on as if they are sports stars. But homelessness is one of the world's greatest problems and for many people, like these players and spectators, it is never far away. At any moment, millions of people could find themselves homeless for millions of reasons. Just a few metres away from this stadium, thousands of people are struggling to survive on the streets.

Homelessness destroys the lives of millions of people all over the world. And it haunts everyone who witnesses the horror for themselves. Sometimes, you see the horror in the streets – people begging or queuing for food. But closer up, you also see the horror in their eyes. They feel despair and often become suicidal. They have lost everything including self-respect. They have no friends or family. They're excluded from society, with nowhere to live and nothing to eat, and no access to health care. Sometimes they are stripped of their identity – as if they don't even exist.

The horror is something you can never forget. The homeless people living on a dump in Nairobi who work all day sorting out rubbish to earn enough to buy a scrap of bread. The abandoned children living in the sewers of St Petersburg who try to keep warm at night hugging the pipes from the buildings above. The endless lines of homeless people queuing round the block in San Francisco for a small bowl of soup, in a country better known for over-eating. Women who are driven from their homes because they have been raped by soldiers during civil war. Orphans abandoned on the streets of our cities who soon become recruited by criminal gangs.

Sometimes, homelessness is also a nightmare – the nameless bodies lying in a morgue after a police raid to remove homeless people from the centre of one of the world's greatest cities, people dying of hunger and cold in the same streets where millionaires shop for their luxury goods, not even seeing what is happening in front of their eyes, not aware of all the desperate people killing themselves or accidentally overdosing on drugs, only metres away. In every society, wealthy or poor, homelessness can often equal hopelessness. But together we can put an end to it once and for all, by deciding to act.

* * * * *

Faced with statistics like a 100 million people and this terrible waste of resources, most people's reaction is anger – sometimes even rage.

Most people usually ask the same questions. Why is homelessness such a huge problem? How did this tragedy happen? Why did we allow it to get so bad? What is the government doing about it? Why don't the big corporations do something about it?

Sometimes, I think the problem is that homelessness has never become a political issue in the same way as taxes or pensions or schools. There are no votes to win from people who are probably not even registered to vote in the first place because they have no address or identity.

In many countries, homeless people are officially 'invisible'. In Mexico, for instance, hundreds of thousands of people have no access to important public services like health care. They are known as 'the people who do not exist'. And if they don't exist, who will look after their interests?

The simple fact is that instead of arguing about the social, economic and political causes of homelessness, and blaming other people, governments and business, all of us should take responsibility for homelessness. After all, we have created the problem, and only we have the power to solve it.

*****

In the heart of this darkness, there are signs of light. Around the world, there are a lot of innovative organisations, including social enterprises, committed to tackling the homelessness problem. There are also many caring individuals who recognise that they have the power to make a real difference – even if it's only helping one single person, or volunteering one day a month or donating a couple of dollars. Some individuals even give millions of dollars to homelessness causes.

Governments, charities and religious organisations used to be the primary providers of support to the homeless (setting up soup kitchens, shelters, etc.), but that traditional approach did not succeed in getting people off the streets and into employment and housing. We needed a more innovative approach, one that would address the problem and transform attitudes to homeless people, not just among the general public but also governments and large corporations, the media and anyone who wielded any influence. We needed to make homeless people the centre of every solution, motivating them to reintegrate into society and create positive change in their own lives. We needed to empower the most powerless people on Earth.

In the 1990s, street papers rose to the challenge. The idea was to create a highly readable paper for homeless people to sell on the streets. In the process, they would not just earn some money but also boost their self-esteem and engage with the community around them. The ultimate objective was to find themselves somewhere to live and a job, and the philosophy behind it was 'a hand-up not a hand-out.'

In 1995, these publications joined forces to create a new organisation called the International Network of Street Papers (INSP). A movement was beginning to gather momentum. Then at a meeting of the INSP in 2001, the 'crazy idea' of the Homeless World Cup was conceived...

* * * * *

To illustrate what homelessness is all about, I usually discuss what it is like to be the poorest of the poor in the world's richest country – and compare it with what it is like to be homeless in one of the poorest.

Whether it's the USA or India, South Korea or Ghana, Nigeria, Poland or Spain, homelessness destroys the lives of millions of people all over the world.

What makes the difference in the USA and many other countries is when someone does something about it, instead of just talking about it. And Lawrence Cann, the President and founder of Street Soccer USA (SSUSA), is one of the people who does more than most.

When Lawrence and his brother Rob (now Chief Operating Officer of SSUSA) were children, they found out the tough way what it meant to be homeless when their home burned down, destroying all their family possessions. But the Cann brothers knew even then they were lucky compared to many other people suddenly finding themselves in the street. 'We lost everything,' says Lawrence, 'but it wasn't a big deal because we were able to move in with our grandparents.'

Soccer has also played a major role in the lives of the brothers since they were children, and when Lawrence got involved with a homelessness project in Charlotte, North Carolina, while he was a student, he quickly realised how sport – and particularly soccer – could create social change. After he graduated, Lawrence worked in a soup kitchen, but he believed that – more than anything – soccer could make a real difference by 'changing the context' of homeless people's lives, getting them involved in serious training and learning how to be part of a team, sharing the same hopes and targets.

Lawrence founded SSUSA in Charlotte in 2004, and it 'snowballed from there' and soon became the pilot for a nationwide street soccer programme sending teams to the Homeless World Cup.

Within ten years, the 'sports for social change' organisation has grown from one project to a 16-city nationwide league. In Greater Charlotte, it has reached out to more than 20 per cent of the 'chronically homeless' and achieved a 75 per cent success rate – e.g. positive changes such as addressing a substance abuse problem or mental health issue, securing full-time employment or moving off the street.

According to Lawrence, the sense of belonging, mentorship and structure that SSUSA provides is the difference between people hanging around on the street and successfully re-integrating into society. As a core part of its programme to incentivise players, SSUSA has sent a team to the Homeless World Cup since 2005 and organises the annual Street Soccer USA Cup. As well as SSUSA teams, over 50 business and community teams play in an 'open' tournament at the annual event, which is held in high-profile, iconic locations including Times Square in New York. The national network includes 25 Sport for Development programmes based in social service agencies across the country serving homeless youths and adults. These programmes aim 'to transform the context in which participants live from one of isolation and marginalisation to one of support and encouragement.' And the driving force behind it all is soccer because it is an easy sport to organise and also inclusive in terms of physical ability and skills, as well as very scalable at local and national level.

SSUSA emphasises the evidence-based approach to its projects and has conducted studies right from the beginning, to measure the difference it makes in peoples' lives and under-served communities, including homeless families and people in recovery. And according to Lawrence, more than 90 per cent of the thousands of players who take part in the street soccer programmes have positive outcomes in terms of self-esteem, emotional self-regulation, increased social networking, the ability to trust others, and mental/physical health.

Seventy-five per cent of the people involved in the programmes get jobs, move into housing, complete a rehabilitation programme or further their education within a year of joining the programme. The philosophy promoted by the network means that every player plays for 'more than winning or losing.' Everyone is encouraged to play to better themselves, to better their community, and better the world.

Lawrence also stresses that the organisation does not expect instant success. It's important to recognise all individuals are different. Some players drop out of the programmes, but many of them also return later on. It can take a year before players show signs of progress, and SSUSA wants 'sustained change' for its players, not only short-term results. And partnership is key to how it works in every city.

Many cities in the USA have different policies for homeless people, and New York is one of the most progressive, believing shelter is a basic human right. The authorities also provide homeless people with shelter designed to meet their needs at different stages, starting when they come in off the streets for initial assessment and ending when they're ready to live in their own home. Different shelters have different 'rules' and conditions, and this provides 'incentives' for people who see they can 'move up the ladder' and helps avoid too many people becoming dependent. Lawrence thinks rapid rehousing is a good idea for families but it is also very costly and can be a 'revolving door' for people who don't suit the system.

Even though New York may be successful in addressing the homelessness issue, its approach may not be suitable for other US cities, says Lawrence. Similarly, many countries have successful policies which may not translate to other countries.

Self-empowerment is also important to SSUSA. Its mission is to improve health, education and employment outcomes for the most disadvantaged people in society by using sports to transfer the skills they need to achieve these outcomes for themselves. It also seeks to raise awareness about the challenges of poverty in the USA and celebrate the talents and abilities of homeless people, to change stereotypes and misconceptions among the general public, using different media such as film and social media.

Over the last few years, homelessness and social exclusion have become much worse in many US cities, with many families affected as well as the 'chronically homeless'. In New York, for example, an estimated 50,000 people are involved in homeless programmes, including 20,000 under-age children. Like everywhere else, homelessness is a symptom of a breakdown in society.

The economics of homelessness are also a major concern. It costs a lot to get one homeless person off the street, but according to Lawrence, the key is prevention. 'I'm a big supporter of public policy,' he says, 'but it takes a long time to work and we need other lower-cost, longer-term grass-roots solutions, including sports for social change. We focus on community sport and the young, because they are our future.' Lawrence has always loved soccer, but homelessness is something he refuses to accept, and that is what drove him to set up the organisation, and prove that soccer can get homeless people off the streets. 'Some people felt we shouldn't make it too comfortable for homeless people or they'll have no incentive to move on to build lives of their own. But homelessness isn't comfortable no matter how you slice it. The goal isn't to have happier homeless people. It's to have fewer of them.'

Lawrence still remembers what it feels like to be homeless – and what it means to be poor. At age 19, while still at college, he worked as a translator at a hospital in Enongal in Cameroon. 'I saw poverty there that was worse than anything I had ever seen in my life, and it changed me,' he says. 'You can read about poverty all you want and think you get it, but after you see it around you in real life, it makes you want to help.'

* * * * *

Not everyone is chosen to play for their country at the Homeless World Cup, but the players who do play are not always the most obvious candidates. 'We have old guys who stink – their soccer ability ranges from zero to excellent,' said Lawrence when he went to his first Homeless World Cup in Scotland in 2005. But what distinguishes them all is 'a desire to move forward from homelessness. If there's a hunger for change,' he explained, 'we can help them beat the homeless time horizon, where they are just living day-to-day.'

As part of the programme, social workers work with every player to set individual objectives – for example, lose weight or quit smoking, or learn about nutrition. For team members still recovering from drug or alcohol addiction, any relapse means suspension from the team. It's a powerful incentive, says Lawrence.

* * * * *

Nineteen of the first 23 US players who went to the Homeless World Cup were no longer homeless immediately after, and Lawrence estimates that at least three-quarters of the players in the league at any given time eventually get off the street – men like Zenas Fuell, who wanted so badly to get into the team that he agreed to do a psychiatric test first. Eventually, Zenas was able to move off the street and got a job at a pizza parlour. 'Does he still play?' I ask. 'No,' replies Lawrence. 'He's no longer homeless.'

Ray Isaac was one of the stars of the 2005 USA team in Scotland, and now works as an outreach worker at Street Soccer USA. Lawrence feels a special sense of kinship with Ray – like Lawrence, his home burned down when he was younger. Ray hasn't looked back since joining the programme. 'I thought that it was off the wall I made the team,' he tells me. 'Suddenly, I found myself going to Scotland, kicking a soccer ball, and all my problems didn't seem like problems any more.' 'I'm convinced that homeless soccer is one of the most cost-effective ways to create social change,' says Lawrence. 'People wonder why we're teaching homeless people to kick a soccer ball.

Our goal is not to have happier homeless people. It's to restore their human status and change their expectations of themselves.'

* * * * *

It's not so long ago the USA was bombing Cambodia during the Vietnam War, but nowadays the countries are at peace. The USA is still the world's most powerful country, and Cambodia is one of the poorest, but when it comes to homelessness, both countries have more in common than people may think – and both teams play a big part in the Homeless World Cup every year.

As I move around from stadium to stadium on Day One in Mexico City, I meet Paraic Grogan, an Irishman now living in Australia who has managed the Cambodia team since the Homeless World Cup in Melbourne in 2008.

Paraic tells me all about the players who have come this year, including Chan 'Ton' Sophondara, 'the smallest player with the biggest heart', who is already emerging as one of the stars of the tournament, after only a couple of games. 'He's taking on players that are six foot high and just going for it,' says Paraic, who first went to Cambodia nine years ago and fell in love with it right from the very first moment. But Paraic was also so moved by all the poverty he witnessed that he helped set up the 'Happy School' which now provides some of the players for the Homeless World Cup, in partnership with other well-known charities in the capital city, Phnom Penh. Two years later, in 2005, Paraic went back to Cambodia to set up Happy Football Cambodia Australia, and the team made its début in the Homeless World Cup in Melbourne in 2008. There are about 100 young people enrolled in the programme at any one time, all of whom are signed-up with one of the partners. Next year, the programme hopes to take in 60 more participants, but 'everything depends on the funding,' says Paraic.

According to Paraic, the aims of Happy Football Cambodia are simple – to give disadvantaged children and young homeless people in Phnom Penh and beyond 'the opportunity to play the beautiful game in a safe environment.' Many young people slip through the cracks, he explains: 'They are among the 10,000 street children who make their living scouring the rubbish dumps for plastic to sell, or the many young people who beg or steal or even prostitute themselves, just to survive another day.'

I've always wondered how Paraic managed to set up the organisation and why he thought of using soccer as a platform, so closely in tune with the aims of the Homeless World Cup. 'When I first went to Cambodia,' says Paraic, 'I noticed the kids playing football, but I also noticed there were not many places to play – at that time there were only ten football pitches to play on, which cost about ten US dollars per hour, in a city where most people earn just a dollar a day.'

When Paraic moved back to Australia and found out that Melbourne was to be the host city for the Homeless World Cup in 2008, he saw the opportunity to take the players into an entirely new league – an international tournament, playing in front of tens of thousands of supporters, and the global media.

That first taste of the Homeless World Cup in 2008 was the 'journey of a lifetime' for the five young Cambodian players and two support staff who made it to Melbourne. Most of the players had never been on a plane, train or tram before, and suddenly they are on 'live' television, representing their country at soccer.

The team won a couple of games, beating Sweden and Sierra Leone, but according to Paraic, what mattered most was the experience. 'For the first time in their lives,' Paraic wrote at the time, 'these players were not just poor street kids from Phnom Penh, they were heroes wearing the Cambodia jersey with pride. For two weeks they were professional footballers, and their only concern was training and getting their picture taken by fans.'

When they went back to Cambodia, the impact of the tournament was analysed in a report which concluded: 'After attending the Homeless World Cup, we noticed a change in the children. They were so happy, proud and much more confident. They became the leaders of the kids in their community and organised football matches with their friends in the slum. They had such a positive attitude and that influenced other children as well. They had pride in themselves and in their country, and that is something that we very much want to encourage.' Another report said: 'The children are trying hard to learn more, to live independently, to share their ideas and what they learned from the culture of the Homeless World Cup. They have gained more creative ideas in sharing and helping younger children to do all the right things and change their behaviour. They teach the younger children about discipline and how to play football and team work while competing with other teams.'

*****

One of the Cambodian players who starred in Australia, Sam Yi, has since gone on to be a coach at Happy Football Cambodia, and has signed a two-year contact with a leading Cambodian Premier League team. In Melbourne, however, no-one imagined that Sam would emerge as a leader – he was so shy and quiet. 'Like many players, he was slightly overwhelmed by the experience,' Paraic explains. 'The other players teased him and one day he burst into tears, but as the tournament went on, he gained in confidence, embraced the whole experience and ended up one of the stars of the team.'

According to Paraic, a film producer following the progress of the players in Melbourne told him that Sam was so quiet, the documentary about the team would be 'a silent movie' but a few years later, Paraic almost fell over in shock when the young man made a fluent and articulate speech to an audience of businessmen in Phnom Penh. 'Despite that speech, he's still quite shy and quiet,' Paraic tells me, 'but he knows that to be a coach, sometimes you have to speak up to be heard.'

At one time, Sam almost lost his job as coach because he didn't speak to the players enough. 'If you don't start talking, Sam, you're out in six months,' he was told. But today he is earning good money, as a semi-professional player and coach. 'He leads by example,' says Paraic. 'He realised he had to change his ways and become more aggressive to win the respect of the players, without going over the top, and now he's made the most of it and has a new career.' In fact, he has progressed so much he's managed to negotiate an increase in his salary, more than doubling his earnings to over 12 dollars a week, in addition to his income (about US$120 a month) as a player – a huge step up from earning a dollar a day just a short time ago.

* * * * *

After Melbourne, team Cambodia went to Milan, where they were coached by Jimmy Campbell, a businessman now resident in Phnom Penh who once had a trial for top Scottish team Celtic. That same year, one of the players, Chan Rithy, emerged as a coach of the future, under the guidance of Jimmy and Vibol Chao, the country manager since 2006.

Rithy's job as a coach hasn't always been easy, however. Paraic describes how he was once told by another coach that Rithy had been showing a 'bad attitude' at training, and was asked to have a word with him to find out the problem. Like all the other coaches, Rithy has to turn up on time and work hard for his money, but when Paraic approached him, expecting he would have to play the role of the 'bad cop', he saw at once something was wrong. 'My father died yesterday,' Rithy explained. He'd fallen from the scaffold at a building site, at just 41 years of age, leaving his family nothing. Overnight, Rithy had become the head of the household and its main source of income, earning a few bucks a week as a coach, and Paraic was amazed he'd even turned up at work that day.

When Paraic went to Rithy's home before the funeral, he realised how poor the family was, living in a shack beside the river, with no running water or power. But all day, even though they were in mourning, they went out of their way to make Paraic feel welcome. He may have spent several years in Cambodia, but Paraic was still treated as a guest of the country.

Since then, Rithy has continued to work as a coach and managed to complete a university degree in business studies. And now his brother Sophondara follows in his footsteps three years later, with another younger brother in the wings who the coaches believe has the potential to be best of the bunch.

* * * * *

Watching Sophondara play in Mexico City today, it is easy to agree with his manager, Paraic. He's very quick and skilful and is agile enough to compete with players stronger and bigger than him. Most importantly, he plays without any fear. He is an inspiration, on and off the field. After starting most games on the subs bench, he has quickly become the first name on the team sheet.

For Sophondara and his team-mates, being at the Homeless World Cup will be an unforgettable experience which will hopefully transform their lives. It is also a personal challenge. They are light years away from the world that they know, and this is the first time they have been in the media spotlight, watched by so many people. They deserve all the cheers that they get.

Life back in Phnom Penh is very different. Sophondara lives in a shanty-town shack with his brothers, and their mother has been under huge financial pressure since their father died three years ago.

To help the family survive, Sophondara and Rithy get up at three in the morning to help their mother set up her stall. At six o'clock, they go back to bed for a short while before getting up again later for school or for work.

Rithy's continued involvement as one of the coaches reflects the 'holistic approach' of the programme, as Paraic explains: 'Sam and Rithy have both made the most of their chances. We're trying to invest in these guys and skill them up – we want them to be role models as well as players and coaches. There's a much bigger picture.'

The emergence of players as coaches employed by our national partners is a phenomenon that none of us anticipated when we first set up the Homeless World Cup, but Paraic's words echo the experience of many other countries: 'It's an organic process we never expected to happen,' he says. 'The average kid in Cambodia has no idea what the outside world is like, so when the players go back and tell all the new kids their story, it's truly inspiring. And when they go on to be coaches, the young players listen.'

* * * * *

The stories of Street Soccer USA and Happy Football Cambodia Australia may have started on opposite sides of the planet, but every year the two teams come together at the Homeless World Cup and every year, a new generation of players and coaches emerges. Becoming homeless in the USA or many other Western countries may not seem as tough as being orphaned and abandoned as a child in Cambodia, where there's no form of welfare for people in need of support, but in reality, there are a lot of parallels – they are all among the poorest of the poor in their society and all deserve an opportunity to change their lives and shine at an event like the Homeless World Cup.

* * * * *

My own experience with homelessness dates back to Edinburgh in the late 1970s, when I first became involved in community papers. In 1993, I co-founded *The Big Issue in Scotland* – the first time people told me I was crazy – in partnership with Tricia Hughes, inspired by the example of the original *Big Issue* set up by John Bird in London. The basic idea was to produce a professional paper which homeless people would sell on the streets, like any other publication. The vendors would keep most of the cover price, thus earning some money and reducing their dependence on charity. It was more than an alternative to begging, however. In the process of selling the paper, the vendors would be out there, engaging with people and boosting their own self-esteem. As they gained more confidence, they would then begin to re-integrate, and eventually find themselves somewhere to live and a job. The first edition – 25,000 copies – was a sell-out, and sales later peaked at 140,000, but along the way we faced a lot of challenges and media hostility. One local paper was particularly negative about homeless people, regarding them as garbage that messed up the streets and kept tourists away. One day, it published a front-page 'exclusive' which targeted an individual vendor, calling him a 'con man' because they had followed him 'home' and believed he was not in fact technically 'homeless', even though we knew that he was 'vulnerably accommodated' (in other words, he could have become homeless at any time because he had so many other issues to deal with). The character assassination shocked us all and made the man feel terrible because he thought he had let everyone down, but it was hard to defend ourselves against such a powerful media organisation.

This was a turning point, however, in the history of the *Big Issue in Scotland*. We met the vendors to discuss how to respond, if they faced any public attack, and decided to turn things around in a positive way. And the outcome was the next edition sold out the next day as soon as it hit the streets. We had won our first battle together.

This was a low point in relations with the media in Scotland, and one well-known journalist even complained that he had to 'climb over the homeless to enter his club'. Another asked: 'Why don't the homeless go home?' But in many countries, many homeless people have been murdered, so a couple of media cynics are not a big issue.

* * * * *

At about the same time as we launched *The Big Issue in Scotland*, several other street papers sprang up around the UK and the rest of the world, based on a similar formula. And in 1995, we formed the International Network of Street Papers (INSP). By 2005, this had grown from 16 to 42 papers, with a combined circulation of 25 million and thousands of homeless people earning a living through sales.

Later on, as President of the INSP, I tried to focus on the issues that united the organisation, rather than let any differences tear us apart. Some members were leftist and others leaned more to the right or were deeply religious. But we never lost sight of the fact we are stronger together and ultimately share the same objectives, and this in turn strengthened the Homeless World Cup as it started to get off the ground – we wanted homeless people at the centre of what we were doing, whether they were on the streets selling their papers or representing their country at soccer.

* * * * *

Many years later, here we are in Mexico City, as homeless people reclaim the streets of the city. Homelessness is still a major problem but we're starting to gather support from the people who matter, including the general public.

A few minutes after my meeting with Paraic, I bump into one of our Mexican hosts, who takes me to see all the trophies they've made, and the medals we present to every player every year. As I gaze upon the glittering trophies, I realise how simple the original Homeless World Cup seems compared to these magnificent creations, commissioned by Telmex, our new global partners. Then I realise how much I treasure the original trophy, even though it is battered and bruised after almost ten years on the road. In 2003, we asked some homeless people in Glasgow to design the first trophy, with help from an artist. It's made of scrap materials sprayed with metallic grey paint, but I have always loved it, not only because it's a symbol of what we've achieved since 2003 but because it was made in the streets by the people who live there and know what it's like to be homeless. And the trophy will always belong to all the homeless people in the world.

When it was being presented in Paris in 2011, one of the players cut his hand on the edge of the trophy, and held it up in triumph, smeared with blood. Several times, people suggested we get a new trophy, but it's hard to imagine replacing the Homeless World Cup, even if does get smeared with more blood in the future.

My dream, however, is when nobody plays for the trophy, when the 'one homeless person too many' is no longer homeless – no longer a shameful statistic.

3

Homeless to Heroes

Q: What about the impact of the Homeless World Cup?
A: It's all about the players. Does a million people sound like a lot?

Sunday, 7 October 2012: This morning is a relatively quiet day for media, after the intensity of the opening day, but soon after breakfast I meet a reporter from Chile whose home town Santiago will be hosting the tournament two years from now. Fernando also shows up in the media tent with his oversized brown-leather notebook, but now that the first day is over and everything seems to be going OK, I am feeling much more energetic and happy to discuss whatever anybody wishes.

'What kind of impact do you have in economic terms?' Fernando asks.

'Homelessness not only wastes lives but money,' I tell him. 'In New York, for example, it costs $40,000 a year for every homeless person living in the street, adding up the costs of services like health-care, police and social workers, etc. In England, it costs about $30,000 a year. So, if we get 1,000 players off the street, we save tens of millions of dollars – and that's just the tip of the iceberg. The total cost of homelessness around the world is billions of dollars a year, no matter how you add it up. Add on 100 million opportunities lost, not only for homeless people themselves but the society to which they could be making a real contribution, and the end result is hard to imagine.'

* * * * *

The economics are important but the most important aspect of the Homeless World Cup is the impact it can have on individuals – in social, psychological and also physical terms. Nothing matters more than helping people get the opportunity to change and feel that they are part of the community.

The impact on the media and general public is also important, but above all, I love to see players go back to their countries to become the next generation of leaders, or just go back to school, and make up with their loved ones, friends and families. Thousands of players take part every year, and change their lives as a result. Research by independent academics* has found that nearly 80 per cent of the players significantly change their lives – kicking drug or alcohol problems, finding employment and somewhere to live.

From 2003-2008, we polled players after the tournament and came up with the following statistics:

- More than 90% of players polled reported a 'new motivation for life'.
- About 85% improved their housing situation.
- About 75% 'significantly changed their lives' by finding regular employment or opting to develop their education.
- Of those with drug or alcohol problems, over 50% had success in addressing their dependency.
- Many players have also gone on to become professional or semi-professional coaches or players.

Initially, we found it very hard to believe the results. But as the years went by, a pattern began to emerge and the impact was consistent in virtually every respect.

The impact on the players goes beyond the statistics, however, and lasts long after the tournament reaches its climax. The players go back to their homelands as heroes – living proof of the transformational power of soccer. They return to society as change-makers and role models. They inspire other people to transform their lives, and influence public opinion on homelessness and poverty issues. Many of the leaders of our national programmes were homeless at one time, or first came into contact with the organisation as players.

The transformation starts as soon as the first ball is kicked but as the players suddenly find themselves treated as sports stars by thousands of fans, it is easy to forget about the journey they have taken to arrive at this magical moment – and the journey that still lies ahead.

* * * * *

The Homeless World Cup also has an impact on society at large by changing attitudes to homelessness and homeless people (for example, negative stereotypes), especially in cities where the tournament is held.

The impact also goes beyond the tournament itself. In addition to the 'headline' data and individual examples, it can also be measured in terms of the number of successful social enterprise programmes run by our national partners. In Western countries, most of our partners focus on inclusion

– finding somewhere to live, addressing drug or alcohol dependency, education or employment. In developing countries, the focus is on job creation, education and community building.

In every country, the initial steps are similar, however – and very simple. For example, in the Netherlands, the Life Goals Foundation talks to homeless people in the streets or a shelter and asks if they want to play soccer. The players then begin to talk about their personal issues and work out individual solutions.

In Sweden, Gatans Lag has focused on addiction. The Sweden coach in Mexico City is Keijo Orava, who knows what it's like to be homeless – he's a former player who once had a problem with drugs and now helps other people with similar problems. Our partner in Russia, New Social Solutions, organises tournaments for homeless people and drug and alcohol addicts. Another key objective is engagement with the media so they will not ignore homelessness issues or describe them in negative terms. Our Russian friends express very clearly the spirit of the Homeless World Cup:

> Football is extremely effective at integrating excluded groups back into society. Taking part is not just good for keeping fit and leading a healthier lifestyle. It is an opportunity to work systematically, as part of a team. In the process one establishes new social contacts and a more positive outlook on life.

Street Soccer Scotland was founded in March 2009, 'inspired by personal experience of the power of sport and football to create real change and a desire to provide a unique response to the social disadvantage prevalent in Scottish society'. The organisation soon began providing weekly drop-in street soccer sessions in Edinburgh, and started growing from there, engaging over 4,000 people in regular sessions. 'We use street soccer as a trigger to energise people who are socially excluded, combined with personal development and training to empower them to change their own lives for the better.'

Our partner in Greece is Diogenes NGO, named after Diogenes of Sinope, the ancient Greek philosopher who found himself homeless. The Athens-based organisation focuses on homeless people, poverty and substance abuse, as well as asylum seekers and illegal immigrants. It organises soccer-based activities as well as cultural events and actively pursues 'social inclusion for all' in a country suffering from chronic social and economic problems.

In South Africa, the focus is on schools and job creation, and our partner there works with the government and business corporations to find employment opportunities for homeless and excluded people taking part in their soccer-based activities. South Africa Homeless Street Soccer also works closely with schools, using soccer to encourage the students to stay on at school, and reaches out to street youth in partnership with another organisation called Oasis (Reach For Your Dreams).

In Uganda, Girls Kick It works with marginalised women, using football to bring them together to develop a sense of community and simply meet other women like themselves, as well as become more economically independent or continue education.

In Indonesia, Rumah Cemara use soccer to overcome discrimination towards people living with HIV/AIDS and engage both HIV-positive and HIV-negative players.

The scope of all these very different national programmes never ceases to amaze me, but the best way to appreciate the impact is to listen to the stories of the individual players themselves...

* * * * *

It's 10.00am and getting close to 30 centigrade already, and as I walk towards the players' tent, I see Lukes Mjoka, and smile because his smile is irresistible and seems to light up everything around him.

He may be smiling now, but Lukes had a tough start in life. He was born in Cape Town, one of six children with three different fathers, and when he was just four years old, his mother 'dumped' him with his granny. Instead of going to school like the other kids, when he was six, Lukes had to work in his grandmother's shop, and when he was seven, he ran away from home to 'look for a new life in Cape Town', sleeping rough in the streets.

Soon after, in a train station, two men approached Lukes and took him off to teach him how to beg. At first, this new life didn't seem too bad to Lukes – it was better than working for granny. 'They said that I could work with them, going to houses to ask for some food. Some people feel bad about begging but for me it was something for nothing, some small change for bread. I could do what I wanted. I was living the life I deserved.'

The guys who had befriended Lukes then taught him how to break into cars. When the older boys broke the side windows, Lukes was small enough to squeeze through and steal whatever he could find inside the car, including radios. The older boys also told Lukes they would protect him. And soon they also introduced the young boy to drugs – sniffing glue. 'It was interesting, something I'd not done before. Begging all night in the streets, maybe wearing only a tee shirt, you get very cold, and sniffing glue made me feel better.'

At eight years old, Lukes wanted to 'fit into a group and forget' about everything and everyone else. Living on the streets, sleeping under a bridge – he thought this was a better life than anything he'd ever had at home. 'On the streets, we're like a family. It's more comfortable.' He thought this was his future, begging and stealing to get enough money for drugs. 'It was an easy life. I never found it challenging.'

After eight or nine months living on the streets, he went to live in a children's home called The Homestead. Kids heading back from school had told him that this would be better than life on the streets, but at first he was reluctant. 'For me, it just wasn't a choice,' he explains. 'The children's home was not the solution for me. On the streets, I could get things for free!'

The young boy's dreams of being a success in life were shattered, and he had no hope of being part of 'normal' society. But gradually Lukes was persuaded to give the children's home a try, and as soon as he went through the door, he felt welcome – and also started going to school in the morning. 'I realised the importance of going to school. It showed me the reality of life, and taught me if I carried on living the way that I had done, I'd end up in jail or be killed. It opened my eyes and gave me something to look forward to in life, mixing with positive people, learning how to keep away from negative people.'

Life was getting better all the time – until his aunt arrived. She had been looking for Lukes all over the city, showing people his photo, but when she took him away from The Homestead, he cried because he didn't want to leave the place and go back to the life he'd had before, sitting around playing cards or helping in the family shop. 'From the very first minute, I decided to leave. So I slept there that night and the next morning, ran off again. And they understood this time that I didn't want to go home – my home was The Homestead.'

When he left the children's home at 18 years old, after finishing school, Lukes went to live with his brothers, including one who'd spent seven years in prison. Soon after this, his mother died, but Lukes says that he never saw her death as a loss because he didn't really know her at all as a child.

Life also didn't work out with his brothers, because of the pressure of six people living together in only two rooms. They had not grown up together and started to fight. 'My brother was meant to be my role model,' says Lukes, 'but I couldn't depend on him any more.'

Some friends showed Lukes how to 'make an easy living', robbing people, breaking into houses. 'We didn't care if people died or not,' he confesses, 'as long as we got all their money.'

Lukes also wanted to prove himself as a man, and please his sisters by bringing some bread to the table. So he started selling drugs again – this time crystal meth.

Dragged into a life of crime and violence, Lukes started drinking heavily as well as taking drugs. 'The drinking turned into girls, from girls we turned to guns, and from guns we turned to robbery,' he tells me.

His new family was the neighbourhood gang, and they used to meet at his place to count all their money – the other guys had parents who would not approve of what they were doing. 'But I got too deep into the negative living by being in the gang and I couldn't see any way out. That's when I decided to become a Drug Lord, getting my own stock and running my own operation.'

For three years, Lukes was dealing drugs and also becoming a regular user. Through all this time, he managed to avoid any criminal charges – he would bribe the police and some of them were customers.

Lukes says this was the 'easiest life' he could have. He was 'successful', had a motorbike and even employed other people. Today, he jests that he was an 'entrepreneur', but there's an element of truth in that – running his illegal 'business' sharpened his management skills.

Then something happened that would change his life forever: The Homeless World Cup.

The road to Rio was not a smooth ride, however. In 2010, Lukes was caught with four kilos of crystal meth. The police confiscated the drugs and drove him back to Khayelitsha, where one of his close friends – who had also been involved with drugs and violence – was killed in a shooting. This made him realise he had to leave his old life behind, and Lukes believes God saved his life when he made the decision to change.

Soon afterwards, he bumped into a childhood friend who had played in the Homeless World Cup in Milan in 2009. His friend persuaded Lukes to go to the trials for the next Homeless World Cup in Rio the following year, telling him that playing soccer could be the break that he needed.

Even though he now had a part-time job in a restaurant, and was still using drugs, Lukes qualified as a player because he had been living on the streets during the last two years. 'I had been looking for that one big opportunity to change my life, and soccer was the key, the motivation.'

Lukes went along to the trials at the same time the FIFA World Cup was being held in South Africa in 2010, and was one of the players selected to attend a three-week training camp, to prepare for the next Homeless World Cup in Rio, later that year. For the first time in years, Lukes completely quit drugs, and along with all the other players started learning life skills and all about drugs and HIV/AIDS. 'Is that the life I want to lead?' he asked himself. 'Taking drugs all the time?'

Then Lukes was selected as captain. 'That lifted my confidence. Being part of the team was a big privilege and to play in the Homeless World Cup was an honour for me.'

Next stop was Rio de Janeiro: 'Going to Brazil really opened my head up! I learned that everything is possible. It's up to individuals to change their own lives. You can't go around blaming others, and you have to stay away from negativity. It's up to me to point the finger at myself, not other people.'

Lukes also made a lot of friends in Rio, including Pupo Fernandes, the manager of the Brazil team. 'I lived in a cloud for 11 days in Brazil and really enjoyed being able to communicate with different people from different countries – sometimes just with body language. That alone was a life-changing experience.'

Meeting so many people with a similar background was also important. 'One of the things that I learned from the Homeless World Cup was that my problems are not the biggest,' he says. 'One guy from India told me all about what life was like for him there, and I started crying, even though my own life was like his. And he said, 'Don't cry! It's just how it is.' I will always remember that moment.'

Before Lukes went home, he asked Pupo if he could move to Brazil and work with him, because he was in love with the country and saw the impact he could make in people's lives. 'Mr Cliffy' (Clifford Martinus), the director of South Africa Homeless Street Soccer (SAHSS), knew what Lukes was thinking and told him he would help him to achieve his dream – as long as Lukes kept his side of the bargain. 'When the tournament ended, I saw this as a stepping stone, and decided to make the commitment – go back and change my life. The only way out was to stop taking drugs. I spoke to Mr Cliffy and I told him I was definitely not going to disappoint anyone, especially him, and also didn't want to disappoint myself.'

Back in South Africa, Lukes knew it was entirely up to him what happened next, so after Cliffy helped him find somewhere to live, he started teaching life skills and was chosen as a coach for the South Africa team heading to the Homeless World Cup in Paris in 2011. 'The organisation has been a pillar of strength for me all along. I was trying to be on my best behaviour to see my life change, using my past experience to give back to the community. Working as a coach has made my relationships stronger and made it possible for me to achieve my dreams.'

Lukes also continued to dream of Brazil. 'My goal was to be there. I didn't want to wait for it to happen but tried to empower myself so that when it eventually happened, I would be ready.'

In Paris, Lukes met up with Pupo again. 'He could see the progress I was making,' says Lukes. 'I was giving something back to the community, to youth, to kids the same as I was just a short time ago.' Then, the next year, in Mexico City, Pupo made arrangements for Lukes to go to Brazil, and a few months later, Cliffy bought him a ticket and Lukes flew to Rio.

Lukes started coaching in schools in Sao Paulo and helping out Pupo. He also got his dream job as a chef. 'I'm happy I'm living my dream,' Lukes said later. 'The Homeless World Cup opened the door to success and gave me a once-in-a-lifetime opportunity to make a change in my life and be part of something positive. Thanks to Mr Cliffy, my life will never be the same again.'

Soccer to some people may look like 'kicking a ball around', but for people like Lukes it means something much more than sport. When he was trying to kick drugs and also quit smoking, he would pick up a ball and kick it and kick it until he was so tired, he did not want to smoke any more. 'I was so in love with soccer, and that's how I've been able to develop myself, and why I am employed today and work as a coach.'

Looking ahead, Lukes can see himself being involved in the street soccer programme for years. 'My wish is to see other people who play in the Homeless World Cup encourage others to have hope in their lives. I want to be an example to others and show them there really is hope. A ball really can change the world.'

Later, Lukes moved on to do community development and grass-roots coaching, teaching kids from disadvantaged communities for an organisation set up by Cliffy. 'My future plan is to coordinate a programme that will run across two of the world's greatest countries – Brazil and South Africa. It will be an exchange programme where guys who have played in the Homeless World Cup will live in each other's country for a few months, sharing their experience and giving something back to the community. I want to give hope to the hopeless.'

* * * * *

They say that if you want to change the world, start with yourself and the rest of the world will soon follow. And time and time again I have witnessed how players have managed to transform their own lives and then change other people's lives, as if there is some kind of exponential effect.

For example, one of the players Lukes works with is Glandel Robain, who played in goal for South Africa and carried the national flag at the opening ceremony of the Homeless World Cup in Poznan the following year.

For eight years, Glandel didn't have a job and spent most of his time on the street, taking drugs and robbing tourists. Every day he woke up thinking, 'I have got to get a tourist, I have to got to get someone.' When he did get money, he would give some to his wife (who had been diagnosed with cancer in 2007) to feed her and their children, but he couldn't stay with them because there was never enough for them all. The street became his home. 'I would go back with money,' says Glandel, 'then go away again for four or five months, back to the street.'

Glandel had always loved soccer and one day he went to a soccer event organised by Oasis. 'Cliffy saw potential in my goalkeeping,' Glandel explained. 'When he and Oasis came into my life, I became a different person – changed my whole way of thinking.' But even though he was clean (not taking drugs), his wife and children didn't believe him.

When Glandel was selected to play for his country, he tried to tell his wife that he'd been chosen for the team and that he wasn't telling lies – he had been training for the last two months and was checked every week to make sure he was clean. But his wife still wouldn't listen.

Eventually, his wife got in touch with Oasis to check out his story, and came to the airport with all of their children to see the team off. 'I never thought I'd reach such a point in my life,' says Glandel. 'And I promised to bring a ball back for my kids.'

According to Glandel, 'Cliffy gave me all these very positive messages and I knew when I went home that the door would be open.'

Later, Glandel's wife had a successful operation and underwent a course of chemotherapy, and when he went back to Cape Town, a friend of Cliffy's offered him a job.

Giving up drugs wasn't easy. But playing football every day and spending time with other people keeping away from drugs helped Glandel stay clean. 'Willpower also helped,' Glandel adds, smiling.

Now, whenever he has money in his pocket, Glandel goes back to the streets to meet up with his old friends still living the same kind of life, and gives them money, saying it is better for them to get money from him than to rob someone for it. 'It also means I influence them,' Glandel says. Four of his friends later signed up to play with Oasis, and Glandel still carries on playing as much as he can.

When Glandel carried the flag into the stadium in Poznan, he wondered where he was – it was such an emotional moment. And during the tournament, he was a father figure for other players. 'I am older,' he says. 'And that means I'm responsible for some of the younger ones. I keep an eye on them and check out what they're doing, and they also treat me with respect – the team pass the ball with respect.'

For Glandel it is all about respect, and respect for himself is the first step to making a change in his own life and also the lives of the people around him.

* * * * *

As I head for a drink in the media tent, I meet Lisa Wrightsman, a former player who is now coach of the USA Women's Team. Lisa comes across to say hello and straight away I see how much she loves every moment of the Homeless World Cup – it shows in her ear-to-ear smile.

There are thousands of players whose stories deserve to be told and Lisa's story does not just explain where she's come from but speaks for those thousands of others whose lives have been changed by a ball. We often talk about how players change 'from homeless to heroes' and Lisa – like Lukes – is a shining example. The two of them may come from opposite sides of the planet, but their lives have run in parallel, and their paths have crossed thanks to the power of soccer.

* * * * *

At age 12, Lisa fought a battle with cancer – and won.

At age 18, she won a scholarship to Sacramento State, where she became a college soccer star and then turned semi-pro.

Several years later, in 2009, she was out of control. She didn't know what she was doing. She talks about it later as a feeling of 'impending doom' – as if she wanted to destroy everyone and everything in her life.

* * * * *

One day, in a parking lot, a Sacramento policeman forces Lisa's arms behind her back and charges her with robbery and possession of drugs. For six months, she's been spiralling into addiction, starting off with alcohol and moving onto methadone then crystal meth. She's homeless now. For four days, she's been sleeping in her car. The car won't start. Like Lisa's life, it's now become a wreck. She spends the next week in jail, sober and straight for the first time in as long as she remembers.

She has lost everything. She has no faith in anyone or anything. Her whole life is falling apart. She is hopeless and helpless, and handcuffed. She presses the crisis button in her jail cell and is soon put on suicide watch, 'because I couldn't imagine a life that I was happy in,' she said a few years later in a TedX talk.

The root of Lisa's problem is addiction: 'The only way to get off methadone was to get arrested and thrown into jail.' But there was 'life after homelessness', Lisa knows now.

Just one year later, in 2010, Lisa is one of the stars of the USA Women's Team at the Homeless World Cup in Brazil. The following year, she's presented with the 'Women's Social Impact Award' by Street Soccer USA. By that time, she is also the founder of the Street Soccer USA Lady Salamanders programme in Sacramento, reaching out to homeless and excluded women in the area and showing them how soccer can transform their lives. And that is just her part-time job – she also works at a vocational college and coaches the USA Women. 'I can't turn my back on it now,' Lisa tells me. 'If I walked away, something would bring me back here.'

* * * * *

Lisa started playing soccer when she was just three years old. She loved the game and dreamed she would play for her country. Life didn't work out exactly as Lisa imagined, but soccer changed her life when she was most in need of help, and now she has become an inspiration to others.

The journey has been difficult. And going into rehab in 2009 wasn't the first time she'd tried to go clean. In the past, she had made unsuccessful attempts, once living in her mother's place for 30 days, not eating or sleeping, before she started using again. Another time, she tried to get physically fit again, running up and down the hall of her mother's apartment, until she was too tired to move.

Using drugs was a 'comfort' for Lisa but not using drugs was a struggle. After she got out of jail, she went into rehab. 'I had to get some help,' she says. 'I didn't know enough about it. I just knew I had an addiction.'

Going into rehab was also the first time in a long while that Lisa felt safe – and also felt understood. 'There were people around me who knew how I felt and what I thought, and I knew that I was the only person responsible.'

The daily routine was a big help and Lisa did not need to fret any more about food or where she would sleep for the night. Most people take such simple things for granted but for Lisa, it meant that she was 'getting back to normal'. Meanwhile, she was focusing on other things like going back to work, to 'overcome the barriers that keep you from getting employed.'

She then spent two years at the Mather Community Campus in Sacramento, and during that time re-discovered the power of soccer. Her case manager, Chris Mann, was also the coach of the Mohawks, Sacramento's street soccer programme, and he persuaded Lisa to start playing again, even though Lisa resisted at first.

At that time, there was only a men's team but that wasn't what bothered Lisa. She had played soccer most of her life, but she still had mixed feelings about playing again, despite the fact she loved the game. 'But playing soccer taught me how to get along with people again,' she says.

At college, Lisa had been one of the stars of the team, but her off-field activities started to become a major problem. 'I played well and I partied really hard,' she explains, 'but after college, there wasn't the same kind of structure, and I started partying more.'

Lisa dreamed of going pro, but when the US Women's National League suddenly folded, the opportunity seemed to be lost. 'I put all my energy into my soccer,' she says, 'and not so much into my studies.'

For a time, Lisa worked as a personal trainer and carried on playing, but as soon as she was out of work, she started using drugs – and drinking and driving. 'I wasn't passionate about things any more. I was missing something, so I filled it with drugs. I had no motivation. No energy. I was one of the "untouchables" at college, because of my abilities as an athlete, but in the real world I no longer had that identity.'

The consequences soon became more serious, not just for Lisa's self esteem but also her love of the beautiful game. 'I felt I could do what I wanted, but it kept getting worse, and a year without a job or playing soccer was the worst. There was nothing to anchor me.' Then, mostly because of her spiralling spending on drugs, Lisa also went bankrupt.

The drugs soon started taking Lisa even further down – painkillers then methadone and crystal meth. 'I got so scared I wouldn't be able to stop it, and my body started to need it. Methadone's highly addictive, and I didn't know about addiction or how to go clean. I thought I could stop on my own, but I had no tools to deal with the sobriety, or dealing with the fact that I had trashed my life. 'I'd had a lot of opportunities at college, and now I had nothing. I knew it was my own fault, but I still wanted to destroy everything around me. I started to withdraw from methadone, but it was so bad, I started using crystal meth, and couldn't sleep or eat. I felt really crazy. I thought the government was watching me from satellites.'

Lisa also describes how her mother moved out of her own home to let Lisa use it to go through cold turkey. But after 30 days, she started using drugs again. 'I thought I saw the bigger picture, and I wanted to save the world from all of these problems. But I turned into this crazy person, watching it happen, and I just couldn't stop. I would focus on one negative thing, then I'd go on the Internet and get overwhelmed by all these negative thoughts I had no control over. I was frightened but I also couldn't stop it – I was obsessed with finding out what's wrong with the world, and I really just wanted to find out what was wrong with myself. But I was looking in the wrong place. I was so far from reality, it was scary.'

* * * * *

And this was how Lisa ended up in a parking lot, hanging out in her car till the cops came and took her to jail. 'My car had died. I was high. I had drugs on me. I had no ambition to leave.'

A nearby restaurant had reported a break-in, but when the cops appeared, Lisa thought they were coming to help her – to jump-start her car. Then the next thing she knew, they pinned her arms behind her back and took her away to the station to charge her. 'What are you doing?' the cops asked. 'Weird things!' said Lisa. 'You're crazy!' they said. 'Yes I am!'

The charges were later dropped – the robbery had been a case of mistaken identity – and Lisa went straight from the jail into rehab and a period of 'sober living,' then moved on to the transitional programme which eventually led back to soccer. 'They had a football programme but I didn't want to go near it because soccer had led me to a dead end. When I got sober, I thought it was a good opportunity to start afresh, to focus on school and employment. Did I want to play soccer? No way! I thought it was just a distraction. I needed a job.'

Gradually, however, Lisa rediscovered her great love for soccer, and also how much other people love soccer. She also watched a documentary about the Homeless World Cup called *Kicking It*, narrated by the actor Colin Farrell, which also inspired her. 'Initially, I didn't want to risk that by playing again, but Chris convinced me, so I went along to one of the practices – and after only one second, I loved it! I hadn't really enjoyed anything so much since I'd been sober!'

But love was not the only reason, Lisa says: 'I realised that soccer was my freedom. That was when I was free.'

Soon after this, in 2010, Lisa played for Sacramento at the Street Soccer USA National Cup. She was the only woman in the team, and did so well she made it to the women's team at that year's Homeless World Cup in Brazil, the first time that the USA had sent a women's team. 'Brazil was an incredible moment,' says Lisa. 'I really felt empowered, and felt that I had something I could offer other people.'

Lisa was amazed at what she saw in Brazil – the spiritual home of the beautiful game. She suddenly realised how much soccer mattered to so many people, and the importance of playing together as part of a team.

Lisa also knows better than most that the Homeless World Cup is not all about winning but giving the players the chance to bounce back from defeat, and that everyone learns more from losing than winning. 'I also noticed that the women's teams seem to come closer together as the tournament progresses,' says Lisa.

In Rio, Lisa also faced the challenge of getting everyone to feel an equal member of the team, including one young woman with mental health issues: 'She struggled to deal with all the stimulation, but when she played, she was fine. She wasn't very socially engaged, either, but when we came together as a team, she was different.'

Even though she didn't want the responsibility of being a leader, Lisa's Rio team-mates seemed to follow her. She may not have known it herself at the time, but Lisa was a natural born leader.

For Lisa, going to Brazil was like a spiritual experience: 'After Rio, I had a new purpose in life. I saw how people loved the game and also the impact of the Homeless World Cup. That's why I love the game, and think it's the most powerful sport in the world – so many people are just as committed to soccer as they are to religion.'

* * * * *

After Brazil, Lisa felt very strongly she had to do something to help other people, using the power of soccer. She also realised that what she had learned on the field could help her a lot in her job, and she wasn't 'ashamed or embarrassed' to talk about playing in the *Homeless* World Cup – she felt proud of what she had done and had nothing to hide.

Soon, she was drawn into coaching and helped start up a women's team, initially playing indoors twice a week, moving furniture around to create enough space for a game. 'At first, I didn't want to coach, but felt I had to try,' says Lisa. A few of the players had children, but instead of that being a problem, the children became their 'opponents' in practice, which in turn helped the families to bond. 'The parents and their kids have lots of trauma,' says Lisa, 'and relations are strained because of drink and drugs. But suddenly they're playing together and communicating better.'

As time went by, the standard of soccer also got better, and the goal became sending a team to the USA National Cup – and for some players also the Homeless World Cup in Paris in 2011. 'It was epic!' says Lisa. 'The players all wanted to go there but I told them it's not just your skills on the field but who you are that gets you selected.'

The Sacramento project started up without any resources to speak of – just a couple of balls. When they went to the National Cup in New York, many of the women hadn't travelled away from their home town before or worn a shirt 'that said something positive' on it. They had never represented anything or anywhere before.

The team had some experience of training, but none of them had ever played a proper game before. 'They were crying, so emotional,' says Lisa. 'They may not have known how to play but they felt like real soccer players and they supported each other.'

Despite losing all of their games, two of Lisa's players were selected for the USA women's team in Paris in 2011, and Lisa went to Europe as the coach. 'That was pretty huge for me. I was insecure about being a coach, but it wasn't about my ability as a soccer coach but my ability to motivate and build the team. It also made me realise I'm capable of doing much more than I think.'

What mattered most to Lisa when she took the team to Paris was to make sure every team-mate had a positive experience. She still has her job at the college and coaches the local team part-time, focusing on winning new sponsors and public support. 'It would be great to make the Sacramento programme full-time. We could have a big impact on the community, partnering with other local agencies. People soon get tired of all the talking. More action is needed.'

Lisa will never forget where she comes from. 'Looking back, I realise that I was an addict long before I had a drink or used drugs at all. There's so much wreckage in the past, but I have now built a foundation for myself. Even now,' she says, 'there are still traces of destruction and unfinished personal business. You can't make up for things that happened in the past but you can be more positive about what you do now and what you will do in the future. You can prove you don't want to do that any more, and lead people in a more positive direction, without asking for anything in return. I'm constantly surprised at the effect we have on women and their kids.'

Eight players in the current Sacramento team have 32 children between them, and the kids want to be soccer players just like their mothers. One of the sponsors donated some uniforms and as soon as the kids put them on, even several sizes too big, they also feel like 'real' soccer players. 'The mothers don't need to be pros,' Lisa says, 'just committed to playing.'

When Lisa played soccer at college, she was reluctant to lead from the front. But now she can't say 'no' to getting involved in the fight against social exclusion. When Lisa first learned about the Homeless World Cup, she thought it was a joke and imagined she'd never be homeless – or play in a 'homeless' event. Now she dedicates her life to the programme. 'There is life after homelessness,' Lisa concludes. 'There is life after alcohol and drugs, and I needed to change. I was going to end up in jail or I was going to die.'

* * * * *

As I walk towards the players' tent with Lisa, she introduces me to one of the USA men's team – Donnie Nicholson from New York City (via Japan and West Germany, England and Texas).

Donnie is pouring with sweat after playing his heart out against South Korea. You never know how any game will turn out, but the USA won eight to one and the players are all feeling proud of themselves. Lisa smiles and tells me that Donnie reminds her how she felt on Day One in Rio – and how he doesn't know yet how much he will change in the course of the week.

Donnie looks to me as if he's well equipped to cope with the experience. It's taken him two years to bounce back from life on the mean streets but now he has another mountain to climb – his first ever media interview. The BBC World Service has arranged to speak to Donnie 'live' on radio in less than five minutes, but even though he's never done anything like it before, he knows exactly what he is going to say. 'Soccer saved my life,' says Donnie, gulping down more ice-cold water. 'Without it, I would probably be dead now.'

'I played to kick cocaine,' he adds. 'I played to no longer be homeless. I played for my country at the Homeless World Cup.'

Our media team have been briefing Donnie, telling him what to expect. They also need to know if he's happy to answer more personal questions. About the problems of being bipolar. The loss of his mother. Cocaine. Being homeless. All alone in New York. Is it OK to ask about drugs and his family? 'Anything!' Donnie says, wiping the sweat from his brow.

Ten seconds later, the phone rings. It's London. He's on.

And as if he's been doing 'live' broadcasts for years, Donnie is soon up and running. He describes how he was born in Japan, on a military base where his parents were posted (they were both in the Air Force). His parents were divorced when he was four, and he and his sister spent most of their time with their mother, including stints in Germany and England. In 1988, when Donnie was 13 years old, his mother was posted to Texas, and Donnie started having psychological problems.

Fast forward 12 years: Discharged from the Navy after testing positive for methamphetamines, Donnie moved in with his mother, and started hanging out in clubs and bars. In 2003, his mother died of cancer, and Donnie's habit started catching up with him: 'My cocaine use had become a major problem even though my family had not caught on. Later that year, I admitted myself to a state hospital where I was re-diagnosed as bipolar and slowly began the nightmare of hospitalisations and changes in medications.'

Donnie then moved in with his grandmother, but she died in 2005 and Donnie drifted from apartment to apartment, and was 'hospitalised multiple times, willingly and unwillingly', until April 20, 2010, when he was discharged for the last time and swore not to take any more medication to treat his bipolar disorder.

Three months later, on July the Fourth, with nowhere to call 'home', Donnie boarded a bus to New York, and went cold turkey overnight, turning his back on cocaine. 'I thought I'd hit rock-bottom till I saw what rock-bottom was,' Donnie tells the BBC reporter. 'But soccer saved my life...'

'You're a natural, Donnie,' says one of the media team, as Donnie describes how he made it to Mexico City, and the interview comes to an end.

He may have seemed a natural on radio but Donnie isn't feeling at his best today. He couldn't sleep the night before he checked in at the airport, and didn't sleep during the flight from New York. And he hasn't slept since. He also has a wound which refuses to heal, and has to change the dressing several times a day. But it won't spoil his week here in Mexico City: 'A little hole in my chest isn't going to keep me from playing after all that hard work to get here.'

It's taken Donnie two years to get into the USA team. Last year, the tournament in Paris came too early for Donnie but now he has finally made it: 'When the names for the USA team going to Mexico City were announced in Times Square, and mine was included, I had what is best described as an out-of-body experience. It was only two hours later that the tears came – tears of joy.'

At the opening ceremony, Donnie and his team-mates were inspired by the reaction of the crowd, as they marched through the packed city streets with the Stars & Stripes proudly held high in the air as they entered the plaza, filled with thousands of cheering spectators.

They know they only have one chance to play for their country in the Homeless World Cup. That's what it says in the rules. So this is their moment to shine.

Donnie is just one of many hundreds of thousands of people who have taken part since 2003. He is also only one of hundreds of players from dozens of countries who will play in the tournament this year. And like every single player, the end of the week seems a long way away – not just the Finals at the climax of the tournament but the long journey home to a future that could still go in any direction.

* * * * *

One year later, Donnie flies to Santiago in Chile, the host of the Homeless World Cup in 2014. He is the 'official photographer' for the USA team playing in the Copa America, a tournament designed to give the city a taste of street soccer before the 'real thing' the following year. He also makes a documentary about this adventure called *World Cup Project Chile*. Within a year, Donnie has found a new job and is no longer homeless – he got the keys to his apartment soon after returning from Mexico City. Donnie has achieved a lot thanks to the power of soccer, but as he says himself, his journey is only beginning.

And for hundreds of players in Mexico City and hundreds of thousands of others all over the world, the Homeless World Cup is the first step on that journey.

* * * * *

Speaking earlier to Lisa Wrightsman brings back lots of memories of Rio and also reminds me how women today play a much bigger role in the Homeless World Cup as both players and coaches.

One of the 'ambassadors' of the Homeless World Cup is the Brazilian soccer star Michelle da Silva, who was 'discovered' at the tournament in Denmark in 2007 by French soccer legend – and anti-homelessness campaigner – Eric Cantona.

Michelle was born in 1990 in the infamous *favela* portrayed in the film *The City of God*. All her life, Michelle has lived for soccer, on a journey out of poverty through sport, and in Denmark she soon made her mark as a player.

In 2007, Michelle was one of very few women who made it as players in teams which were still dominated by men – it was not until Melbourne the following year that we staged the first women's event.

During a training session, Michelle was singled out by Eric as one of the most talented players – a speedy and powerful striker. And Eric's judgement was confirmed when she won the Best Female Player award at the end of the tournament. But as well as competing on the field with the men, Michelle was also determined to do her best off the field, turning her life around as soon as she went back to Rio.

Soon after Copenhagen, Michelle was selected for the Brazil women's under-20 national team and went on to play in the 2010 South America Cup. She was not only beginning to fulfil her potential but overcoming all the obstacles laid in her path since her difficult childhood in Rio.

Michelle says: 'The Homeless World Cup is a major life experience. You create friendships and set the right attitude to succeed in your life and in football.'

Three years later, when Michelle turned up in Rio, I could see at once how much she'd changed. She had the confidence that comes from being recognised and knowing there are people who support her. And she also never lost sight of where she had come from and how other women like her were still living there, struggling to survive from day to day.

Today, Michelle is playing for a team in São Paulo called São Jose, a well-known professional club that has won major trophies. No matter what she does in future, however, I will always remember Michelle as a player in Denmark, receiving her award from the Crown Prince of Denmark. An outstanding player and a brilliant example to others.

* * * * *

Another ambassador is Ginan Koesmayadi, one of the founders of our Indonesian partners, Rumah Cemara. Ginan played in Paris in 2011, when the team made its début and he won the Best Male Player award. Since then, he has been an inspiring example to the rest of the team, but life for the young man has never been easy.

Ginan started using drugs when he was only 14 years old. At this point, he felt the whole world was against him, but after a few years, he decided to take back control of his life. 'I had grown tired of living on the streets, doing petty crimes to support my dependence on drugs,' he says. 'When I was 20, I asked my family to get me into rehab. But I encountered yet another bump on the road when I was told that I'd contracted HIV, possibly because of the needles I used to inject.'

Ironically, however, that's when Ginan turned his life around: 'The biggest barrier for someone who is diagnosed with HIV is self-doubt,' he explains. 'When you limit your own ability because you are HIV positive, then you are doomed to failure.'

After three years in rehab, Ginan and four friends founded Rumah Cemara: 'We want society to treat us just like other human beings – neither privilege nor social stigma is needed,' says Ginan. 'We would like to change the mindset that thinks we are useless and bad.'

Before Rio, Rumah Cemara was chosen as our national partner in Indonesia, but due to lack of funding, the team could not go to the tournament that year. Instead of sitting back and waiting for something to happen, Ginan did a sponsored walk from Bandung to Jakarta – a distance of over 200 kilometres – and his patience paid off when donations and sponsorship funded the team's trip to Paris, where they quickly became a crowd favourite and finished sixth overall.

When asked about the secret of the power of soccer, Ginan quotes French author Albert Camus: 'Everything I've learned about human morality and duty, I've learned from football.'

And that is the impact we seek to achieve at the Homeless World Cup, for every single player and spectator.

* * * * *

Like Ginan who is following the action on the Internet back home in Java, another former player and ambassador, David Duke of Scotland, is thousands of miles away, watching the games 'live' on YouTube. Now the CEO of Street Soccer Scotland, David is already beginning to think of the next Homeless World Cup in Poland. And as he sits in Edinburgh, watching the Scotland team losing 10-1 to the 'Boys from Brazil', he feels frustrated that he can't be there to help them. Like any soccer manager who used to be a player, he makes every tackle and kicks every ball. And not so long ago, he was a player the same as the rest of the team.

Today, he is head of an organisation which employs 20 people, as coaches, counsellors and general assistants. He also holds an Honorary Doctorate from Queen Margaret University and is a regular speaker at international sporting and business events.

It's an incredible achievement for someone who was once very close to despair, and the fact that he now has a high-profile job and promotes street

soccer all over Scotland is a major by-product of the Homeless World Cup
that we never envisaged – not even in our wildest dreams did Harald and
I think the players would one day be part of a large global network which
revolves around soccer, creating opportunities for other homeless people,
and even full-time employment.

The key to the success of these national organisations is that players go
on to be leaders in the programmes which reached out to them in the first
place. The leadership comes from empowering people rather than simply
providing a ready-made answer. 'Football changed my life,' says David. 'I
was homeless in Glasgow, but getting involved with the Homeless World
Cup gave me structure, something positive. I had nothing to do and nowhere
to be, and suddenly I was needed.'

As a Global Ambassador for the Homeless World Cup, David's commitment grew deeper and deeper, and he expresses that commitment through his
job, speaking to the players in a language that they understand at the same
time as building his personal network – his address book is a *Who's Who* of
celebrities, including Sir Alex Ferguson, the former manager of Manchester
United, who has given David great support over the years, as well as sound
advice. Leading business figures also act as mentors and increasingly call
him to ask for advice in return. New partners such as Microsoft come forward every year to get involved, not only to fund future projects but learn.

✵ ✵ ✵ ✵ ✵

It's a long way from a hostel for the homeless in Glasgow to the stage at a
five-star hotel in Los Angeles, where next week he will speak alongside CEOs,
gold medallists and government officials at the Doha Goals Forum, but what
lies ahead for David is a much greater challenge. 'Every morning, as soon
as I open my eyes, I ask myself: How can I make today better? How can
tomorrow be better? And next year?' says David.

We have met one Monday evening when he's rushing home to pack for
his flight to LA in the morning. It's been hard to catch him – he's been working in Glasgow since early today, advising a youth soccer project in Scots-
toun, based on the same field where he used to play as a child. It used to be
harder to go back to Glasgow. 'I used to avoid my old haunts,' he explains.
'I didn't want to meet the guys I used to hang out with. They're doing all
the same things we all used to do, but I've moved on since then. I've got
responsibilities.'

For David, that is critical. In 2004, drink took over his life – he lost his
job and home in Glasgow when he fell behind with his rent. 'I couldn't get

out of my bed,' he says. 'I would binge drink for weeks, to forget and escape, then I found myself out on the street.'

Not sure where to turn next, he ended up spending the next year in a hostel for the homeless in Broad Street (now closed), where people 'out of it on drugs' or recently let out of prison with nowhere to go hung around in the middle of nowhere, mixing with dealers and prostitutes, getting mugged every now and again for whatever possessions they had. 'It was horrific,' says David. 'I used to lock the door and try to sleep.'

After going to sessions to address his addiction, he managed to come off the drink, and one day saw a poster on a notice board about a soccer Challenge Cup for homeless people organised by *The Big Issue in Scotland*, to select a team to represent Scotland at the next Homeless World Cup in Sweden. David had always enjoyed playing football at school and had also played for Celtic Boys Club, so he jumped at the chance. 'I loved the idea of playing for Scotland,' he says, 'but I just wanted to play again.'

David almost missed the trial – he'd had a drink the night before and didn't want to go, but two friends dragged him out of bed and forced him to go. 'I will always be grateful to them,' he says, 'because if I hadn't, I would never have played for my country. It was a fantastic high, better than anything you could ever get from drink. And that was the beginning of me distancing myself from alcohol. I had a new purpose.'

In Sweden, David loved the atmosphere as well as the football. He learned the Swedish word for friend (*vanner*) and wrote it on his forehead, and had Sweden and Scotland flags painted on his face. 'People came up to me in the street and shook my hand and asked me for my autograph.'

Scotland reached the semi-finals in Gothenburg, losing five to one to holders Austria, but for David the experience was better than winning. And along the way, the Scotland team defeated the mighty Brazil – a result he will never forget.

As well as the excitement of the soccer, David was moved by the stories of players he met. 'They really inspired me,' he says. 'To see the strength and courage of these players made me realise they were worse off than myself, so when I came back, I wanted to change my life.'

When he touched down back in Scotland, however, he faced a completely new challenge. After the 'high' of the Homeless World Cup, he confesses he struggled to cope, and returned to the hostel in Broad Street, feeling more down than ever. He had started addressing his problems with drink, and had won several battles, but drink was still a difficult issue and after his inspiring time in Sweden, he simply felt flat.

Nowadays, Street Soccer Scotland sets goals for all for the players in advance, but at that time, the programme was still under-funded and had no professional set-up.

It was several months before David moved out of the hostel, and picked up the keys for his new home, but he learned a lot and soon became determined to pass on that knowledge to others. Today, when people come to his nationwide street soccer sessions, he knows how they feel and he knows how much football can help them – including the regular training and teamwork, as well as the prospect of the Homeless World Cup. But back then, there was little support.

In 2004, however, David was determined to build on his achievements in Sweden. He took official coaching courses and studied at Anniesland College, then got involved coaching youngsters in Glasgow. 'Football keeps them off the streets,' he said at the time, 'and away from temptations like drinking and drugs. We teach them some manners, show them how to work together as a team and respect each other.' And this is now what David does for thousands of homeless people all over Scotland.

After coaching children's soccer, David gained the confidence and the experience needed to take on the challenge ahead. 'Football gives people the skills they need to change their own lives,' he explains. 'It gives you self-esteem and motivation.'

The next year, David was appointed Assistant Coach of the Scotland team playing in Edinburgh at the Homeless World Cup, working under former professional coach, Ally Dawson (coaching Scotland again ten years later). Media coverage put David under the spotlight again, and the team performed well in their capital city, but more was to come...

*****

For the next two years, David continued to coach the team part-time and worked for *The Big Issue Scotland*. But at that stage, there was no real financial support and no national network, and David was a volunteer who spent time every Wednesday and Sunday at sessions in Glasgow, with trials in other cities once a year when the team was selected for the Homeless World Cup. After Cape Town in 2006, when the team finished ranked 33rd, David was approached by *The Big Issue Scotland* and given a challenge: 'Win the Homeless World Cup.' And David accepted the challenge – and delivered the trophy the following year, beating Poland in the final.

Being on the front page of several national papers attracted more sponsorship money, but even more important than winning the trophy was that

David was now put in charge of the organisation, and got other cities in Scotland involved on a regular basis. As well as selecting and coaching the team, he gradually built up a network of contacts in government, business and sport.

David understands what the players expect. He knows that sponsorship means much more than the money he needs to pay wages – it also means the simple things like getting good-quality shirts for the players so they feel proud to play for their country.

In 2009, David founded Street Soccer Scotland, with initial support from the Homeless World Cup. At first, David only worked part-time, but over the years he has brought in a series of sponsors to help him establish a professional organisation.

David has achieved a lot since Gothenburg, but never forgets where he comes from. For him, responsibility and self-esteem are critical. Today he is responsible for 20 employees, and a role model for players. 'It was my lack of self-esteem that made me drink so much,' says David. 'It isn't easy and you need a lot of discipline. Sometimes, people need to change the people around them, in order to change their own lives.'

And David has not only transformed his own life but now gives other people opportunities to follow in his footsteps, on the soccer field and far beyond.

*****

Meanwhile, David's latest group of players, under the experienced leadership of ex-Glasgow Rangers professional player Ally Dawson, are playing in the sunshine of Mexico City. And when Scotland beat Ukraine in another nail-biting encounter, winning seven to six in a penalty shoot-out, a young man called Sallah Mboob is the match winner, scoring the equalising goal in the final seconds of the game then stepping up to take the winning penalty.

As Sallah scores the winner, his team-mates rush out to embrace him. It's a moment to savour – he's earned it.

Two years ago, Sallah decided to change his life – to leave behind a life of gangs and drugs and start over. It was a lifestyle that had cost him his relationship with his family and got him in serious trouble with the law. So when he was offered a fresh start and the chance to reunite with his family in Scotland, he took it.

Since moving to Scotland, Sallah says he's left all his old ways behind. Street Soccer Scotland has played a major part in helping him. Sallah got involved soon after moving to Scotland while living in a hostel and has been playing ever since. 'It has boosted my confidence a lot. I have met a lot of people in similar situations and that has helped a lot, too.'

Now making the headlines in Mexico City, Sallah says: 'It's a fantastic experience. For a guy like me, coming where I am come from, it's a life-changing experience. It's all down to Street Soccer Scotland. I have a lot to thank them for. Basically that is why we are here – to change our lives.'

David Duke may not be here in Mexico City today, but I know he'll be proud of what Sallah's achieved, and understand from personal experience exactly how the young man feels – and how much work is still to be done.

* * * * *

Talking to David reminds me of Sweden, and many other players I will never forget, like Claudio and Daryl, Yoshinori Matsumoto, Kevin Wilson and Maxim Mastitski. Claudio Bongiovani was one of the stars of Brazil and his story was one of the most moving I've ever heard. He had ended up homeless soon after his family were killed in a terrible car crash. 'I went out of my mind,' he said, fighting back tears. 'I was like a crazy man, lost, without direction. The worst moment was when I was unable to see my children or my wife because the coffins had already been sealed – they were so badly burned.' It is hard to imagine how Claudio managed to fight his way back from the edge, but with help from the street paper OCAS in Rio, he told me that he 'found new strength from within.'

The Brazil team have a hard act to follow, with the national team winning so many trophies, but they are always popular wherever they go. Before they played in Gothenburg, the players trained under a viaduct, without proper footwear or even a very good ball, but when they played, the crowd screamed out 'Brazil! Brazil!' – treating them the same as their professional heroes.

Daryl was another unforgettable character. Before he played in Gothenburg, he lived in the Canadian backwoods, 'dodging bears and coyotes', and his dream was to go back and build a log cabin. His manager, Paul Gregory, was very quick to realise the power of the Homeless World Cup, and saw how it 'takes people out of their environment and mixes them with others who are different.' Paul is very protective towards all his players but he also knows everyone has to think 'out of the box' and explore new horizons as part of the process. 'It's the power of the group,' he says. 'And I changed too – I never realised the full potential of teamwork and sport.'

England goalie Kevin Wilson provided one of the most memorable moments in Gothenburg – when he was handed the Homeless World Cup trophy, which every single player dreams of winning, he managed to drop it. Was it damaged? Would we have to repair it in time for the Final? As Kevin picked it off the floor, I closed my eyes and waited to see what had happened. Every goalie is supposed to be a 'safe pair of hands,' but Kevin instantly recovered his composure by saying, 'It's better than dropping the ball!'

Homeless since the age of 17, Kevin had been chosen at a trial involving 1,000 players, held at Manchester United's famous Carrington training facility. Legend has it that Sir Alex Ferguson, at that time still club manager, selected the team. I don't know if it's true or not, but in my view, every player was a legend, including the goalie, whose dream was to go back to England to coach. 'I've never played in front of crowds that size before,' said Kevin. 'It's something you never imagine will happen.'

But it did…

For many other players, this was their moment to shine. Two-hundred players travelling thousands of miles. Two-hundred people hoping to return to a new life, inspired by their experience in Sweden. Players like Maxim Mastitski of Russia, who studied social management and worked for the St Petersburg street paper, *Put Domoi*. The Sweden captain Tajmaz David Nilsson, who coached the team next year in Scotland. Ahmet Akday of England, who signed for English team Bromley when he went home from Sweden. Or Yevgen Adamenko, top scorer in the tournament with 53 goals, who signed as a professional back in Ukraine.

Another star in Gothenburg was Yoshinori (65), the oldest player and another favourite. The Japan team went around with a number displayed on their shirts – 52 – and it took me a few days to realise this was the average age of the team. Homeless men are often treated badly in Japan because they are thought to be 'past it' as soon as they start to get older, so the number was also a protest.

Yoshinori ended up homeless after losing his job as a welder – like so many people during the recession in Japan. He said that living in a tent was not a picnic – it was hot as a sauna and everything went very mouldy because of the damp, with ticks and centipedes everywhere. Yoshinori scraped a living picking up tin cans, but he knew there were others much worse off than him and refused to let homelessness beat him. 'If you can handle homelessness,' he told me, 'you can put up with almost anything.'

* * * * *

So many players say things that impress me every tournament, and Sweden also had its choice examples: 'The Big Issue is not a magazine. It's a life saver!' said Mziwamabhele 'Bells' Hlati. 'When you play, you feel like flying,' said Marek Sosczak, the goalie from Poland. 'I feel I am really a star now,' said Argentina's Sergio Pena.

Ukraine's Mykola Serebryansky summed it up for everyone: 'It was unforgettable. I realised that I am not alone. All those other people there with the same problem I have, now so confident and proud of themselves.'

And eight years later, watching the players in Mexico City, the story continues...

* * * * *

Biswajit Nandi and Surajit Bhattacharya didn't make it to Mexico City but both of them are destined to be stars next year in Poland. And their story is the story of the Homeless World Cup.

Biswajit (17) and Surajit (18) may not be brothers but everyone who sees them playing soccer thinks they are – not just because they look alike but also seem to have a telepathic understanding on the field. And this is no surprise because the two young men have been playing soccer together for over ten years on the waste grounds of Sonagachi, the largest red-light district in Kolkata.

Growing up in Sonagachi was a dangerous business for both boys. 'The men don't like to see kids with their mothers,' says Surajit, 'so we had to keep out of sight.'

'I would cry in my room every night,' says Biswajit. 'I was always very lonely.'

When they were both about five years old, they started playing soccer together, wherever they could find a piece of ground. They both dreamed of playing for one of the big clubs, but as they grew up in Kolkata, their challenge was more off the field than on, as other children bullied them because they were sex workers' sons. 'The other kids refused to play with us,' says Biswajit. 'We used to face taunts all the time and were also physically abused. At times I used to get disturbed by this harassment, but I realised that staying calm was the best way to handle a bad situation. When I was beaten or abused, I never fought back. I used to plead with them it's not my fault that I am a sex worker's son.'

The boys were first spotted as stars of the future in 2006, when they played in a match between sex workers' children and other children at the home where they were staying. Their team didn't win but the referee, Biswajit Majumdar, saw their potential. 'I realised that they were gifted and just needed some direction, support and a platform,' Majumdar told the *Hindustan Times*. For almost seven years, the boys turned up in worn-out shoes and faded shirts to train with other boys who made fun of their family background, but the coach told them not to lose focus and the boys later went to the annual tournament in Delhi and were picked for the national team. 'I was shocked,' says Biswajit. 'I have never been abroad before and don't have a passport, but I couldn't stop smiling! I want to win. I want my mother to be proud of me.'

But even though their mothers were happy to see them selected, the two boys didn't want to go to the Homeless World Cup unless they could make sure their mothers were safe. Biswajit wanted his mother to give up her work in Sonagachi and found a part-time job filling tanks with buckets of water. 'I didn't want to go away and worry about my mother back home,' Biswajit explained. Earning money playing soccer for teams in Kolkata has helped, and Nandi's mother no longer needs to work in Sonagachi.

At one time, the trip to the Homeless World Cup was almost cancelled due to lack of funds, and Biswajit and Surajit thought their dream had ended, but after their story appeared in the *Hindustan Times*, donations poured in.

Many of their team-mates tell a similar story, including three young women from Chennai – Thenmozi Meganethan, Pavithra Gunaseelan and Shankari Krishnan – who have won a place in college since getting involved in the Slum Soccer programme. Another player, 19-year-old Pankaj Mahajan started playing soccer three years ago when he took shelter at Slum Soccer after running away from his abusive, alcoholic father, and later became the team captain.

Slum Soccer founder Vijay Barse organised his first football tournament for the slum children ten years ago and called it 'zhopadpatti football' or 'slum soccer'. Soon the idea spread around the country, and the India team made its début in the Homeless World Cup in 2007. 'My aim was not to create good football players,' says Vijay. 'All I wanted was to give the kids a chance to improve their life. For at least two hours a day, they would be away from all the bad influences around them. Many of the kids I started with indulged in alcohol, drug abuse, petty thefts and street-fights. But when they played with me, they were away from all these. And that's what I wanted.'

Biswajit now has his eyes on a place in his favourite Indian club, Mohun Bagan, and played in a trial before going to Poznan in 2013. The dream continues, but for Biswajit, his mother is what matters most. 'When I go home,' he says, 'and see my mother, that will be happiness for me!'

According to Surajit, the children in Kolkata and other cities in India need all the help they can get, but it's not only money that counts. 'We also need respect,' he says.

Biswajit and Surajit are destined to be future stars of the Homeless World Cup, like thousands and thousands of others who dream the same dream – and will also transform their lives, thanks to the power of soccer.

4

Something Magical Happened

Q: How did it start?
A: As a crazy idea...

MONDAY, 8 OCTOBER 2012: Fernando asks the question that everyone asks every year but I try my best to answer as if it's the first time, even though it's a story engraved in my mind I could probably tell in my sleep. I tell him I will try to recreate what we were thinking and how we were feeling at the time of the first Homeless World Cup in Graz, and how the crazy dream eventually came true...

Sunday, 6 July 2003: Everything's going exactly according to plan, as the teams parade around the arena, and the first Homeless World Cup is officially opened in Graz, on the edge of the Austrian Alps. The players, all wearing their national colours, are smiling and laughing as they line up in front of the crowd with their flags held high up in the air, and their national anthems ring out in the city's main square.

Just a few months before, all these players were homeless – asylum seekers, alcoholics, drug addicts or simply people who had lost their jobs and homes. People going nowhere with nowhere to go.

Now, they are the centre of attention in their shiny, new shirts, being treated like heroes. Not so long ago, they were not even treated as real human beings, but now as the players stream into the stadium, they feel like sporting superstars. They are changing in front of our eyes.

Harald Schmied and I have been waiting for kick-off since 2001. I look across at Harald, quietly wiping the tears from his face. Our dream is coming true. The Homeless World Cup is becoming a reality. One-hundred-and-forty-four players from 18 countries have travelled to Graz to reclaim the streets for homeless people all around the world. Thousands of people are cheering as the players prepare for the opening game. Two years of hard work have led to this magical moment and we're loving every second.

Everything is going well, but both of us are also thinking a few steps ahead, and the questions start to multiply inside our heads: Will the tournament be a success? Will the players get on with each other? Will the football be good? Will the crowds turn up? How will the people of Graz respond? What will the media say? How will the players cope with the experience? Most of them have never been abroad before, and many are still fighting drug or alcohol problems. How will they handle the pressure? Will the managers and volunteers also be able to cope?

Will Graz be a one-off event? Will the tournament have any long-term impact?

*****

Nine years later, in Mexico City, as the fireworks explode in the sky, Harald and I still instinctively know how the other is feeling, without even saying a word. It's a long way from Graz and the Homeless World Cup has become an established event, but for us – and the players – it's new every year. 'The opening parade is always special,' says Harald. 'When the players arrive, it is always a very emotional moment. That first time, I felt this incredible energy, and it is still the same today. I still feel emotional as the teams meet for the first time at the opening parade, and dance and sing, communicating via the language of football.'

*****

The road from Graz has been an epic journey for everyone who's ever been involved with the Homeless World Cup, as players or managers, volunteers or employees. Along the way, a million people have been part of the adventure, using the power of soccer to transform their lives and lift themselves from poverty or homelessness. But as the tournament kicked off in Graz in 2003, we didn't have a clue what would happen that week, never mind years ahead into the future.

A few months before the whistle blew to signal the start of the opening game, we wondered if the tournament would happen at all, and Harald wondered if he would still be alive to enjoy it...

*****

The idea of the Homeless World Cup was conceived over a couple of beers in a beach-side bar in Cape Town, South Africa, in 2001.

Harald and I were attending a conference on homelessness, organised by the International Network of Street Papers (INSP). Both of us had been involved with street papers for years – I was the President of the INSP, while Harald was the editor of *Megaphon* in Austria. And after the conference ended, we went out on the town with a few of our colleagues: Ron Grunberg from New York, along with Peter Ten Caat and Jeroen de Rooij from the Netherlands.

The conference had been extremely positive but all of us agreed it would be better if homeless people also attended, not only to speak for themselves but also to share their experience in different countries. Every year, the editors exchanged ideas and talked about sharing resources, so why not the street-paper vendors as well? We had talked before about international exchanges, with vendors selling street papers in other countries, but employment laws and other issues stopped us from taking it further. Perhaps the conference would be the ideal venue for the vendors to meet? 'But they might think it's boring!' says Ron. 'And what about language?' asks Peter. 'There may be a problem with language,' says Harald, with a gleam in his eye. 'But there is one language everybody speaks in every country.' 'What's that, then?' I ask him. 'The language of football!' says Harald. 'Football is a universal language. So why not organise a football match for homeless people?' 'Scotland versus Austria?' I suggest. 'Great idea!' says Harald.

We both think about it for a couple of seconds. 'And Scotland will win,' I say. 'Nonsense!' says Harald.

We shake hands and immediately agree to organise a challenge match between our two countries, then toast the agreement with another bottle of beer.

Two or three beers later: 'Why don't we organise an international tournament and ask along countries from all over Europe?' 'Why not the rest of the world?' 'We could call it...' '...the Homeless World Cup!'

Harald and I both immediately love the idea but the others are not quite so keen. 'You're crazy! It will never work!' one of them says, as the waiter announces they are closing the bar in a couple of minutes.

* * * * *

We all went to our rooms that night thinking everyone else would forget all about it, like so many other evenings when we solve the world's problems. But the following morning, as we sat down for breakfast, we knew this idea was different.

It may have been a crazy dream but we were determined to make it come true.

* * * * *

As soon as we got back to Europe, Harald and I started drawing up plans for the Homeless World Cup. But progress was slow – we both had other jobs so the project wasn't getting the full-time attention it needed. We still believed the tournament could have a huge impact, but without any funds or official support, the project may have stalled before it even had a chance.

Then, in June 2001, we made our first breakthrough. The president of Caritas Austria, Franz Küberl, was speaking to Harald about the idea and immediately understood how it could work. Franz then asked Harald if he could use his connections with other street papers to invite teams to Graz in 2003, when the city would be in the spotlight as the 'Cultural Capital of Europe.' Suddenly, the crazy idea took off again, setting off a chain of events which have had a major impact on the lives of hundreds of thousands of people worldwide.

Harald takes up the story: 'I told Franz we were planning to invite not just a few teams from neighbouring countries in Europe but teams from all over the world. He looked me in the eyes and said, 'Okay, go ahead. We will support you.' And suddenly the Homeless World Cup was beginning to happen for real.'

Harald immediately started to map out the street soccer concept in detail – how homelessness was closely linked with living on the streets and how playing soccer in the centre of the city was a way of reclaiming the streets, a metaphor for overcoming homelessness. And today that is still what the Homeless World Cup is about.

Over the next few months, we split responsibilities between us, with Harald focusing on Graz and having talks with UEFA (the Union of the European Football Association), which eventually paid off when they gave us much-needed financial support, as well as their invaluable official endorsement. Meanwhile, I coordinated with our international colleagues via the street papers network, and Harald started trying to persuade his home city to make our project one of its showcase events in 2003.

The Homeless World Cup was one of 500 projects that applied for funds in Graz, so Harald had a tough job convincing the powers that be. 'OK,' he said, 'you've got your operas and ballets. Why not homeless people in a soccer competition in the centre of the city?'

It may have been a highly original pitch, but Harald's presentation didn't seem to be working at first. The committee members didn't seem to recognise the benefits of homeless people getting involved in their cultural festival.

But Harald had a few tricks up his sleeves – a bag full of street papers from countries all over the world. 'The people of Brazil will see Graz,' he declared, pulling out a copy of the street paper from Brazil. 'The people of England will see Graz,' he continued, pulling out *The Big Issue.*

Thirty papers later, he had made his point and won the backing of the committee, including financial support. As a bonus, we were also given access to the media centre set up by the city, as well as help from other public agencies.

Soon afterwards, at the 2002 INSP conference in Madrid, we announced that we had European backing and the plans at once started to gather momentum, working out the format of the tournament, the rules and the travel arrangements, plus 1,001 other details.

Then, we started going backwards...

We had been confident of winning European Union (EU) support but in January 2003, just a few months before kick-off, the offer of money was suddenly cancelled.

Then a few weeks later Harald had a heart attack.

* * * * *

The phone rings in my Edinburgh office. It's Harald calling me from Austria. We haven't had a chat for a couple of days, but we've been working very closely together for months. 'You aren't going to believe this,' he tells me, sounding his usual jovial self. 'I'm in intensive care!' 'What?' I say, not sure I've heard him correctly. 'I've had a heart attack!' 'You're joking!'

Fit and healthy Harald? Clean-living Harald? Two days ago, he suddenly collapsed, while playing football. No warning signs. No wonder he's been quiet for a couple of days. 'But there's no need to worry!' he says. 'No?' I say, still thinking this is Harald's perverse sense of humour. 'Bernhard will take over from me, starting tomorrow.' 'Bernhard who?' I ask, struggling to put names to faces. 'Wolf.' 'Bernhard Wolf? 'I will give you his telephone number.'

Fifteen minutes later, I believe him. He's really in intensive care. He's really had a heart attack. It isn't his warped sense of humour. But there's only four months until kick-off and 50 per cent of our management team is in hospital: Harald.

* * * * *

All logic told me we should cancel straight away. But then I asked my friend Layla Mathers, the INSP secretary, what she thought: 'There is something about all of this which I feel is significant and therefore I've concluded that we should just proceed, which is totally crazy. So what do you think?'

If Layla said no, I was ready to cancel. 'You're crazy anyway,' said Layla. 'Do the opposite of what appears to be totally sensible and make things happen. It's what you people do.'

Decision made.

* * * * *

The next four months saw many highs and lows but eventually, everything fell into place. Harald's doctor advised him to rest but he couldn't resist doing something to help, although Bernhard took over most of his duties.

Meanwhile, we were still short of money – as always. But the city fathers in Graz were so disappointed by the decision of the European Union not to give us the funding we needed that they raised the cash from several local government departments and also brought in private sponsors.

Another major boost came from UEFA soon after. Harald had been talking to UEFA for months and they also came forward to back us. Football has often been criticised in modern times for being a 'rich man's game' which has lost touch with its grass roots despite the fact that many leading players come from underprivileged backgrounds. And that is partly why UEFA backed us. 'We were committed to supporting initiatives in the community and also because we think this tournament will genuinely help tackle exclusion,' said UEFA's chief executive at the time, Lars-Christer Olsson.

In January the same year, we also made a breakthrough on the sponsorship front, during the World Economic Forum (WEF) in Davos, when Nike gave us 50,000 euros – and even more importantly, help to develop the 'brand' and our network.

It had been a long and sometimes painful journey. But all roads led to Graz. And we were ready for kick-off.

* * * * *

'Coming to the Homeless World Cup every year is like coming home for Xmas,' Harald tells me as we sit in the media tent, nine years later in Mexico City. 'It's always different – different venues, different players. I am proud and very happy that the Homeless World Cup is still going, and attracting so much international interest. Looking at the players' faces, they are always new but they always behave in very similar ways. There is always the same great atmosphere, same friendship and warm-heartedness. These guys are from the street and when they play here, they are brilliant!'

Harald says that Graz was 'our first child – our baby!' And very soon, he says, we started to feel responsible for it, and determined to make it grow bigger and better. At the time, we never spoke about carrying on after Graz. Maybe it would just be a once-in-a-lifetime event, or maybe we would hold another tournament four years later, like the FIFA World Cup. 'But three weeks afterwards,' he tells me, 'you had been thinking and thinking, and I saw the look in your eyes, and I knew that you would carry on. I also knew I wanted to be part of it, no matter what happened. And now we're in Mexico City.'

We had a vision and a dream for Graz, but since then it has grown from only 18 teams to 60 teams, plus many more partners in countries all over the world. Great football stars have also been involved, and influential people like Archbishop Tutu have also made big contributions, along with major sponsors such as Nike and Telmex. 'We had a feeling people would love it,' says Harald, 'but there have been a lot of ups and downs, and money problems right from the start.'

According to Harald, even his home town of Graz did not welcome the players 100 per cent – perhaps because the tournament was something they had never imagined before. 'One official was worried that the Homeless World Cup would be bad for business, but we managed to convince him that the opposite would happen.'

As we sit together, thinking of the lead-up to Graz, it's still hard for Harald and me to believe that it turned out to be such a major event, in terms of sporting drama as well as its impact on players and public perceptions of what homeless people are like. 'There were so many paths to walk, and many people to persuade,' says Harald, getting up to go and cover Austria's next game for national TV. 'We also had to raise a lot of money. But we had a vision, and after the first event turned out so well, we knew that it had huge potential.'

Harald looks at me. It's almost ten years later but we both still believe in this crazy idea. 'What's the secret?' I ask him. 'The players make it work,' says Harald. 'Simply the players.'

* * * * *

In those early days, Harald played a critical role in the growth of the Homeless World Cup from a dream to a real-life event, and he still manages to come to almost every annual tournament, despite all his other commitments.

Harald later explains why he first got involved with street papers, and what still motivates him now: 'A few years ago, I read a book called *Globalization from the bottom up* which talked about the conflict between the rise of global multinationals and the globalisation which was also emerging because of the Internet – a communications revolution from the bottom up. The Homeless World Cup became a symbol of this and a platform for change. And what motivated me was helping to make sure that globalisation was not just a negative thing. The gap between the rich and poor is getting bigger, so we have to counteract this.'

For Harald, soccer was the other inspiration from the very beginning, and the network of papers that joined us: 'The street papers are still very much part of it all, but the Homeless World Cup has become something else. It has developed an identity all of its own.'

The business world also had lessons for Harald, who first worked as a teacher then a journalist. 'Street papers were perfect for me, working with like-minded people and writing. But I always thought you also needed business solutions and business methods to make it sustainable, so even though I was working in the social sector, I did a few business courses. Maybe if I'd started out in business, I would have arrived at the same place, the other way round.'

* * * * *

Even a heart attack didn't stop Harald from playing his part in the birth of the Homeless World Cup. For me, the news came as a shock, but for Harald it was just another natural event in life, even though he was relatively young at the time, and also much fitter than most other people I knew. 'I had my heart attack ten years ago,' says Harald later on, 'and I certainly didn't expect it! The very day it happened, I left the house and told my wife I felt 18 years old again, I felt so good. But I was pushing myself too hard, working too late at night, trying to do everything at once. I felt the pressure, and my body told me, "don't do this to me, I am not a machine." So I had to change.'

Harald still pushes himself very hard, but sometimes he has to step back. 'Having a heart attack is always a major event,' he explains, 'but in fact I was lucky. The heart attack did not cause any damage, but it taught me a lesson. You have to be positive and have a zest for life, learn how to live with it.'

When Harald left hospital, there were only six weeks till the tournament started, but by then, the toughest times were behind us. Now we could focus on the soccer and the teams.

* * * * *

For Harald, Graz is still a precious memory, like when we watched the Netherlands team being mobbed by local fans outside the stadium and asked for autographs. 'So that will be the homeless people, then?' both of us said at the very same moment. And we still smile together remembering that special moment, because it made us realise the idea was beginning to work.

Harald also remembers one of the players in Graz whose story really touched him at the time. He was an older guy from the US and hadn't seen his daughter for the last 15 years, but Fox News made a documentary about him, and his family got in touch with him after they saw it – something that would never have happened if the player had not been in Graz. 'There are always a couple of tears in my eyes whenever I am touched by the spirit of the Homeless World Cup,' says Harald.

* * * * *

What made the first event such a success despite all the obstacles put in our way was that everyone was equally determined to make it all work, even though some colleagues running street papers laughed at the idea to start with. Umberto, the editor of the street paper in Milan, even confessed that he 'hated' the game – but everybody loved the whole idea of an international tournament and giving the players a platform. Ron Grunberg, the editor of *Upward* and *Big News*, who brought the USA team to Graz, initially thought the idea was absurd. But no matter what anyone thought of 'The Beautiful Game', the critical factor was that all of us were united in our attitudes to homelessness and part of a network that knew how to influence public opinion – and make the magic possible, against all the odds.

* * * * *

Within a few days of the kick-off in Graz, we knew we had created an event where homeless people were perceived in a completely different light. They were no longer homeless but heroes. And that is exactly the point. It is all about changing perceptions – how homeless people view themselves and how other people view them.

From Day One in Graz, the local people's attitudes to homelessness started to change, and this was reflected in the smiles of the players. The stigma of homelessness was gradually being removed, and the crowds were beginning to buzz with excitement, the same as crowds at any other major sporting event.

The players won the hearts and minds of everyone who came along and showed what sport was really all about. The Switzerland team, for example, conceded a total of 65 goals, but every time they scored a goal, the stadium erupted. They may have been recovering addicts and they may have lost all of their games, but the crowd was on their side, cheering every time they appeared on the field to the magical sound of their cow bells. The bond between the players and the crowd was getting stronger every day. Barriers were coming down. Perceptions were changing. All the teams – including Switzerland – were winners.

*****

As the tournament gathered momentum, we had to get extra TV screens so more fans could watch in the square. Homeless people were becoming the talk of the city, applauded in the streets and interviewed by media from all around the world – over 20 broadcasters and more than 90 journalists registered for the event. 'You forget they're homeless people,' said a Reuters photographer one day in Graz, 'as soon as the camera's on them.'

Before the tournament, the *New York Times* published a feature on the Homeless World Cup which attracted a lot of attention and encouraged other media – including HBO and ESPN – to cover the event. HBO produced a documentary on Team USA which won lots of praise from the critics, while the Polish director Mirek Dembinski recorded the build-up before adding footage from Graz, for his film called *Losers and Winners*.

As the week went on, the cameras were everywhere. The media had fallen in love with it all. Their view of homelessness was being transformed, and suddenly, the homeless players found themselves making the headlines.

*****

The players were also beginning to change as the spirit of the Homeless World Cup spread through the teams. 'You've got to take the homelessness out of people's heads and you can do that by involving them in teams,' said the Manchester United coaches Dave Bell and Louis Garvey, the managers of England's squad in Graz.

England eventually got through to the final and it was self-belief and determination not to return to a life on the streets that got them there. For one of the young England players, however, the chief goal was simply to find a new reason for living. He had tried to kill himself only a short time before, when he ended up homeless, alienated from his family and friends. Feeling worthless. In total despair. 'Now I am here,' he told me in private, 'and I've never experienced anything like this, so I will go back home and promise you I'll never try suicide ever again, because I know that whatever happens

I will always retain self-respect. And it's down to the people in Graz who applauded and made me feel human.'

*****

Yuri Kuzmin, the 42-year-old captain of Russia, was also deeply moved by the welcome he got from the people of Graz. Yuri was a victim of the economic crisis which had hit his country five years before, losing his business (a shoe shop) and forced to move out of his flat. 'I tried not to think about being homeless,' Yuri explained. 'Life continued. I tried to find work and I still had my girlfriend and circle of friends.'

After Yuri heard about the Homeless World Cup, he decided to give it a try. 'I'm an adventurer,' he said. 'Anything new is always interesting and I started playing football for the very first time in my life. It was quite traumatic but also amazing to see what playing could achieve.'

Selected for the Russian team and then appointed captain, Yuri was proud to be part of it all. Apart from meeting other homeless people from countries all over the world, it was the international atmosphere that moved him the most. One day, in Graz, an orchestra from Latin America was playing in the square when one of the musicians dedicated the next piece of music to the players from Russia – he had studied in St Petersburg some years before. 'We tried to hide our tears,' said Yuri. 'I will never forget this.'

*****

The USA team made a big impression from the start, including Harris Pankin with his mass of unruly hair, scraggly beard and Lennon-style metal-rimmed glasses, which he wore throughout all of the games. According to his manager, Harris always arrived first at training – and always grumbled that no-one else showed up on time. Sometimes, there were very good reasons for not showing up. One day as he was heading for a session in New York, one of the players was beaten up so badly that he ended up in hospital and had to miss training. Another player, trying to recover from cocaine and heroin addiction, had to go back to rehab.

Like many players, getting a passport – or even trying to prove who you are – can also be a struggle, and one of Harris's team-mates needed a lawyer to twist a few arms. Another with a drinking problem had to go to great lengths to convince his counsellor he would not have a relapse while playing abroad. But all of them made it to Graz.

Harris used to be lead singer in a punk band and was homeless for over three years before going to Graz. He was also one of the most passionate and bad-tempered players – a perfectionist who said he got much more upset with himself than the rest of the team.

In Graz, he became so immersed in the action that he seemed to forget where he was, chasing after referees, demanding penalties and running after every ball as if his life depended on it – never giving up for one single second as the crowd sang, 'Harris! Harris!' to inspire him on to even greater efforts. At the end of one game which finished 5-5, thus requiring a penalty shoot-out to decide the result, the crowd demanded Harris take the kick. And he didn't let anyone down as he strolled up to bang the ball into the net, igniting the roar of the fans.

The USA team boss Ron Grunberg knew so little about this strange game called 'football' when the Homeless World Cup first appeared on the radar that he asked if players had to wear a helmet. But by the time he got to Graz, his attitude had turned around completely. 'To talk just about the soccer doesn't do it justice,' he said at the time. 'For me, it was a transporting moment. It was unimaginable and unforgettable. Some people say the money should have been used to feed people. Man doesn't live by bread alone, however. Sitting eating soup three times a day is mind-numbingly boring, but you can change through some form of active engagement, and that is what happened in Graz.'

*****

Another US player I will always remember is Rory Levine, a survivor of the terrible events of 9/11. For Rory, the journey to Graz began two years before when the building where he used to work, in the shadow of the Twin Towers, was reduced to rubble after the deadly attacks on New York.

Rory was one of the lucky ones. He was late for work that morning. But if he'd got to work on time, he may not have survived. Even though his life was spared, Rory was suddenly out of a job. And because he had no regular income, he could not pay his rent and was evicted, ending up on the streets.

As the world grieved for the victims and their families, Rory was simply forgotten – like the millions of other invisible people classified as 'homeless' in New York and many other North American cities.

Then Rory was chosen for Graz, and his life started turning around: 'We won our first game and I felt overwhelmed,' Rory said. 'It was exhilarating. People were actually cheering us. The media were following us, their cameras were flashing and their microphones were pushed toward us.'

Rory was the centre of attention with his trademark bandana and toothpick. And he soon became an unlikely trend-setter, too: 'All these kids started wearing bandanas,' said Rory. 'And after a couple of days, I saw them with toothpicks as well.'

The USA team did well in Graz, winning three of their preliminary group games – but also winning many hearts and minds: 'We destroyed the stereotype of the homeless person,' said Rory. 'We didn't look homeless, we were proud, we looked smart and the people watching us thought we were cool. And we were. We were athletes.'

Soon after he returned to New York, Rory left the shelter and got a new job and a home in the Bronx. 'The tournament gave me a new perspective,' Rory added. 'After Graz, I thought, I can beat this homeless thing.'

* * * * *

Football fans are always testing each other's knowledge of the game they adore. Another star in Graz, Mark Elliot, posed one of the most difficult questions of all when he stood in a packed bar in Glasgow years later and asked: 'Who's the only Scottish football player who has ever scored a hat-trick (three goals in a game) versus Brazil?'

Silence for a moment as everybody racked their brains and went back into ancient sporting history in search of the answer.

'Denis Law?' someone suggested, invoking the name of one of Scotland's greatest football legends.

'No,' said Mark, pausing for effect. 'It was me!'

Mark's greatest sporting achievement was one of the highlights of Scotland's appearance in Graz. Scotland played Brazil twice in the early stages, losing both games, but Mark will never forget his famous hat-trick or the experience of playing in the very first Homeless World Cup.

His story is also a lesson in how you can suddenly find yourself homeless – and how you can turn things around.

Mark became homeless at 16 years old. His parents had divorced four years before and his mother got involved in an abusive relationship that ended with her early death. Living with his father and his new stepmother did not work out, and Mark ended up in one of Glasgow's hostels for the homeless – large impersonal places run the same way as prisons – where it was easy for any young man to get sucked into drug abuse, bullying and casual violence.

'It was horrible,' said Mark. 'Bell Street Hostel was the worst experience of my life. But it opened my eyes to homelessness. It was full of old alcoholics or young guys full of heroin. And nothing in between.'

Mark did not have any huge personal problems before he went into the hostel, but he soon became very depressed and 'sank into a deeper and deeper hole.' Even though he was tempted by drugs, 'just to escape from reality,' he chose a different path: playing football in a street league organised by the Queens Cross Housing Association. Then he was selected to play for the national team in the Homeless World Cup – an experience he later described as 'surreal.'

'I was just a homeless boy from Glasgow,' he explained, 'and later I was catapulted into the limelight. I was given superstar status and was being treated as if I was a real football star, with people coming up to me in the street and asking me for autographs. I felt seven-foot high.'

Mark quickly realised he wasn't alone, and that he was better off than many of the others. 'I learned a lot. The whole experience altered my life. I suddenly had motivation, confidence and a reason for not lying in bed all day. And I came back from Graz and started to look for a job as a coach.'

Soon afterwards, Mark got his coaching certificates and went on to teach other young players: 'After my experiences, I'd like to put something back.'

* * * * *

Mark Elliot would be quick to acknowledge that the legendary Brazilian striker Ronaldo was a slightly better player than he was. But just like Mark, Ronaldo also wanted to give something back, coaching the Spain team preparing for Graz.

Modesto was one of the players who treasured that visit the most. For him, the Homeless World Cup was the start of a new life – and the end of five years living on the streets of Madrid with his 'homeless' cats and dogs.

'Bad luck and a bad head' had caused Modesto's problems, including his gambling. 'My head can bring me bad ideas. I didn't want to be kidnapped by them any more.'

At that time, there were no shelters or hostels for homeless people in the capital city, but Modesto admitted that he did have his freedom and rarely met any hostility from other people. 'They knew that I wasn't a thief,' he explained. 'They trusted me and sometimes even asked me to look after their market stalls. I felt that I was part of the community, even though I didn't have a proper home.'

The 'community' of football was the answer for Modesto in 2003 when he was selected to represent Spain in the Homeless World Cup – an unforgettable experience that gave him strength in ways he had never expected.

Something unexpected also happened after he got back from Graz: 'When I returned, the police had taken away my possessions, which I had hidden in the park. All I had in the world were the friendships I brought back from Austria. Everyone spoke their own language but even if we didn't know one single word, we all managed to understand each other.'

Like most other players, Modesto had never been out of the country before or flown on a plane. 'And suddenly, my dreams were coming true, because of football.'

The Spain team thought the other teams looked taller and stronger than them, and they wanted to prove – to themselves and the others – that they were just as good. 'We didn't want to look like poor people. No way! We were football players representing our country who just happened to live on the street.'

Ronaldo's visit was a big boost to the Spain team before they departed for Graz, but Modesto was not overawed by celebrity status and knew that many professional stars came from very poor backgrounds and were not so different from him or his team-mates: 'David Beckham lives in a palace in Madrid and he plays football with other people who live in palaces, but if his circumstances had been different, he might have been playing in the Homeless World Cup.'

* * * * *

The Denmark team was visited by soccer legend Pele before they departed for Graz, and were also inspired by the world's greatest player. Pele also came from a very poor background. He grew up in the streets of Sao Paulo, playing football with a sock stuffed with newspaper, tied up with string, so he knew what it meant not just to overcome adversity but also what it meant to represent your country.

Pele would have smiled to see Brazil at the Homeless World Cup, and recognised a little of himself in the players. As the tournament got underway, several people noticed the Brazil team were playing without any boots. Thinking they could not afford proper footwear, the fans bought them boots, but even though the players seemed happy to get them, in their next game, they played in their bare feet as usual. It was what they were used to and they also believed that it helped them play better.

Brazil were disappointed when they lost the semi-final to their Austrian hosts after a penalty shoot-out, but they won the hearts and minds of the people of Graz. Like their Brazilian friends, Modesto and his team-mates also missed out on the coveted trophy, but they were just as proud to represent their country as Beckham, Ronaldo and Pele – and were treated the same as their heroes by fans. 'The Homeless World Cup was a once-in-a-lifetime experience,' continues Modesto. 'You feel so special when you go out on the pitch. You feel this huge wave of support.'

Modesto may have only been 'a homeless man who lived in Madrid' but people stopped him in the street to shake his hand and ask for autographs.

After Graz, he went back to Madrid and moved into a hostel with his girlfriend and two-month-old son. 'I want to be like everyone else,' he said. 'I want to keep my family together. I want my son to be proud of me, to see me as a winner – a man who has played for his country and works for his dreams. I want to feel alive. I want to be like other human beings. We all have goals to reach.'

* * * * *

For Harald and me, one of the highlights in Graz was sitting together to watch Scotland and Austria play. It was how it all started. The dream had come true.

His doctor had told him to rest, but Harald joined me every morning for meetings and also did interviews during the day. He told me he was probably working at half normal pace, but according to my calculations, that would be a lot more than the average person.

The Scotland-Austria match is a thriller. The crowd roars and just for a moment, I forget it is only a game. 'Come on, Scotland!' I shout at the top of my voice, as if this is the greatest match in history. 'Go-o-o-a-a-l-l!' I scream as Scotland take the lead. 'It's only a game, Mel,' says Harald, as Scotland win two goals to one.

* * * * *

The standard of football in Graz was amazing and the crowds played a huge part in building the atmosphere right from the start. Some teams were more competitive than others, and that helped them focus on issues like teamwork and fitness. Others came along for the experience.

The atmosphere throughout the week is truly inspiring, and Harald is delighted it has also been so entertaining. His only criticism is my German – it was my job to declare the tournament open and despite hours of practice, I messed up completely.

I have only one thing to say in defence: 'In Graz, we're breaking all the rules of football, and I am breaking all the rules of German.'

* * * * *

Everything is going very well, but the day before the Finals, the trophy goes missing en route from Edinburgh to Graz.

I know this is not the most critical issue but the trophy is more than a symbol of winning the Homeless World Cup – it belongs to every team and every player, and we want it in Graz for the Finals.

After frantic phone calls, we discover that the trophy is stuck in a warehouse in Brussels – there's been a complication with the paperwork. So what do we say? 'We have more than 90 journalists and 25 broadcasters showing this 'live' round the world, and it wouldn't look too good for you if the trophy was not here in time for the finals. There are thousands of fans here. Just think about the disappointed faces of the players. It could be a PR disaster.'

But that isn't how we do things.

We have an idea: 'If you can get it to Salzburg tonight, we can get it to Graz by tomorrow, and instead of a disaster, there will be a hero's welcome, for you and the driver!'

And the next day, the trophy arrives just in time, delivered straight to Harald's home at five in the morning. 'When I woke up and opened the door, there it was,' says Harald. 'When I saw it for the first time, that was special. And my two young boys came out and said it seemed the greatest trophy in the world – and it was!'

After two years of planning and one week of action, it's time for the Finals...

* * * * *

Eighteen-year-old Nigerian Angus Okanume is excited as Finals Day reaches its climax. The semi-finals have been thrilling and the action has been non-stop since the very first game. England edge the first semi-final, scoring the winner against the Netherlands with only two seconds to go. Austria then beat Brazil in a nail-biting climax, winning a penalty shoot-out. The Brazil players burst into tears as the crowd cheer them off at the end of an all-action thriller. Then the rain starts.

Angus is used to the rain. But last year was the first time he had ever seen snow. 'And there is lots of snow in Austria during the winter!' he says.

Born in 1985 in Onisha, Angus entered Austria illegally two years ago. He had fled his native country because of a flare-up between local Christians and Muslims. Fearing for his life, he paid illegal traffickers to get out of the country and ended up in Graz, where he was in the care of Caritas, a charity backed by the Catholic Church. On the day of the Finals, he was living in a shelter for asylum seekers, still waiting for his case to be reviewed – not unusual in a country where such cases can sometimes take up to ten years to resolve.

Life in Graz hasn't been easy. 'I had to deal with lots of new things like the food,' he says. 'Some people also have negative attitudes – they do not see you as a person but only that you are black. Or they might suspect you are dealing with drugs.'

The best time that Angus has had since arriving in the middle of Europe is making new friends at the Homeless World Cup, as a member of the Austria team who have just won their way to the Final, all of them asylum seekers just like himself – now the favourites to win the inaugural trophy. 'Meeting other players from different nations has helped me learn what homelessness is like around the world,' says Angus, gazing out over the pitch where his team will soon be having their showdown with England. 'Playing here has given me great motivation. As an asylum seeker, you have to be patient and wait for your status to alter. But I have found confidence now and am sure opportunities will open up.'

Harald is proud of his national team. 'The tournament has not only helped to change the image of homeless people but also asylum seekers, showing what a contribution they can make to Austria.'

Just one game to go but Angus and his team-mates are ready for anything now, even if it snows in the middle of summer.

* * * * *

The players are ready to take to the field, but just before kick-off, with the stands packed with hundreds of people, the rain starts to pour down on Graz. Play can't go on – the concrete surface is too slippery. 'Should we postpone till tomorrow?' we ask each other, knowing that the atmosphere created in the stadium will never be the same again the following day. But will the fans stay for the climax?

Then the fans give us their answer. Every single person refuses to move. They will stay until the rain stops, no matter how long it continues.

Eventually the clouds lift and the Final begins. It's a close match and both teams are determined to win. But the host nation comes out on top in the end, beating England by two goals to one. And the crowd is ecstatic.

Before the trophy is presented to the Austrian players, every single player who has taken part receives a special medal – the start of a tradition that continues till today. Switzerland is another very popular winner, taking home the Fair Play Trophy, which is also still awarded every year.

Then the moment everyone is waiting for – as the Austria team lift the trophy and all the teams start dancing in the centre of the stadium, before a lap of honour in front of the still cheering fans. The song *We are the Champions* booms out of the speakers as the players hug and celebrate their moment of triumph. The flashbulbs pop like firecrackers. Everyone stands up and joins in the clapping and dancing. Everyone's a winner. 'It's only a game,' I tell Harald, as his countrymen show off the trophy and the first Homeless World Cup refuses to come to an end.

* * * * *

The first Homeless World Cup is over. The players go back to the village, and the singing and dancing continues for hours, as everyone celebrates into the night.

The next day, I wake very early and go for a solitary walk round the city, to gather my thoughts. The stadium is already being dismantled, as life in Graz goes back to normal. But my life and the lives of all the people involved will never be the same again. The event has been a great success and the whole team is feeling elated. Thanks to the power of soccer, the lives of homeless people are being transformed. The media have changed their view of homeless people from zeroes to heroes, and sent their message all around the world.

Harald and I have been able to see our dream become a reality. The Earth seems to tremble for a couple of seconds as I walk through the glistening streets of the city, still wet from the rain, with the mist rising into the air.

Something magical has happened. And we know a ball *can* change the world.

5

Why Soccer?

Q: Why soccer?
A: It's the universal language...

TUESDAY, 9 OCTOBER 2012: There are 1,000 ways to answer the question. But the simple fact is we believed from the start that a ball really can change the world.

If it hadn't been a 'soccer' story, Graz would not have captured much media interest. If we'd simply organised a conference on homelessness, and even if we'd put some homeless people centre stage before the media, the response would have been disappointing. But because it was a soccer competition called the Homeless World Cup, the media were curious and turned up in force. 'Soccer is a great way to get different people involved, regardless of fitness or age,' I tell a reporter from England who joins the ever-present Fernando and me, as we walk towards the Zocalo early one morning. 'And soccer can lead to profound psychological change. When you're homeless, living on the streets, you only think about today, and how to survive till tomorrow. You are only concerned with yourself, not with anyone else. But when you play soccer, and pass the ball to someone else, you're starting to relate to other people. You're suddenly becoming an integral part of a team.'

I then explain how when players meet other teams at the Homeless World Cup, they realise that they are not alone. Homelessness is also very different from country to country, but homeless people have one thing in common – exclusion. They know what it is like to be rejected by society and made to feel as if they are not part of the 'team.'

Soccer is what brings the different countries together. Even though they may not understand what other players are saying, they speak the same language – the international language of soccer. And that changes people's perspective on life. You can see it in front of your eyes at the Homeless World Cup every day.

'What about other sports?' asks the reporter.

'Most people enjoy playing or watching soccer. But soccer doesn't work for everyone, in terms of social change. Not everything we do will work for everyone and many other sports can also be very effective. We have a huge impact on players all over the world, but we're not the only solution.'

'So how does it work?'

Homelessness can be a very complicated issue for each individual affected but our solution is the same in every country: the power of soccer.

Soccer is a simple game as well as the most popular sport in the world. You don't need any special equipment. You don't need to be any good at playing, to enjoy it. All you need is a ball.

The great appeal of soccer is that anyone can play – old or young, male or female, big or small. You don't need to be skilled or athletic to enjoy it, and any number of people can play, wherever there is space to kick a ball around.

When you're homeless, you're alone and isolated. But when you play soccer, you escape for a time, and suddenly find yourself part of a team.

This is an important psychological shift because when you pass the ball to somebody else, you are beginning to connect with other people, who have had the same experience as you. And very soon, the team becomes a family.

When you become homeless, you quickly lose your self-respect and confidence. But the experience of being in a soccer team helps to re-build self-esteem and reintegrate into the wider community by being part of something special that you share with other people. You start taking one simple step at a time. And the first step is to go and kick a ball around.

There are games and training sessions in locations all over the world every week, run by organisations that work hand in hand with the Homeless World Cup and share the same philosophy of using soccer as a catalyst for change. When they turn up for games, many players are counselled and all are encouraged to get fit and healthy. Soccer coaches also help with technical aspects, developing the players' skills, building team spirit, and creating a disciplined atmosphere where everyone can play an equal part. Sometimes, just having somewhere to go at a regular time every week can make a huge difference. It's something to look forward to and also makes it easier to steer away from negative environments.

As players get more involved, they improve their fitness and develop their skills. Many are invited to participate in national trials, to select the team to represent their country at the Homeless World Cup. Different countries use different methods to choose teams. Some have knock-out tournaments for teams from different areas or cities and the winning team then represents its country, while other countries hold trials and select a team of individual players from various places who may not even meet until they set off for the tournament – maybe not until they check in at the airport.

Players only have one opportunity to play in the Homeless World Cup, and then move on to build better lives for themselves and inspire other people to follow. It is all about creating the next generation of leaders, so every organisation becomes self-sustaining.

A few extremely talented players at the Homeless World Cup have been signed by professional and semi-professional teams. Some have gone on to be coaches. But players are not just selected because they are brilliant at soccer. Many players are also selected because they are good for the team.

* * * * *

As well as the experience of many different languages and cultures, plus hours of brilliant non-stop soccer action, head referee Iain McGill loves the fact that different people get together every year at the Homeless World Cup, including officials and players. 'We are very aware we are part of the players' experience,' Iain explains.

The referees (all volunteers) can 'make their day' but also have to make sure that everyone plays by the rules. Many players have a problem with authority, gained from their lives on the street, so when they meet the 'Man in Black', they sometimes react. And that is when the referees have to be human as well as professional, ensuring the highest of standards and treating the players as equals. 'Above all,' says Iain, 'we must treat the players with absolute, total respect.'

According to Iain, 'The players have an overwhelming desire to do well. After all, they're playing for their country, and the games are 'live' on TV, and their families may also be watching, so we have to help them all manage the pressure.'

Iain also confesses that the men in the middle can sometimes be wrong. Once, when he didn't award a goal to one of the teams, a player on the other side politely informed him he'd made a mistake. 'It was an act of outrageous honesty,' says Iain.

It's hard for referees to be professional for every single game in every tournament, and Iain says the hardest games are when the result is extremely one-sided. 'If one team is losing by a very wide margin, you have to focus even more,' he says. 'But if the game is very close, it's easier – you can't take your eye off the action for one single second.'

The Homeless World Cup means a lot to every single player. 'Up close and personal, we see it in their eyes,' Iain tells me. 'There's always lots of pressure, but it's always an honour.'

* * * * *

What makes it most rewarding for Iain and the other officials is when someone comes up to them during the tournament, greeting them like long-lost friends and asking them if they remember their names. Maybe they are coaches now or volunteers. 'You look at them and suddenly, you recognise their faces, and remember they were players once, in Cape Town or Melbourne or Rio, and now they have jobs and a home of their own, and the Homeless World Cup was the turning point for them,' says Iain. 'To know that you have played a part in their experience, even a small part, is brilliant – even when it's one of the players you may have sent off.'

One player given the blue card (our version of the red card) in Rio, Camilo Gonzalez, did not only walk up to Iain years later and greet him like a long-lost friend, he also announced he would be an official in Chile, for the Homeless World Cup in 2014.

Being sent off may have been the low point for Camilo in 2010, but the high point was the 'Player of the Tournament' award, when the young man got a standing ovation at the end of the tournament on Copacabana.

Camilo's story is a typical tale, with a twist. At 14, he had run away from home to pursue his dream of becoming a professional soccer player, after being scouted by a leading team in Chile. But his parents didn't want him to go for a trial, because he was too young and still at high school, so Camilo left home and soon after found himself homeless.

Six years later, he made his appearance in Rio and after he went back to Chile, he was signed by Santiago team Magallanes. Then everything went wrong again...

Only 12 months into his contract, Camilo suffered an injury that ended his career. 'In one moment, it was over,' Camilo told journalist (and Homeless World Cup veteran) Danielle Batiste.

But in retrospect, Camilo thinks the injury was also a blessing in disguise: 'I think that's when my mindset changed,' he added. 'As a teenager, I only lived for football. Now, I realise that other things are also important – including my wife and my child. I now know how important family is and have a new motivation in life.'

Soccer may not be the most important thing in his new life, but Camilo still loves it and now has his official referee's badge. 'After Rio, I wanted to give something back,' Camilo told Danielle. 'When I couldn't be a player any more, I decided to become a referee. That way, I am still involved in the game, and I hope to be able to inspire other players who are in the same position I was once in.'

Camilo was the first former player to become an official, and for Iain, that's exactly what the Homeless World Cup is about. The Chilean is now an invaluable part of the referee team – including South African referee Jabulane Nkosinathi Mahono, best known as 'Shoes', the man who sent Camilo off during the Rio event. 'It will be hard for me to referee a game instead of playing,' said Camilo, 'but I want to do the best I can. The players deserve a great experience, just like I had.'

Camilo's achievement is also a tribute to the people who work for the Homeless World Cup every year, and in Iain's view, Camilo is also the future of the Homeless World Cup, because one day he'll pass on his knowledge to others, completing the circle.

* * * * *

'How do players qualify to play in the Homeless World Cup?'

To qualify, the players must have been homeless at some point in the two years preceding the tournament, based on the criteria of individual national partners. For example, in most Western countries, the definition of homelessness is simply that the person does not have a permanent home or is living in a shelter for the homeless or enrolled in a drug rehabilitation programme. Political asylum seekers also play for many Western nations. In many Asian, Latin American or African countries, the major issues are unemployment, poverty and social exclusion, or the players may be victims of violence, rape, famine or war. The most important issue is that players are the 'poorest of the poor,' and good ambassadors, not only for their countries but also homeless people everywhere.

* * * * *

'Is street soccer different from ordinary soccer?'

The games are played on small pitches (22 metres long by 16 metres wide) in temporary stadiums erected in the centre of cities. Each team has eight players – with four players on the field at any one time and four rotating replacements. Matches last 15 minutes (seven minutes each way plus one minute at half-time), and the games are packed with action, with lots of goals and last-second winners. Each team plays an average of 13 games during the week – a total of well over 300 games. The tournament is structured so that every team plays every day and also plays a 'Final' on the last day of the tournament, against another team of a similar level. At the end of the tournament, every player is presented with the same medal, and every team also goes home with a trophy. Everyone's a winner and has something to play for, and everyone plays every day.

'Is it very competitive?'

The teams vary widely in terms of ability and in their attitudes to competition. Some are keen to win while others are more interested in the experience of being there. Friendship and sportsmanship matter for everyone much more than winning or losing, and games are often highly emotional both for the players and fans.

The players may come from opposite sides of the world but they're also united in their love of the beautiful game, because it has enabled them to turn their lives around, and because it is simply a great game to play.

The games are exciting and fast, with no let-up for players or fans. You can see players struggling to move at the end of the game, even though they've only been on the field a few minutes. The crowd are often sitting on the edge of their seats – it has a magnetism and a special magic about it. We've changed the rules over the years, but it's still the same basic game.

* * * * *

'What happens after the Finals? What happens during the rest of the year?'

When the tournament ends, the hard work continues in countries around the world, 365 days every year. As soon as all the managers and coaches return, they start the whole process all over again, organising training sessions, providing support for the players already enrolled in their programmes, and scouting in the streets for the next generation of players.

The tournament is always a great celebration of the work done by our national partners but the greatest impact takes place on the street every day.

* * * * *

Sometimes, the best way to answer the question, 'Why soccer?' is simply to describe a game which sums up the spirit of the Homeless World Cup, whether it's a thrilling encounter or an underdog winning against all the odds, or maybe an unlikely fightback, with seconds to go. Or simply an example of a homeless person winning the hearts and the minds of the crowd.

The annual event is a very emotional sporting occasion but it goes a lot deeper than soccer. It is also about how the players 'rewrite the rules of the game.' Some games are end-to-end classics but others simply demonstrate what it means to be human.

One of the greatest sporting rivalries in history is Germany versus the Netherlands, so when the two teams met in Graz in the first Homeless World Cup, everyone anticipated yet another epic encounter – like their meeting in the final of the FIFA World Cup in 1974, when the Germans broke the hearts of the Dutch.

The Homeless World Cup is different, however. The Dutch won both games easily.

Then something wonderful happened...

When the whistle was blown at the end of the second game, the Netherlands goalkeeper raced to the opposite end of the pitch, hoisted the German keeper onto his shoulders and did a lap of honour around the arena. The whole crowd cheered and stamped their feet. This was what the Homeless World Cup was about.

* * * * *

One of my personal highlights was Scotland winning the trophy in Denmark, beating Poland in the Final. The Scotland team had played well in the earlier rounds but I thought just reaching the Final was the end of their journey. Poland had easily beaten the host country, Denmark, in their semi-final, and no-one gave Scotland a chance.

Perhaps it is part of the national psyche, but the underdogs seemed to grow several feet taller and blew their opponents away, taking full advantage of a new rule which demanded that at least one player stay inside the opponent's half throughout the game, to prevent teams being over-defensive. Although I am meant to be neutral, it was almost impossible to hide my excitement, as Scotland held out for the win. I was sitting with the Crown Prince of Denmark at the end of the game, talking very calmly, but inside I was almost exploding with joy.

* * * * *

Another unforgettable match was in Gothenburg in 2004, when Argentina met their traditional rivals Brazil. As both teams came onto the field, the crowd were expecting another tense match between the two 'best' teams in South America, but the players had exchanged shirts before the game started and played in their opponent's colours rather than their own. When they realised what had happened, everyone watching applauded the teams for their gesture – embracing the spirit of the Homeless World Cup.

* * * * *

Soccer stars are often criticised for acting like playboys and being out of touch with the people who pay them – their fans. But many of the biggest names in soccer come from very poor backgrounds and some of the world's poorest countries, so they know what it's like to have nothing – and many of them also want to give something back. Over the years, I've been lucky to meet some of the world's biggest stars, like legendary Manchester United player Eric Cantona, who coached the teams in Denmark.

The Copenhagen tournament happened the year after Cape Town, when the Homeless World Cup took a quantum leap forward in terms of global coverage and scale. It was hard to follow the razzmatazz and spectacular setting of Cape Town, but Eric did his best.

Eric is not just a soccer legend but an actor and a passionate campaigner on behalf of homeless people, so I was delighted when he said he would join us at one of our media meetings. Nicknamed 'King Eric' by Manchester United fans, Eric made headlines throughout his career, and was widely regarded as the *enfant terrible* of football. But when one of the journalists in Copenhagen asked him about one of his more controversial incidents, when Eric had been banned for several weeks, he refused to answer any further questions, and sat with his arms crossed for the rest of the session, staring straight into space.

Twelve years before in England, speaking to the media after his infamous ban, Eric famously said: 'When the seagulls follow the trawler, it's because they think sardines will be thrown into the sea. Thank you very much.' These enigmatic words were quoted all around the world, but this time, the French soccer legend had nothing to say. Not a word.

As I sat there, answering the rest of the questions, I wondered what Eric was thinking. Did he want to talk about homelessness rather than soccer? Did he want to generate more controversial headlines? Was he tired of being asked the same old questions?

Eric has a lot to say about poverty and homelessness issues. In early 2012, he even announced he was running for President of France on a homelessness ticket. It may only have been a publicity stunt to 'stand up for the millions of families who have been forgotten' and raise funds for his favourite homeless charity, but millions of people responded. He's a passionate supporter of what we are doing, and has been a Global Ambassador for the Homeless World Cup since 2007. People like him change the world.

* * * * *

After Eric's strangely quiet media session, he sat down to chat with the players, and right away Eric seemed more like himself – and the players responded.

They may have been star-struck but the players related to Eric because they sensed he understood exactly how they felt and how much they loved soccer. He treated the players as equals.

'Who's the best French player ever?' asked one of the players.

'Michel Platini?' the player suggested, referring to another soccer legend who became UEFA President.

Eric thought for a moment then answered: 'I once played Platini at tennis. I beat him!'

The day before, Eric had trained with the players, and during a penalty shoot-out, one of his efforts had been saved by the Germany keeper. 'You were one of the world's greatest penalty takers,' another player asked him. 'But did you miss deliberately?'

Silence for several seconds. I can see Eric puffing his chest out as if getting ready for action. He seems twice normal size. 'Cantona *never* misses a penalty. Ever.'

No need to say anything more.

The goalkeeper suddenly jumps from his seat, smiling ear to ear and waving his hands in the air, and the room fills with cheering and laughter. For the rest of his life, the keeper can tell people he saved a penalty by one of the world's greatest players. That's what the Homeless World Cup is about – the opportunity to change your life and take part in something you'll never forget.

* * * * *

Many famous players have supported the Homeless World Cup since the start, including Eric's Manchester United team-mate Rio Ferdinand, plus several players who have won the FIFA World Cup, including Emmanuel Petit (France), Marco Materazzi (Italy) and Romario (Brazil). Brazilian players bring a special magic wherever they go, like Neymar (who was one of the pin-ups in Rio in 2009) and the one-and-only Pele, who met the Danish players in 2003.

Another player who has recognised the power of the Homeless World Cup is one of Sweden's best-known and most popular players, Henrik

Larsson, who is also an ambassador for Gatans Lag, our partner in Sweden. Henrik sent a personal message to the Homeless World Cup in Mexico City, expressing solidarity with all of the players:

> **Soccer is the best game in the world. Respect one another. Have fun and play well. The Homeless World Cup is soon over, but the memories will be there forever and the friendship as well.**

Henrik's words were warmly welcomed by the players and coaches, but how many of them knew about the tragedy in Henrik's life? Star players are sometimes attacked for their 'glamorous' lifestyles, but behind all the glitz, there can often be something much darker.

In 2009, Henrik's brother Robert was found dead a few hours before Henrik played against Denmark in Stockholm. Henrik only heard the news after the end of the match. He had tried his best to help his brother win his fight with addiction, but in the end, it was impossible. Henrik told the *Summer Speakers* radio programme in Sweden: 'I've always had the power over my life and my career, but when it came to my brother's addiction, I was powerless.'

Henrik may have been unable to help his own brother, but he continues to support Gatans Lag, knowing better than most people how hard it is to overcome addiction, and also knowing more than most the power of sport.

These thoughts are all at the back of my mind as I chat with a reporter in the media tent, trying to express what the Homeless World Cup is about and the magic of soccer. The reporter says he's got enough facts for his story and asks for a final quote to round it all off. I have said something like this 1,001 times before but I know it is always worth saying again: 'From Afghanistan to Zimbabwe, everyone loves to play soccer – and the Homeless World Cup demonstrates that a ball really can change the world.' I know these words don't carry the same weight as Henrik's but somehow I think he'd agree.

* * * * *

As I bid the reporter farewell at the end of our talk in the media tent, I am thinking of all sorts of things, including why we started all this in the first place. I also remember that 12 months ago, I was standing in the shadow of the Eiffel Tower, as the tournament came to its climax...

Paris that year was a memorable tournament for various reasons, particularly the iconic venue. And one of the stars of the tournament was Emmanuel Petit – who not only has a medal for winning the FIFA World Cup for the host country France in 1998 but also scored in the Final.

Emmanuel won everything during his playing career, but like Henrik Larsson, he also knows exactly what it's like to lose a brother. He is also a bit of a rebel in the sometimes ugly world of soccer, where players can often earn more in a day than their fans earn in several years. But no matter how famous he is, Emmanuel is a model ambassador for the Homeless World Cup and also made a huge contribution to the success of the Paris event, coming along every day to speak to the players, signing autographs, posing for photos and answering every enquiry with incredible patience.

Emmanuel is also a 'political' player, believing that the world of soccer mirrors the state of the world as a whole, with too much money at the top and not enough at grass-roots level. He also criticises the 'football elite' who currently dominate soccer, giving nothing back to the game and happy to buy success rather than earn it.

Another big supporter of the Paris event was the Arsenal manager, Arsene Wenger, who got involved right from the start and made homelessness the *cause celebre* for his players that year – not just to raise money but to make them more aware of their responsibilities as highly paid professionals. As Arsene himself said, 'every single person makes a difference' when it comes to major issues such as homelessness.

*****

In Paris, I also reaffirmed my belief in the Homeless World Cup and was reminded why we started the event in the first place. During the tournament, there was a conference on homelessness and I was invited to speak, but instead of helping to promote constructive dialogue, the debate got very heated, and divided people rather than bringing them closer together.

Conferences can be very useful but I also remember how Harald and I decided to put homeless people at the centre of what we were doing, instead of simply talking to like-minded people. Sometimes I think there is simply too much talking, not enough action. Too much research and not enough policy changes. The idea of the Homeless World Cup is that everything we do revolves around the players, changing the world with a ball, not with speeches and data. We let the soccer do the talking.

In Paris, the players and managers did not have enough time for a conference. They were too busy training and playing their matches. They were totally focused on soccer, and practical outcomes.

Another thing in Paris I will never forget is the players' parade on the opening day, as the police closed off the boulevards around the Champs de

Mars, stopping the traffic to allow 500 homeless people to march through the streets, with their flags in the air, like a scene from the French Revolution.

* * * * *

Another Scotland victory, beating the favourites Mexico one goal to nil in a nail-biting final, brought the Paris event to an end, with Kenya taking home the women's trophy, also beating Mexico. But soccer itself was the winner.

As I watched Emmanuel presenting the players with medals, I realised his life could also have been very different. Emmanuel was so shocked by the death of his brother Olivier, who collapsed and died in 1988 while playing soccer, that he almost quit the game before his career had begun. Ten years later, as he clutched his winner's medal in Paris, his brother could not have been far from his mind. But like so many other soccer fans, I'm glad he didn't quit and later went on to become such a powerful spokesman for the Homeless World Cup.

* * * * *

Every day, I try to catch some of the action, and one of the highlights today is a penalty shoot-out between Haiti and Austria, after the teams draw in regular time. The drama is amazing but it's not just the emotions of the players that grab me – it's also the fact that the Haiti team made it to Mexico City at all.

When I sit down with Haiti team manager Boby Duval, he describes the incredible journey his players have made since the terrible earthquake in 2010, and the impact of one disaster after another, in one of the world's poorest countries – 200,000 dead, plus more than two million homeless.

After another earthquake in January 2012, thousands of people who'd lost their homes set up their tents on the soccer fields used by Foundation L'Athletique D'Haiti, Boby's soccer-based programme in Haiti, which supports about 2,000 children at six different sites island-wide, not just providing soccer but food and education. Everyone needed a safe place to stay, but Boby told the people that if they wished their children to continue playing soccer, maybe it was better to move the camp elsewhere. It was a tough call for the people but they took a vote and made a unanimous decision to move, and the site was cleared of every single tent within 24 hours. Boby tells me that out of the rubble, there are plans to build Haiti's first professional 12,000-seater soccer ground, appropriately called the Phoenix Stadium, in Cité Soleil.

The first time Haiti went to the Homeless World Cup was Brazil, where the women's team finished in third place, and their star player that year was Gerthrude Saint-Jacques, from Cité Soleil, where about 400,000 people live in appalling conditions: 'The slum is a very dangerous place,' she told me. 'I live in a tent which is ripped so at night we sleep where we can. I've been playing football since I was six years old. I love to play. I'm overjoyed to be in Rio – it's a miracle.'

In Paris the next year, Haiti won the Women's Plate, beating hosts France in the final by ten goals to two. This is the first year that Haiti has sent an all-men's team, and they have been one of the sensations of the tournament so far, winning over the crowd with their incredible talent and raw emotion on and off of the pitch.

The penalty shoot-out with Austria leads to a nail-biting drama. After both teams miss with their first two attempts, Haiti score with their third. When the Haiti keeper saves Austria's third attempt, to win the decider, he bursts into great floods of tears – and one of the Austrian players runs over to hug him and share his big moment.

The action is more powerful than any other game I've watched so far this week, but what makes it so moving is not just the drama I see on the field but the story behind it – and the passion of all of the players, including the keeper, Paul Alex, who's been living in tents for the last 18 months. No wonder he's emotional. 'Sport is a universal language,' Boby says to me later. 'The kids may be extremely poor and barefoot, but when they walk out on the field, I guarantee you could not tell. It's not rocket science – it's the power of soccer.'

*****

Apart from being very good for fitness and developing teamwork, soccer is a game where individuals can emerge as sporting heroes, whether they win or they lose.

In Mexico City, Finland's goalkeeper Jesse Hinkalo emerged as a hero, despite the fact his team lost ten to one to Ukraine on the opening weekend. And Jesse is all smiles in spite of being knocked out by a shot in the face during what he nonetheless describes as his 'best match of the tournament.' Even though he had to wear a neck brace for a couple of days, he came back for games later on in the week, but Jesse has come through much worse in the past. When he was younger, he was knocked down by a car and needed major surgery to fix his broken leg – 17 operations. But he has overcome this – and much more besides – to become a sporting hero at the Homeless World Cup.

* * * * *

Every year, the Homeless World Cup conjures up magical moments, and images that stick in your mind, like Edinburgh in 2005, when the Ireland team were sent to meet the President of the Football Association of Ireland, David Blood. 'Gather round, boys,' the President told them, as they all wondered why they'd been summoned. 'You're doing Ireland proud, boys, every one of you. And the FAI has decided to recognise what you've achieved.'

None of us who stood there knew what to expect and I will never forget the looks on everyone's faces as David Blood opened his bag and presented an official FAI cap to all of the players, shaking their hands, one by one. The players were completely overcome with emotion. Like their heroes, they had won an international cap for representing Ireland. They were trying to change their lives, and now their efforts had been recognised. There were tears in everyone's eyes, me included. This was what the Homeless World Cup was about – not just the cap but what it symbolised and how it made these players smile and hug each other, sharing the moment.

* * * * *

Top referee Hary Milas believes that what makes the Homeless World Cup so special is that soccer is easy to play – and inclusive. 'You don't even need to know how to play,' Hary tells me. 'You just get included, and inclusion is very important. It's the game that brings people together from all walks of life, all countries and all sorts of previous issues, and for those 14 minutes, while you are playing, you forget the past and your problems. You are sending out a very clear message to say you are now moving forward in life – a game of soccer can help change the world.'

* * * * *

As I sit here in the sunshine of Mexico City admiring the skills of the players, I think about how soccer transcends all the problems we have in the world. For a moment, as the ball hits the back of the net, we forget all our troubles. We are one with the rest of the crowd. We're in love with the beautiful game.

Highlights from the Homeless World Cup (2003-2016)

The first event in Graz (2003) ends with a win for Austria – a team of refugees playing their hearts out for their new homeland. (Photo: Mauricio Bustamente)

The co-founders of the Homeless World Cup in Poznan (2013): Mel Young (left) and Harald Schmied (right).

The Homeless World Cup has been held in iconic locations all over the world. Clockwise (from top left): Mexico City (Photo: Ozzy Dror), Melbourne (David B Simmonds), Cape Town (Mark Wessels), Glasgow (Anita Milas), Santiago (Mauricio Bustamente) and Paris (Mauricio Bustamente).

Archbishop Desmond Tutu joins the players for a kickabout in Cape Town (2006).
Photo by Brenna Bales-Smith.

When football legend and Homeless World Cup ambassador Eric Cantona (right) coached the teams in Copenhagen (2007), some of his magic rubbed off on the players.

Daniel Copto (left), founder of Street Soccer Mexico: 'Today, we have thousands of people involved in our programme.' (Photo: Peter Barr)

Martin Asamoah (right), manager of Ghana: 'The Homeless World Cup changes people's lives and I believe it will continue to change people's lives, and help to put an end to poverty.'

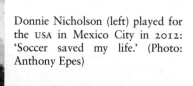

Donnie Nicholson (left) played for the USA in Mexico City in 2012: 'Soccer saved my life.' (Photo: Anthony Epes)

Lukes Mjoka (right) played for South Africa in Rio de Janiero (2010) and coached the team in Paris (2011): 'I want to give hope to the hopeless.'

In every game throughout the tournament, the action never stops. (Photos top and above right: Ozzy Dror)

The players are treated like stars by the fans.

The passion of the players takes the breath away – united in their love of sport and proud to play for their country. (Photos: Top right: Andrew Kelly, Centre right: Ozzy Dror, Centre left: Mauricio Bustamente)

The team behind the scenes make sure the players are treated as heroes – volunteers in Glasgow (2016).

The referees come every year as volunteers – from countries all over the world. (Photo: Mauricio Bustamente)

The trophies are treasured by all of the players, including Russia (top right), winners in Cape Town (2006), Kenya (above), winners in Paris in 2011 (Photo: Esme Deacon) and Afghanistan (centre) who won in Melbourne (2008).

The Players

The Homeless World Cup destroys the stereotypical image of homelessness. Homeless people are people. Our players are footballers. Over the next eight pages are portraits of players who took part in the annual Homeless World Cup, standing proud. We could have had thousands of these pictures but these are brilliant representatives.

All photos by Mauricio Bustamente

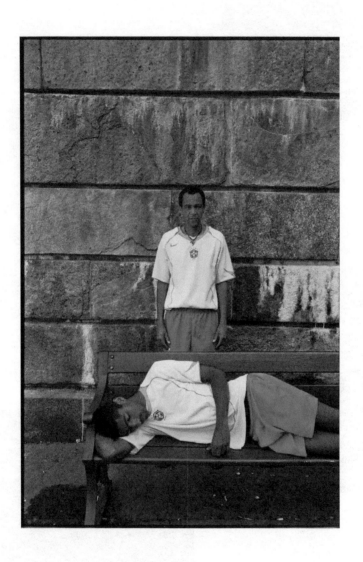

6

From Russia with Hope

Q: Which countries have the worst homelessness problem?
A: If you are excluded from society, homelessness does not have borders.

WEDNESDAY, 10 OCTOBER 2012: It's a difficult question to answer. Through the years, I've got to know a lot about homelessness in countries all over the world, but I couldn't describe it all over a coffee and cake with Fernando in the media tent, before play has even begun. 'Homelessness is all about exclusion and alienation,' I tell him. And perhaps the only way I can begin to describe it is by telling a story about two countries thousands of miles apart, where millions of people have been treated for decades as if they are not even human – or do not exist.

* * * * *

On the surface, Russia and South Africa seem like very different societies – not just in ethnic terms but also their economies and political systems, as well as global influence. But both societies have recently experienced a quiet revolution, sweeping away once-dominant ideologies – communism and apartheid – and going through a difficult transition in the aftermath. Communism tried to make everyone 'equal' and in the process created elites, while apartheid denied 'non-white' people equality, but both societies are still in recovery mode, and the lasting effects of the old regimes still appear now in the homelessness and poverty figures.

In Russia, there are many homeless and 'invisible' people who have been left behind in the wake of recent changes, including many former soldiers and political prisoners, abandoned by society – treated as if they don't even exist because they have no 'official' identity. In South Africa, despite the end of apartheid, there are millions of people still living in townships where many young men feel that crime is the only escape route, and hungry children struggle for survival in the streets, their only real 'families' the criminal gangs who adopt them and use them as pawns.

But even though the situations in the two countries may appear as different as their climates, the end result is more or less the same. For different reasons, people end up living in the streets, excluded from society, including public services like welfare and health care, alienated from the 'ordinary life' most people take for granted. Homelessness and poverty, exclusion and alienation – they have no borders.

* * * * *

What does 'exclusion' really mean? How does increasing alienation damage society? How does tackling alienation help create a better society? What can we do about increasing global inequality?

These are tough questions to answer. Most people see the evidence of damage all around them. They also see increasing inequality and alienation, creating a divided world of haves and have-nots which could lead to economic disaster – and mutual destruction. But to answer these questions, a good place to start is to understand how very different countries – Russia and South Africa – face very similar challenges.

* * * * *

Early on today, I have another interview – for CCTV news in China. As the camera crew walk away, I see Arkady Tyurin heading towards me. My mind drifts back to when we first met in St Petersburg, years before the Homeless World Cup started, and I realise that if I simply told every journalist Arkady's story, they would understand exactly what the Homeless World Cup is about. And as he shakes my hand as if he will never let go, I remember his moment of glory...

* * * * *

Saturday, 30 September 2006: Arkady Tyurin looks on with pride as the Russian national anthem resounds through Grand Parade before the Final of the 2006 Homeless World Cup in Cape Town. His players stand together, arm in arm, singing their hearts out, knowing that if everything goes according to form, Russia will soon be crowned the champions of the world.

The stadium is packed and the final is live on South African TV – a first for the Homeless World Cup. Russia's surprise opponents are the Kazakhstan team who have played well throughout the tournament, but Russia are unbeaten and are favourites to win.

Arkady was homeless once, in Novosibirsk, Siberia, where he was born. He now lives in St Petersburg where he runs the football club for homeless people and also manages the local street paper, *Put Domoi (The Way Home)*.

Winning matters to Arkady. His rationale is simple. If Russia win, the media will cover the triumph extensively. A Russian victory at any sport always makes headlines. But if Russia win the Homeless World Cup, the media will also have to talk about homelessness – still a taboo subject in Russia. Maybe attitudes will change.

I can see the intensity in Arkady's eyes as the anthems reach a climax and the photographers and film crews take up their positions at the side of the pitch. The referee prepares to blow his whistle. I can tell that Arkady wishes he could kick every ball but he is just the manager – there's nothing more he can do now but watch. The result is all down to the players who are not just representing themselves but thousands of other homeless people across Russia – thousands of invisible people who would fill the stadium many times over.

Forty-eight teams have battled their way through the week, and now it's down to two proud nations, aiming for glory – two neighbouring countries who not long ago were both part of the Soviet Union. In the semi-finals, Russia beat debutants Mexico five goals to nil and Kazakhstan beat Poland three goals to one, but it's hard to predict who will win.

The game begins. Will Arkady's dream be fulfilled? Will the players deliver the catalyst needed to make homelessness a major issue back home in Russia?

It's great to win, but Arkady knows that the feeling will not last forever, and next year a new generation of players will follow, and start the quest for victory all over again: 'Immediately after the Final in Cape Town, I told myself, you always have another chance to win. It doesn't matter. Yes, we reached the Final. But the game never ends.'

* * * * *

I fell in love with Russia when I visited St Petersburg the first time, in the mid-1990s, and watched our friends melting the ice to make soup for a queue of people freezing to death in the streets, before they went inside to write the stories for their paper *The Depths* from an office where the electricity only came on every now and again, using what looked like the first computer ever invented. In St Petersburg, I also saw the sewers where the street children lived, moving around between the underground tunnels and rooftops, stealing warmth from central heating pipes. And I heard the horror story of the homeless people, rounded up and taken away from the city, left to die in a forest. This was the reality of homelessness in Russia then. The collapse of the Soviet regime had been dramatic and sudden, and it was ordinary people who suffered.

*****

As I watch Arkady, urging his side on to beat Kazakhstan in the final, I realise how much Russia and St Petersburg have influenced my thinking. Homelessness will not go away overnight. The first step is to get across the message, and this is what Arkady dreams of, as Russia beat Kazakhstan one goal to nil in the Final.

Almost immediately, media enquiries start pouring in from Russia and beyond. Everybody wants to have a piece of the action, as the Russia team return as sporting heroes. Arkady is able to talk about homelessness to people who have never even thought about it before. There is still a lot more to achieve but this is his moment of triumph.

*****

Six years later, I catch up with Arkady in Mexico City, and realise that he has been to every Homeless World Cup from the very beginning. When the project was only a dream, Arkady said he had 'no doubts at all' about getting involved, despite the fact *The Depths* was in crisis at that time and in danger of closing.

But Arkady is not a man to give up very easily, and maybe that is partly because he has been through a lot in his own life. 'I had my own experience of homelessness,' he tells me. 'I slept rough for almost two years. But all my problems were created by myself.'

Arkady used to be a journalist, working in TV and papers, but lost his job and ended up living on the streets. In 1995, while he was still homeless, he bought a street paper for the very first time, and this roused his interest so much that he soon joined *The Depths* as a freelancer, later becoming the editor and executive director of the project – never forgetting for one moment what it was like to be homeless himself.

For Arkady and many other people, exclusion is what homelessness is really all about. 'If you have ever been homeless for only one night,' he says, 'you will feel what it's like – you are treated like an alien, a criminal. You don't have ID, no-one cares. You're dead, below the line.'

I ask him what has changed since the end of the Soviet era, and what it was like then. 'In Soviet times, the authorities managed people by dividing society, just as they did in ancient Rome or medieval times,' he explains. 'It is all about divide and rule, the gap between the rich and poor. Sometimes the rich feel guilty, but when it comes to actually solving problems, accepting equality is not so easy for them.'

Are the police still as brutal towards homeless people as they used to be? 'The police are not paid much and are not very well trained. A lot of vendors still pay the police – for protection. Put two weak members of society together and they will be against each other. St Petersburg has always been a place of extreme contradictions,' Arkady continues, 'but you need "opposites" to organise a movement. It's a magnetic place – it sucks you in. You're always very close to eternity when you are there, and you need to be strong to survive. I can't say I love it but I can't imagine living without it.'

* * * * *

All of us involved in the Homeless World Cup believe in the power of football. Arkady jokes with me that he prefers hockey, but he also recognises how street soccer has a huge impact on people, especially at international tournaments like the Homeless World Cup.

After Cape Town, Arkady thought the result would mean people in Russia would pay more attention to homelessness issues. But what happened after? 'We believed that winning would make a difference but the media continued attacking the homeless as soon as they forgot about our victory, because they were such easy targets. They made fun of us. They called us drunken clowns – a waste of money. So, since then, we have changed our approach.'

Arkady contrasts this with Street Soccer USA and its more positive relationship with the national media there. 'The USA also has a homelessness problem, but people there want to do something about it, and charities also contribute a lot. The media do not attack the homeless, like in Russia.'

In 2010, Arkady saw for himself the big difference between the two countries, when Russia won the USA Cup in Washington DC. At the time, Arkady joked about the team's collective age: 'We're 220 years old as a team and 44 years sober,' he was quoted by a local reporter, surrounded by his players, doing high-fives and hugging each other, as he described his own experience of living on the streets – and his struggle with booze. The media were always very positive during the tournament, but this only highlighted how negative the press could be in Russia. After Cape Town, Arkady decided to focus on soccer and building up a Homeless Football League, involving 20 teams. 'I don't know how we managed it,' says Arkady. 'We had no money, but we set up the League and we still send a team to the Homeless World Cup every year.'

In recent years, the organisation in Russia has got some help from businessmen in Novosibirsk who have funded a programme for addicts. They also got their first taste of the Homeless World Cup when they visited Melbourne to see the event for themselves. Another businessman from Vladivostok also means Arkady 'is not alone any more' in his struggle to reach out to Russia's excluded. 'There is a crisis in Russia,' he tells me. 'We have had some very bad times but we're still alive, still showing we can be human beings in Hell.'

* * * * *

Arkady is one of the most memorable characters involved with the Homeless World Cup, and it would never be the same without him coming every year, but I remember how he almost never made it back to Russia after taking the team to Brazil in 2010. During the tournament in Rio, he was standing at the edge of the water on Copacabana, where the organisers set up the stadiums right on the beach, when he was suddenly swept out to sea by a giant freak wave. Even though he's a very strong swimmer, he couldn't fight the current to swim back to shore, but 40 minutes later he was rescued – when a helicopter pulled him from the ocean. Luckily, two of the Russia team had noticed him drifting away, and one told the other to keep his eyes glued to where Arkady was while he went off for help.

For everybody else, the incident was one of the most dramatic events of the week, but Arkady still plays it down: 'While I was floating away,' he says, 'I wondered if my wife would ever know that my death was so stupid.' But when I met him later on that same day in Rio, he didn't even mention it...

* * * * *

Arkady tells me that Mexico City will be his last Homeless World Cup. 'I am stepping down after ten years,' he confides to me during the week. 'Now, I am just a spectator.'

It's hard to imagine next year without Arkady but he says that he won't change his mind – yet. 'Sometimes, I think about stepping away, but then something happens to stop it, as if I was meant to be here.'

I empathise with Arkady. Sometimes, the pressure can get to us all. And we all feel like taking a break every now and again. Maybe fate *does* play a role in the story, as so many people in Russia believe. Every year, there are similar problems. The tournament will never go like clockwork but every year it always seems to work out in the end and the sun shines, even when the tournament was hosted in Scotland in 2005. 'If the sun can shine in Edinburgh,' says Arkady, 'there must be something powerful on our side!'

* * * * *

South Africa was Arkady's 'moment of glory' in some ways but for him and many other people, simply another big step on the journey, for the players and everyone else.

For Richard Ishmail, the head of the Local Organising Committee (LOC) in Cape Town, the Final was the last time he would ever see a game at the Homeless World Cup...

Less than four months before he was murdered, Richard was sitting a few yards away from me at the Final in Cape Town, with a huge grin all over his face. Down below at the side of the field, I saw Arkady shouting instructions. Arkady knew it was only a game and that soon he would start getting ready for next year, but for Richard it signalled the end of a week he would never forget – or be able to experience in Copenhagen next year when a trophy was named in his honour.

Richard was a truly inspirational figure who made the Homeless World Cup in South Africa such a spectacular success, helping us to raise it to entirely new levels in terms of international exposure and impact. During the year leading up to the kick-off in Cape Town we grew very close, but when he died, I learned much more about him than I ever knew during his life.

In South Africa, the years since the election of President Nelson Mandela had been a time for optimism, but in the build-up to the Homeless World Cup in Cape Town, I began to learn from Richard that despite many positive changes, the struggle for true social justice was only beginning.

Richard was the managing director of the *Big Issue Cape Town*, the street paper acting as host for the Homeless World Cup. Cape Town was a very different tournament from the previous three events, all held in Europe. It was also only four years before the FIFA World Cup in South Africa, so interest in the country – post-apartheid – was greater than ever, and several countries in Africa (including Kenya, Rwanda, Nigeria, Zimbabwe and Zambia) joined the Homeless World Cup family during the year. We were working with a partner far away that operated in a different social, cultural, and business environment. This was also the last year that the street papers organised most of the teams – in later years, separate organisations were founded to focus on the soccer. All of us working for the Homeless World

Cup in Europe were aware that the tournament was not just entering a new era in its development but also taking us out of our comfort zone.

Richard and his team in Cape Town did things at their own pace, in their own way. So, to reassure myself that everything was going according to plan, I visited a few times to check up on progress.

Every day, as darkness began to descend, Cape Town was transformed. Day and night were like two different cities entirely, and every day at 5.00pm, everything stopped for a party. Sometimes we would go into one of the shanty towns – places where tourists were never invited. There were no lights and the darkness was only relieved by the fire. You could not even see what was happening only a few yards away. On one occasion, right in the middle of eating our food, we were suddenly told: 'Time to go!' I never found out what the drama was about but we left at high speed, no questions asked.

Richard worked extremely hard – we all did – but he also liked to party hard. He also organised an extremely successful fund-raising dinner, supported by leading South African footballers, including former Leeds United player Lucas Radebe.

Richard also helped me understand the situation in South Africa, explaining that although people may have more freedom since the end of apartheid, the process was still not complete. 'There are no whites in the shanty towns' was one way of describing progress so far.

Richard also talked about the role of the ANC (African National Congress) during apartheid and how it might be easier to be in opposition to an evil regime, but harder to organise now that they were running a democracy. There was still appalling poverty and widespread inequality.

We also talked about the Homeless World Cup and how a real movement was building which crossed political boundaries. Richard believed that the organisation could learn a lot from the structure of the ANC, sticking together around common values and maintaining discipline at all times. He thought the biggest threat to our organisation would come from countries setting up their own events and not coming to the annual tournament. 'They don't understand what a movement is and they don't understand discipline,' Richard declared.

When I asked Richard what life was like under apartheid, he talked from the heart, but I always suspected there was more to his story than he ever revealed at the time. He often seemed to be on the brink of telling me something important about himself – something I would not find out until he was dead.

Richard was an energetic, passionate man, full of life. He was determined to make the Cape Town Homeless World Cup a success, despite all the obstacles placed in our way, including a shortage of funds. This was the beginning of the Homeless World Cup as we know it today. The event was on a bigger scale – more teams and spectators, bigger media presence, two arenas instead of just one, and a much higher profile in terms of VIP backing, with Archbishop Desmond Tutu and President Mbeki giving us their blessing, and one of the world's greatest footballers, Eusebio, kicking off the tournament on September 24th.

When he visited the tournament, Tutu made a huge impact on everyone, especially the players. Greeted by adoring fans and blaring vuvuzelas, he said:

> All over the world, we've got to end homelessness. Everyone should have a home. It's a right and not a privilege. People treat the homeless as if they're sub-human. In order to overcome this discrimination, we have to unite against homelessness as we did when we fought apartheid.

Support from major figures was important but Richard Ishmail played a key role in making the tournament such a spectacular national and international success.

* * * * *

Six months later, after the tournament ended, someone called from Cape Town to tell me that Richard had died. He had been stabbed inside his home by 'unknown assailants' and a few minor items were stolen – his watch and his cell phone. No sign of a break-in, however. Richard had a habit of inviting people into his home.

A few hours later, his house mate returned and discovered him bleeding to death, barely alive. He was rushed to hospital with serious injuries to kidneys, intestine and spleen, and he died three days later on January 9th, shortly after doctors had declared him brain dead.

That same night, Richard's ANC background became public knowledge. ANC spokesperson James Ngculu said that Richard played a huge role in the movement's underground operations:

> We lost a dedicated soldier and his death is a big loss to the ANC. If one looks at Richard's record, it surpasses some of those who stand on mountains and talk about their struggle credentials. His family must remain strong. We want to thank them for giving up their son.

Gradually, more information about Richard's 'double life' began to emerge. During the apartheid era, he had been in *Umkhonto we Sizwe (MK or Spear of the Nation)*, the ANC's military wing. He was recruited while at school and had organised the storing and distribution of weapons. Code-named Comrade Ali, he was a leading figure in the MK's Ashley Kriel unit, the only military unit to survive until the ban on the ANC was lifted in 1990.

The ANC took over Richard's funeral arrangements. On January 17th, two memorial services were held simultaneously in Cape Town and Johannesburg. Richard was a national hero and several leading politicians joined his former comrades to remember him.

The following year, at the start of the Homeless World Cup in Copenhagen, we held a minute's silence in his memory. It was a powerful moment. You could hear a pin drop. We resolved never to forget him – and the Richard Ishmail Fair Play Trophy means his memory will live with us forever.

Richard's murder was one of the dark days of the Homeless World Cup, but as I watch the players celebrate their victory in Denmark, proudly displaying their medals, there is more light than darkness ahead.

Everyone who's ever been involved involved in the Homeless World Cup is transformed by the experience, including Richard Ishmail.

In 2006, Richard wanted to change the world – not with bullets but with a ball.

7

From *Chavos* to *Playboy*

Q: What's a typical day at the Homeless World Cup?
A: Today?

THURSDAY, 11 OCTOBER 2012: An early start. I go down to the lobby to meet up with a film crew from Cactus Productions who are making a documentary about the Homeless World Cup, following the progress of the Mexico players from the time they are selected to their final game on Sunday, win or lose. I enjoy these early interviews, before the games start in the morning. It is also much cooler and quieter out in the plaza at dawn where I've done at least one early interview each day this week.

I have also told Fernando I will meet him this morning, to join me for a 'typical day' at the Homeless World Cup. Will today be a typical day?

As I arrive in the lobby, however, I see Daniel Copto (CEO of Street Soccer Mexico) and Joe Aboumrad of the Telmex Foundation, waiting there with Nick and Alejandro and the rest of the film crew. Everyone smiles as I walk up to greet them. But why are they all here so early? And what are Joe and Daniel doing, helping to carry the camera equipment?

Without an explanation, everyone heads for the subway, including Fernando, and we navigate the labyrinth of underground tunnels which crisscross the Zocalo and squeeze ourselves into a train for a journey to wherever it is we are going...

It's the start of the rush hour, and we fight our way out of the train at a station a few stops away and emerge at Hidalgo, where they set up the cameras in a nondescript plaza surrounded by high walls of grey, crumbling concrete, covered with gaudily coloured graffiti. It's a place that has definitely seen better days. 'This is the birthplace of Street Soccer Mexico,' Daniel says, waving his hands around, as several young men dressed in filthy-looking tracksuit bottoms, vests and battered trainers start gathering around us, their eyes already glazed from sniffing solvents, from the moment the sun rose and stirred them from sleep.

I see Joe kick a ball around with some of the *chavos* and remember the first time I spoke to him, three years ago, when he called me to 'check out the project' on behalf of the Telmex Foundation. I was in London at the time, on my way to a meeting, when an anonymous overseas number appeared on my cell phone, but I answered it anyway, thinking it could be important.

The phone call didn't last long but I'll never forget what Joe said at the end of our brief conversation, when he told me that Telmex had already decided to back Daniel's programme. 'Let me tell you,' he said, 'we're committed to the project 100 per cent. And let me assure you right now, we do not do things by halves.'

And he meant what he said.

Everything has progressed very rapidly since then, and Daniel and Telmex have worked well together to make sure the project succeeds. Today, there are almost 30,000 people involved in the programme, playing soccer every week at one of the nationwide centres, including three in Mexico City itself.

Daniel can take lots of credit for that. He has worked hard to win hearts and minds, and now his dream's becoming a reality.

* * * * *

In 2006, however, Daniel was struggling to survive, beginning to wonder if his vision would ever come true. He was almost out of money, but Daniel was determined to set up his programme in Mexico, where he grew up – using the power of soccer to get people out of the terrible cycle of poverty, violence and drugs.

The year before, he'd been to Scotland for the Homeless World Cup as a coach of the Canada team – an experience which changed his life and also inspired him to go back to Mexico City. In Canada, he had been studying addiction counselling, working several days a week in shelters for the homeless, when a friend asked if he could help out with a street soccer project which was sending a national team to the Homeless World Cup. As a football fan from one of the most soccer-crazy countries in the world, Daniel said 'Yes!' straight away, and several months later flew out with the players to Scotland. 'The dynamic in the shelters was difficult,' Daniel explains, recalling his experience in Canada. 'It was very hard to deal with, but when homeless people got involved in something recreational, it made a big difference. Playing soccer was fantastic for my clients. It changed their whole mindset.'

Daniel didn't know what to expect when the team arrived in Edinburgh but the 'wonderful atmosphere' captured the hearts of the players as well as the coaches. 'Drugs were an integral part of their everyday lives,' Daniel says, 'but now they were thinking about representing their country. For me it was also a life-changing time – I saw the impact it was having on the players and started thinking it could have the same impact on Mexican people, on poverty and drug abuse, and it made me realise my country should be part of this. It changed my whole life plan, and my family's life also, leaving Canada and going back to Mexico. People said I was crazy to do it. My wife said, "I'm not going," and my kids said, "we're not going," but I knew it would somehow work out in the end.'

A few months later, Daniel found himself in Mexico with no job and hardly a cent to his name, his wife and children thousands of miles away, and people still saying 'you're crazy!' But turn the clock forward another six years, and there is Daniel standing in the Zocalo as thousands of spectators wave their flags in the stadium and the Homeless World Cup kicks off in Mexico City to a fanfare of trumpets and fireworks.

It's a wonderful story. But the journey to get here has never been easy. 'It was difficult,' Daniel says, kicking a ball back to one of the young guys who is hanging around at Hidalgo. 'I spent the first six months here alone, and put all my own money into the project. When my family joined me, it got even harder – no job and no money, no prospects. But I really believed it would work.'

Thanks to Daniel's personal investment in the project, Mexico made its début in the Homeless World Cup in Cape Town in 2006, finishing a creditable fourth. Two years later, in 2008, they struggled to raise the funds needed to take part in Melbourne.

By early 2009, Daniel felt the programme was close to the end of the line, then he 'knocked on the door of Fundacion Telmex' and everything changed. He explained to Joe Aboumrad and the rest of his team what the programme was trying to do, then Joe and Arturo Elias Ayub, the son-in-law of Carlos Slim and CEO of the Telmex Foundation, came to Hidalgo to see for themselves, and immediately agreed to fund the programme for the following year. 'When they came here and they saw the boys we're working with, it got them all crying,' says Daniel. 'It was really contagious for them.'

The next year, Telmex asked Daniel to expand the programme throughout the country, with their full support, and everything took off from there. 'Today, we have thousands of people involved in our programme,' says

Daniel, 'but this is a very big country, and we have a lot of poverty – about 80 per cent of the people live under the poverty line.'

The nationwide network that Daniel has built works in partnership with local institutions who are dealing with poverty issues, providing the money to pay for equipment and pitches. 'They also know where the gangs are,' says Daniel, 'and help us to reach them.'

Over the years, there has been a 'profound change' in Street Soccer Mexico as it spread nationwide and matured. Daniel quotes several examples of players who have gone on to be coaches of the national squad or help support programmes in various cities, among the most dangerous places on Earth. 'The young kids in the gangs love playing football,' says Daniel. 'When they come to us, they may not have been working or going to school, but when we get them off the streets, they experience a different way of life. They play regular games, start to study, learn new skills and sometimes get jobs. We are having a huge impact in every state.'

Daniel thinks the programme works mainly because of the Mexican passion for soccer. 'They all dream of being big stars in professional teams, so when they realise that they can be part of a team to represent their neighbourhood, and maybe even go on to play for the national team, they get excited and commit to the programme. They train and make an effort to improve their fitness, and also have an excuse to say "No!" to drugs.'

The nationwide network is something that Daniel has created from his own imagination, inventing leagues and trophies for the players. And the process continues to gather momentum when the players return from the Homeless World Cup and inspire all the young kids who want to be part of it, too.

The fact that there are so many women involved is also a major achievement and they have more than played their part in Mexico's success at several tournaments. Daniel says the secret is to get the team to concentrate on what they are doing. 'The first time in Rio,' says Daniel, 'we told the women they were here to play and compete with the best, not as tourists.' In every tournament since then, a combination of training, group therapy sessions and educational workshops has helped the team fulfil its potential, engaging the women from eight in the morning till nine in the evening. Sometimes, says Daniel, because they are working so closely together, many personal issues arise, and this means all the players have to deal with them together – as a team.

The players are known for their skills on the pitch, but soccer skills are not the only talent Daniel looks for. Everyone has to be part of the team and be willing to learn and improve. 'We want to engage them,' says Daniel, 'but they also have to engage with the rest of the players around them and be part of the community. That is how we create change.'

The Street Soccer Mexico programme continues to grow nationwide. 'Things are happening in every single state,' says Daniel. 'In some states, they take the equipment to places where the people have not seen street soccer before, and new players come to take part in state competitions, and so it grows bigger.'

The success of Street Soccer Mexico – off the pitch as well as in the international tournaments – has not gone unnoticed in government circles: 'We have been building this movement, in Mexico and around the world, so the government now looks toward us to help them develop a strategy for crime prevention.'

In Daniel's own words, he has not only built infrastructure but also a 'movement' which has won over thousands of young kids whose lives have been shattered by violence and drugs. He has also won over some large corporations and government leaders. 'It's hard to get big companies involved, however,' Daniel explains. 'It is really a cultural issue – the emphasis is usually on profits, not people. So we must continue showing them concrete results.'

The involvement of Telmex has had a big influence not just in terms of finance but also credibility in business and government circles. 'This makes it easier,' Daniel explains, 'because more people take us much more seriously now.'

In addition to funding Street Soccer Mexico, Telmex played a key role in winning the bid for the Homeless World Cup in 2012. 'I didn't think the tournament would come here till later,' says Daniel. 'We were focusing on building up the programme, but it all happened faster than anyone ever expected. I remember very early on, I thought about how wonderful a tournament would be if it was held here in the Zocalo. Initially, I thought it would be a national tournament only, but see what has happened?'

For me and Daniel, there are many different symbols of the progress made in Mexico since the programme was launched, especially the many different people who have got involved over the years. Sadly, a few individuals have died, including team doctor Cesar Mora and Luis Miguel Castañeda, an assistant to the women's team who first got involved as a player in Milan in 2009. 'Luis Miguel was a squeegee kid,' says Daniel, 'who lived on the streets, but he did very well as a coach.'

But neither of us can forget when the star of the women's team, Ana Aguirre, was introduced to Carlos Slim, the founder of Telmex, during the first week of the tournament in Mexico City. This courageous young woman from Ciudad Juarez, one of Mexico's most violent cities, was one of the world's poorest people and there she was casually talking to one of the world's richest men, as if this was perfectly normal for her and for him.

Ana later returned to Chihuahua to coach young local players, and the cycle continued. 'A ball did that,' says Daniel. 'Just a ball.'

* * * * *

At Hidalgo, we experience in miniature exactly what the Homeless World Cup is about. As I sit in a chair getting ready for filming, I watch Joe kick a ball about with some of the young men who are hanging around in the plaza. These people are the poorest of the poor. They're 'the people who do not exist'. And the man from the Telmex Foundation is joking and laughing like one of the *chavos*, playing soccer like millions of others who dream of being Pele or Ronaldo. Just for one split second, Joe is one of them, forgetting his surroundings, with a ball at his feet. And for that brief moment, also, the *chavos* forget who he is.

Meanwhile, just a few yards away, there are thousands of commuters pouring into the subway, eyes looking straight ahead, preparing for another day at high school or the office. Maybe they pass by this very same spot every day on the way to wherever they go, thinking of their families and friends, cares and worries, their children and lovers, like millions of people all over the world. And like millions of people all over the world, they do not see the young men in the plaza, kicking a ball around. They do not see the people slowly dying in front of their eyes. They do not see the people who do not exist, the invisible people who inhabit the streets of the city, without any families or place to call home, except other people like them and the hard concrete benches that encircle the plaza like tombstones.

* * * * *

'Why are there so many homeless people?' Alejandro asks, giving the signal for the filming to start, as commuters continue to flow in and out of the subway, and the traffic noise roars in the background as if it is inside our heads.

'Good question, Alejandro.' I am asked this again and again every year and I still don't know exactly how to answer. I know the statistics. I know there are supposed to be 100 million homeless people in the world, how it costs the world billions of dollars a year and affects every country, from the poorest right up to the richest. There are also many simple solutions...

'We can fly to the moon and cure smallpox. We can communicate with anyone, whenever we like, anywhere in the world – to make ourselves billions of dollars or just say hello to our friends. But if we're so clever, why do we still have homelessness?'

'Why soccer?' Alejandro asks.

'The power of sport and the power of soccer can change people's lives,' I say. 'All you need is a ball.'

It's hard not to notice that Joe and the others are kicking the ball around just a few metres away. Anthony and Ozzy, our official photographers, are snapping away, while Daniel is explaining to Fernando how Street Soccer Mexico started here six years ago, in the park around the corner where the *chavos* are no longer permitted to play since the local police banned them from hanging around.

'So, what is the Homeless World Cup?' Alejandro asks, knowing the answer already and hoping I'll say something different.

I have been asked this question thousands of times through the years by all sorts of people, from presidents and billionaires to some of the world's poorest people. 'The simple answer is that we exist to put an end to homelessness, and the ultimate aim of the Homeless World Cup is not to exist – because we want to live in a world where homelessness has been eliminated altogether.'

Alejandro looks at me in silence, as if he is expecting me to finish the sentence. 'Today, however, there are still 100 million homeless people in the world, so our mission continues...'

The figures are scary, but as I watch the young men in the plaza, I know that every single homeless person is an individual tragedy. 'One single homeless person in the world is one homeless person too many.'

'And the tournament in Mexico City?' Alejandro asks next.

'The annual tournament's the climax of the year. But it is only one week out of 52, and as soon as the tournament ends, all the managers start the whole process all over again – scouting for the next generation of players. The work goes on 365 days every year, in the streets of the cities and towns where we live, right in front of our eyes, even though we may not even notice.'

The work goes on so close, in fact, that when the filming finishes, I join Joe and Daniel and play with the *chavos* for a couple of minutes before we have to go back to the Zocalo.

* * * * *

Daniel tells Fernando that he also has a dream: Street Soccer Mexico House. 'This is the legacy I'd like to see from the Homeless World Cup being held here,' Daniel tells him as we stand in Hidalgo, preparing to leave.

Many 'treatment centres' for addicts use outdated and sometimes cruel methods and Daniel wants to build a safe place where the victims of drugs and the homeless are treated as real human beings.

As the *chavos* kick a ball around, some of them already high since daybreak, he talks about the early days here in Hidalgo, building trust with young men who spend all their time sniffing solvents to try to escape from the mess of their everyday lives.

Some of the *chavos* have been hanging around here for up to ten years and it's amazing they have managed to survive. 'It's a long time to die,' Daniel tells me.

The programme has steadily grown through the years, but Daniel wants to focus on the future – and the hundreds of thousands of 'invisible' people excluded from basic public services, as well as the addicts and people escaping from violence and crime. The poorest of the poor. 'As far as the authorities are concerned, these people do not exist,' he says.

Since returning to Mexico six years ago, Daniel has been trying to 'change the culture' – how addicts are treated. 'These guys feel like a piece of shit,' he tells Fernando. 'And you have to keep telling them they are not just a piece of shit, so they can do whatever it takes to get better.'

'We must build trust,' he adds, as we head back for another day of non-stop soccer action in the Zocalo. 'We must empower them.'

* * * * *

Thirty minutes later...

It may only be a couple of miles from Hidalgo, but the Zocalo is like a different planet. The *chavos* in Hidalgo may be living on the edge 24 hours a day, but many of the players in the Homeless World Cup, now proudly wearing their shiny bright national colours, were living in the same place just a short time ago.

There is no violence, guns or drugs. Only the roar of the crowd and the beat of the music, the commentator greeting every goal with a scream that would wake up the dead. I look down at the Mexico players as they warm up in the stadium, with happy, smiling faces, and under the surface a steely desire to be winners. They look so fit and healthy but I know where they come from. I know that last year or the year before, they must have been in danger, living on the mean streets which are more like a war zone, never more than seconds away from disaster. They may have been the same as the people I met in Hidalgo this morning, looking forward to nothing except the next high, trying to forget the low – and even worse – that follows. The players I am watching in the stadium are no longer just 'homeless people' but examples of how people can change their lives, with a ball.

A lot of this year's Mexico players come from Ciudad Juárez, the border town where more than 10,000 people have been murdered since 2006. Through an interpreter, one of them tells me that six of his friends were killed just a few weeks ago. He comes from a city where 'guns are fired as casually as lighting up a cigarette, and life is just as cheap.'

Another player, one of the women, was forced to escape from her village after most of her family were gunned down at a funeral – to bury her brother who'd been killed in a shoot-out. Now she proudly wears her national colours and can't wait for kick-off, determined to play well and win for her country.

The two teams – men and women – have been training in Mexico City for weeks, not just playing soccer but taking part in therapy sessions where they talk about how they can turn their lives round in the future. It may be 'just a game' but soccer has brought them together and given them a common goal as well as the chance to be part of a team – and the chance to sit next to the world's richest man, in the VIP stands, when they've finished their games for the day.

For all these players, some of whom have never been to Mexico City before, this is something they could never have dreamed of a few months ago. And I ask myself if Carlos Slim could also have imagined this a few months ago.

* * * * *

The Homeless World Cup is about much more than soccer but I'm still impressed when the Mexico women's team beat Kyrgyzstan 16-0, with Ana Aguirre one of the stars of the game. I also catch sight of the Mexico men, who beat England by nine goals to two. Harald will also be pleased, I imagine, when Austria win against Russia by four goals to nil. The scores may not matter as much as the experience of being here, but every time a goal is scored and every time a ball is kicked, it represents another step forward for all of the players.

* * * * *

Even though I have another interview soon, and another appointment immediately after, I spend a few minutes in the media tent with my friend Viktor Kirkov, the CEO and founder of the Team of Hope, our partners in Bulgaria. Viktor's team is making its début this year and I want to congratulate Viktor for so many reasons – including the success of his project so far and the fact that he managed to get here so soon after founding the organisation.

Viktor and his coaches have been raising awareness throughout the whole country, not only of the soccer team but also the problems so many young people now face. As a result, many employers offer jobs to the players because they see this as a practical solution and want to encourage the team.

Because they are so popular, the players were also invited to prepare for the Homeless World Cup at the National Sport Palace, and their main sponsor Globul arranged for a four-day training camp at Manchester United's Carrington complex in England before flying onward to Mexico City.

Before they left Bulgaria, messages of support flooded in from the sports minister, the mayor of Sofia and even the President of Bulgaria, and regardless of results this week, Viktor expects a hero's welcome at the airport upon their return – a welcome the players will richly deserve. 'Before they came to Mexico, nobody noticed the players,' says Viktor. 'But thanks to football, they are being reintegrated into society, becoming more responsible and disciplined, part of a team. Now they feel somebody cares, and they want to live up to their expectations.'

The Team of Hope was set up to 'foster positive qualities in young men' and within a short time, the results went far beyond what Viktor dreamed of, with 75 per cent of the players already in full-time employment, and half of them living in flats.

Some of the players have since become 'famous' thanks to a series of documentaries, screened in prime time on Novo TV. That morning, the film crew from Bulgaria also interview me, as crowds of people gather in the Zocalo. 'Quite honestly, I was surprised by how quickly things happened,' says Viktor. But instead of thinking this is the end of his journey, Viktor wants to build 'a professional project which corporate partners will back.'

According to Viktor, Bulgarian society and the national soccer team have had so little to cheer about in recent years that the Team of Hope doing so well has been good news for everyone – generating positive public relations for corporate sponsors which Viktor is confident will also translate into long-term support.

I promise to meet Viktor later to talk about his thoughts on social enterprise and his plans for the future. What impresses me most is that Viktor will never give up or accept second best for his organisation, and seeks to be inclusive, treating everyone including his players and corporate sponsors with equal respect, so that everyone wins – so that everyone receives a hero's welcome.

*****

Before he leaves, Viktor introduces me to some of his players, including Borislav Angelov, better known as Bobby, who like many other youngsters was abandoned by his parents as a baby and grew up in a series of orphanages until he was 18 years old, when he ended up living on the streets of Sofia. 'For about three months, I slept in abandoned buildings,' Bobby tells me. 'It was tough. I never thought I would go down to that level. I was hanging around with the wrong people, and I went into something like a state of depression.'

Bobby also tells me he felt 'lost' when he finished school without enough qualifications, and ended up moving from shelter to shelter, without any sense of direction. He also reveals that he once stole a phone from a guard: 'I needed the money,' he tells me. 'I had nothing to eat. But later I confessed and told the guard I was sorry, and promised to give back the money. I don't want to make any excuses, but I was simply starving.'

At this point, Bobby knew he'd reached a crossroads. 'There are two choices in life – you either take the wrong road or grow up and become a better person,' he says.

One day, in a shelter, Bobby overheard some other young men talking about a street soccer team called Team of Hope, and Bobby was selected for Mexico City. 'These bad things that happened, they limited me somehow and I stopped dreaming,' says Bobby. 'Now I dream of many things – to be involved one day with children like me. I don't want them to go through what I went through. I want to show them another way.'

When he returned to Bulgaria, Bobby got a job and finished school, then took his university entry exam and moved into his own rented apartment. Today, he is living and working in London and has a new partner – and his dreams are beginning to happen for real.

*****

Another member of the Team of Hope in Mexico, Alexandar Pantov was abandoned as a baby and spent most of his childhood in a state institution. When he reached his 18th birthday, he was offered three months temporary accommodation in an old block of flats once occupied by the army, but the

Team of Hope came to his rescue soon after. 'I heard about it from a friend and I could not believe it,' he tells me. 'I love it and want to become more involved.'

Viktor says that many young people like Alex and Bobby leave school without any real education, and quickly develop bad habits. He also believes that the coaches who run Team of Hope are better than social workers. 'Using football,' he tells me, 'they quickly improve the players' behaviours and attitudes. We don't want to change lives. We want the players to change their own lives.'

* * * * *

Next stop: The British Embassy in Mexico City to give my luncheon talk to local business people and politicians. Hidalgo is still very fresh in my mind as I look at the audience waiting to hear me. The contrast between those 'invisible' people with their blank staring eyes and these bright-eyed men and women in immaculate business suits, eager to listen, could not be more vivid. In the space of a couple of hours, I have travelled from one planet to another, but I realise that these two different places are much more connected than they look on the surface. I realise these influential people could make a huge difference to the life of the *chavos* a few miles away, if they understand what I am trying to say and decide to be part of the movement. 'First the bad news,' I begin as usual, quoting the facts again, just like this morning. 'According to the United Nations, there are 100 million homeless people in the world, including three million in the world's richest country...'

As usual when I do a presentation, there are almost no words on the screen, mainly pictures. These are the cues for the stories I tell, showing people sleeping in the streets, children scavenging on garbage dumps. The horror of homelessness. 'Our human brains can't really comprehend such huge numbers, but if all of us did something constructive, we could change the world – with a ball.'

Then I flash up pictures of the tournaments, flying round the world in a couple of minutes, from Sweden to Australia, Copenhagen, Edinburgh, Cape Town, Milan, Rio, Paris and finally this week to Mexico City.

I talk about the change that happens not just in the players but the people who come out to watch them. The changes in the media. The volunteers who help out at the tournament and also experience something transformative, year after year.

The audience seems to be paying attention. Their reaction is the same as many other groups of people I have spoken to over the years. They are shocked by the statistics and the images of people on the brink of extinction, and want to find out more about the impact of the Homeless World Cup. 'Is homelessness a good idea?' I always ask, towards the end.

And nobody ever says 'Yes!'

But as I reach the climax of my brief presentation, and everyone claps, I wonder how these people will be feeling tomorrow, and whether they will go away and make up their minds to do something about it, and whether that means making a change in their own lives or taking the first steps to changing the world.

* * * * *

Next up to speak is Jose Ignacio Avalos Hernandez, who has 'founded or inspired' several social enterprises over the years, including *Un Kilo de Ayuda* (One Kilo of Help), which fights malnutrition in hundreds of rural communities throughout Mexico, and *Mi Tienda* (My Shop), which supplies small, rural shops with products priced lower than traditional wholesalers, so local consumers can buy cheaper, healthier food.

Almost half of Mexico's 106 million people live in poverty, and an estimated quarter of the population survive on a dollar a day.

According to Jose, *Un Kilo de Ayuda* has had a huge impact – child mortality and general health are improving and the project is gaining momentum. 'The government can't do it,' Jose says, 'but social enterprise can.'

I have not seen Jose since the World Economic Forum at Davos, when we'd chatted with the President of Mexico, Felipe Calderón, and his wife, the First Lady, Margarita Zavala, who have both been big supporters of the Homeless World Cup.

Going to Davos in 2003 was an experience that changed my life – and also made the Homeless World Cup possible. I went that year because of my connection with the Schwab Foundation for Social Entrepreneurship. During the week, I was persuaded by Adolf Ogi, the former President of Switzerland, and one of the members of the Schwab Foundation board, to go along to a discussion on sport. After dinner, I was invited to speak by Vivienne Reading, the Commissioner for Sports at the European Union – who unknown to me had been the person in charge when we lost our EU funding for the first Homeless World Cup in Graz. Later on, Vivienne apologised for not being able to push through the funding. 'So the very least I could do,' she said, 'was give you the floor for a couple of minutes.'

And those two minutes were probably the most important two minutes in the story of the Homeless World Cup so far.

Vivienne stood up and introduced me, saying: 'I had prepared some words, but this gentleman on my left has a much better story to tell.'

Unlike Vivienne, I had no speech prepared, but suddenly I had the attention of everyone there, and talked about our plans for the inaugural Homeless World Cup – why we were doing it and what we hoped to achieve.

It was a version of what I had been saying for months, but this time there was thunderous applause around the room. And sitting at one of the tables nearby was Phil Knight, the chairman and co-founder of Nike. 'This is very interesting,' Phil said to me afterwards. 'It's innovative – and also crazy.' Then he told me to contact his Corporate Social Responsibility department in Brussels as soon as I could. Then, in April, Nike gave us 50,000 euros – money which enabled us to bring in teams from South America and South Africa, who until then were struggling to make it.

Like UEFA, ten years later, Nike is just as committed. They weren't frightened to back something new, and they share our belief in the power of sport.

* * * * *

I say goodbye to Jose and head back to the Zocalo with Juan, a government official who is interested in what we are doing. As we navigate the busy streets of Mexico City, we talk about the state of the economy.

Juan says that Mexico's 'tiger' economy is one of the world's fastest growing right now. 'Maybe that is why there's so much traffic,' I tell him, as we grind to a halt.

Juan winds up his window to keep out the fumes. 'But hopefully things will get better,' he says, 'even in the midst of all this chaos.'

The traffic is insane as we get closer to the Zocalo. We're only a few blocks away but the queue isn't moving an inch. I'm comfortable sitting there, having a rest in the cool air-conditioned saloon, but I ask Juan if it would be quicker to get out and walk. 'Are you crazy?' he asks me. 'Relax!'

And perhaps he is right. So I sit back, close my eyes and have a snooze until we get back to the Zocalo ten minutes later, for more non-stop action...

* * * * *

This evening, the players from England, Scotland and Wales have been invited to the British Ambassador's Residence, along with all the managers, the volunteers and local organisers.

The Ambassador shakes hands with everyone as they arrive and says a few warm words of welcome.

Then Arturo speaks: 'Before today, I used to think 2004 was the best year of my life, when the soccer team we sponsor beat Real Madrid and we won every trophy in Mexico that year.' He looks down at his wife, Johanna (Carlos Slim's daughter), and smiles as he corrects himself, just in the nick of time. 'Of course, the very best year was the year I met my wife!' Then, still smiling, he continues: 'But apart from that, this is the best year – the year the Homeless World Cup came to Mexico City.'

The speeches people make on occasions like this can often seem routine, as if they are simply said out of politeness, but I know that he means every word. I have seen him with the players and the smile on his face as he sits in the stadium watching the games. He has thrown his weight behind Street Soccer Mexico and really believes in what Daniel is doing. The Telmex Foundation is making a difference and helping to change people's lives, and Arturo is completely committed to the Homeless World Cup and everything we are attempting to do. He doesn't just like watching soccer and cheering the teams. He loves to see these people being treated like heroes, and watch them grow taller and stronger every day they step onto the field in their national colours.

* * * * *

One of the English players at the reception, goalkeeper Aaron Ranieri, has attracted a lot of attention since arriving in Mexico City a few days ago, because he is returning to the land where he was born. He writes in his journal that day:

> I woke up very excited as I knew that we were playing Mexico today. Everyone knew how important this game was to me, and I was made captain. Just before the game, I felt very nervous but proud. And when I walked onto the pitch, it was overwhelming – the announcer mentioned I am Mexican and I could hear people shouting my name. I wanted to cry but at the same time I am so happy so I smile. After the game I saw a little Mexican boy with his mum playing football. He reminded me of my son and made me think of myself as a little boy in Mexico City, and how far I've come.

Meanwhile, at the Embassy, another England player, Becca Mushrow, the youngest in the women's team, is deep in conversation with Fernando. One of the coaches told Fernando that when she arrived at the airport to take off for Mexico City, she didn't know anyone else in her team. She hardly said one single word on the plane, but as the week went on, she gained more confidence, and here she is describing her experience as if she has been deal-ing with the media for years. Sometimes, you instinctively know how some players will get more involved with the Homeless World Cup, and as it turns out, Becca later coaches the England team, passing on what she has learned to a new generation of players – even though she is still younger than most of the team.

*****

It's been a long day but I still have another appointment. The British Embassy has organised an interview, after the rest of the guests have departed. The local representative of *Playboy* magazine wants to ask a few questions.

I'm exhausted. The events of the week are beginning to weigh on my shoulders. It is late and I just want to lie down and sleep. 'Just one more interview,' I'm told, as everyone else says goodbye and goes back to the city. 'It shouldn't take long.'

I wonder what *Playboy* will ask me. Through the years, I've spoken to just about every news organisation on Earth, but this time I am not so sure what to expect. I tell myself that every opportunity is equally important and has to be grasped, no matter how exhausted I may feel at the moment. I have to tell the story to every single person who is willing to listen, including the readers of *Playboy*. Even if the story is the same every time, and I've used the same words on 1,000 occasions, it's a story that has to be told.

Then the interview starts...

The first problem is that the journalist doesn't speak English, but one of the Embassy staff very kindly assists, translating the questions and answers, while the reporter and I both sit facing each other in silence.

I explain to her how it all started, then run through all the tournaments until we find ourselves in Mexico City. I describe how homelessness affects the different countries in so many different ways, comparing the United States with Africa, and where we are now, just a few miles away from some of the world's poorest people.

As I think about my answers, I wonder what will interest the read-ers of *Playboy*. One of my good friends, the journalist Monica Sanchez, who used to be a leading light at INSP and ran the street paper in Spain at the time, is now a writer for the Mexican edition of *Alo* magazine, so I know there are a million different ways of presenting the issues for all sorts of people.

I remember I am meeting up with Monica and Harald tomorrow but try to continue to focus on *Playboy*, even though my eyes are beginning to close...

Q: What happens to the players after the tournament? Are they still homeless?

A: Over 80 per cent of the players we surveyed go back to their countries and get a job, continue school or find a place to live.

Q: And what about the others?

A: Our success rate could never be 100 per cent, but 80 per cent is a major achievement. The key thing is engagement – touching something in individuals which makes them respond – and providing a structure for long-term support. A place to go. Someone to talk to. A daily routine. Being part of a team.

The conversation continues for several minutes, punctuated by translations from Spanish to English and English to Spanish. We cover a lot of ground – our corporate sponsors, how the organisation is funded, our international network and the role played by Telmex.

I notice the ambassador's husband is tapping his watch at the top of the stairs leading into the lounge, with my wife Rona waiting behind him. It is well after midnight and the interviewer shows me a list of the questions she still hasn't asked, covering another two or three sheets of paper. If she asks every question, I calculate we may be here till breakfast.

Every journalist needs a good quote, so I think for a couple of seconds before I continue: 'We can fly to the moon and cure smallpox. But if we're so clever, why do we still have homelessness?'

I remember I have said this already today, at Hidalgo, and perhaps in my talk at the British Embassy? And I know I will say it again and again until somebody answers the question – and everyone starts doing something about it.

Then the interview ends. And I only hope *Playboy* will tell all its readers the story of the Homeless World Cup, and that homelessness will get as much attention as the glossy ads for fast cars and after-shave, and glamorous photos.

* * * * *

Half an hour later, we go back in the taxi through the still-crowded streets of the city. I shut my eyes and fall asleep and don't wake up until we have reached our hotel. As we walk to the entrance, we see people wrapped up in blankets, asleep beneath the arches of the colonnade that circles the square like a cloister. I count about a dozen people, all of them probably homeless, with nowhere to go.

It's been a long day. And tomorrow my schedule looks even more packed. The words I have spoken still echo deep inside my mind. 'It is better to try and do something. If every one of us did something constructive, we could change the world...'

The work will continue tomorrow – and the day after that and the day after that, until a ball does change the world. 'Where's Fernando?' I wonder, at the end of the typical day. I think I may have lost him when we went to the Chamber of Commerce. 'Have I answered your question?'

8

The Poverty Industry

Q: You work with corporates – are they not the cause of the problem?
A: They are part of the solution...

FRIDAY, 12 OCTOBER 2012: Today, there's time to wander around in the plaza and catch up with friends – and the football.

I also witness one of the most emotional moments of the Homeless World Cup, when Mexico's Ana Aguirre is injured during their match against Chile. It looks as if she'll be out for the rest of the tournament, and so far she has not just been one of the stars of the soccer but also one of the most powerful ambassadors for Mexico and homeless people. When she is invited to the VIP stand to watch the team's next game versus Paraguay, she bursts into tears when her team-mates come onto the field with a banner and stand in a line – hands on hearts – in her honour.

* * * * *

It is only a matter of time before Fernando appears, armed with his brown-leather notebook, and right on cue, I see him approaching the stand, with his signature smile even wider than ever. He sits down beside me as I'm watching the game, and starts to question me about our close relationship with corporate sponsors. It is not the first time that someone has tried to suggest having corporate sponsors is somehow not good for the Homeless World Cup, but I simply point out that the stadium where we are sitting was constructed by corporate sponsors, and that none of this would ever have happened without them.

People sometimes tell me that the 'corporate' presence at the Homeless World Cup – mainly advertising – is somehow at odds with the ethos of 'changing the world with a ball'. Some people even question if we should associate with 'icons' of the capitalist system. But all the corporations which have been such great supporters through the years have helped make it happen. Without their sponsorship, the players would never get the opportunity to represent their countries at an international tournament – the opportunity to turn their lives around. Many of them wouldn't even get off the streets in the first place.

* * * * *

'So if there's so much homelessness, why don't we just build more houses?' Fernando asks next, scribbling away in his notebook as if he is recording every word. 'Instead of homeless people playing soccer, why don't they do something useful?'

I know that Fernando is trying to tease the words out of my mouth. He's playing Devil's advocate, as I would do in his shoes. 'If you want to eradicate homelessness and poverty,' he continues, 'why are you such good friends with big business?'

Fernando is certainly not the first person to ask and he won't be the last. But the questions are not over yet. 'Why don't you force the government to change things?'

These are just some of the questions I'm asked all the time. But I don't blame any reporter for reducing the issues to soundbites. In this age of social media when everyone broadcasts opinions, the complexity of many problems often gets lost in the crossfire.

So where do I stand?

* * * * *

As I look at all the stadiums, filled with fans cheering their hearts out on another spectacular day, I reflect on what our aims are and the 'philosophy' which first inspired the Homeless World Cup, and still inspires us every single day. I realise how much my perspective has changed through the years. My basic principles are still the same as ten or 20 years ago, built around important basic concepts such as fairness, social justice and providing opportunities for everyone to reach their potential, but my views on how to change the world have gradually evolved.

Fernando meets me again as I'm leaving the media centre and we walk together through the crowds of people streaming out of the stands at the end of the day. Then suddenly he asks me: 'Are you a socialist, Mel?'

Even though I am not keen on labels such as 'socialist' or 'liberal', I like direct questions like that. But the best way to answer is to tell him a story...

* * * * *

I am sitting in a minibus, scared to look out of the window.

Without any warning, the bus seems to lurch to the side and I finally get up the courage to look, and immediately start to regret it. Below me, there is nothing but fresh air and thousands of feet all the way to the foot of the mountain. The two wheels on the right-hand side are spinning around in mid-air, while the other two wheels try to pull us back onto the road – but when I say 'road' I am being very free with my language. It is more like a very rough track made of boulders and dust, or a ledge clinging on to the side of the slope. The only way we'll ever get off is by flying, if the minibus had any wings.

I am part of a group from the Schwab Foundation, on our way to Irupana, to meet a social entrepreneur called Javier Hurtado, on the *altiplano* (or Bolivian plateau), in the heart of the Andes.

We're on our way to somewhere once described as paradise, where many of the people have virtually nothing but the clothes they are wearing, and the children don't even have shoes – never mind textbooks or schools. The road to paradise does not exactly live up to its name, but as I gaze into the emptiness below us and the clouds half-way down, and the bus slides even closer to the edge, I imagine that heaven could be around the next corner.

In fact, the so-called 'road' is better known as Death Road. And every year, just as its title suggests, hundreds of people are killed on what is now officially 'the world's most dangerous road' climbing to a height of over 15,000 feet for 40 miles.

When we finally do reach the end of our heart-stopping journey, we are welcomed by Javier and taken for a fabulous meal – plates piled high with mangoes, avocados and peaches, bananas, papaya and cherries.

Javier is proud of what is happening. He founded Irupana Andean Organic Food in 1987, and the social enterprise not only provides better prices for produce but promotes the traditional organic methods of farming and helps prevent the drug dealers getting a foothold, at the same time as ending the dependence on government aid. In 2002, Irupana's social impact in Bolivia was recognised by the Schwab Foundation when Javier won an award as one of the 'Outstanding Social Entrepreneurs in the World'.

A million thoughts are racing through my mind as we are taken on a tour of the plateau. The air is bracing, even thinner than where we have come from this morning. There is snow on the peaks of the mountains around us. I hear the sound of water flowing over pebbles in the river, like music. And I gaze at the cotton-wool clouds in the sky. It is one of the most beautiful places on Earth. So what is the catch?

The people on the plateau are among the very poorest on the planet, struggling to survive on basic farming, even though the land is very fertile and produces such wonderful crops. Whether they like it or not, the farmers sometimes have to make their living from cocaine, growing coca leaves for pennies while the dealers make a fortune on the streets of the US and Europe. They're even stigmatised because they grow the raw materials of drug abuse in 'paradise' which some politicians demand should be napalmed because the farmers 'poison our children'.

The local people chew the coca leaves to help them cope with altitude sickness and feel less hungry, but the economics of the drug trade are to blame for the fact that they often have no choice except to grow coca. For many years, it has been recognised that 'crop substitution' would provide the incentives to stop this, growing crops such as bananas and coffee. But Javier explains that it is never so simple – if the coffee cartels will not pay more for coffee than the drug cartels pay for the coca, then what is a farmer to do? The money earned from coca leaves is virtually nothing compared to the street price of industrial-grade cocaine. Even the buyer who buys it from farmers and takes it to market makes relatively little from his role in the chain of command. This is only the outermost edge of the business – and business it certainly is.

The 'war on drugs' is clearly not succeeding. 'If they want to get drugs off the street, they should pay more for coffee,' says Javier, whose 'intervention' has transformed the lives of people in the area by empowering them with the tools they require, including new technology and distribution channels – and brilliant ideas.

I look around me at the people and see they are happy. When I look at the majestic, snow-capped mountains and see where they live, I can understand why. But on the global scale, they're also very poor, in terms of money and facilities like health care, education and transport.

We find the same conditions all over the world. Poverty and homelessness are everywhere. But who are we to intervene – a sick society addicted to our happy pills and mindless consumption? Should we export our unhappy way of life to this happier world? And is intervention always the answer?

It's easy to say education and jobs are the answer to everyone's problems, but many people who migrate from the country to cities in search of 'improvement' may end up even worse off on the streets. So is this progress? Do we really want more megacities eating up the countryside, unable to cope with their own populations?

'Intervention' is a dirty word for many people because it is often equated with war. Many politicians also tend to dislike intervention because they think free market forces should rule. If you see someone being attacked in the streets, you have similar choices to make. If you intervene, you may be injured, but if you don't, it could be even worse for everyone. And poverty and homelessness force us to make the same almost impossible choices.

The people on the plateau appear to be happy and probably would still have a smile on their faces whether we intervened here or not. But when I think about the billionaires I met in California just a few weeks ago, I remember how deeply unhappy they were, despite the fact the top one per cent of the world's population will soon own more than everyone else put together. Some of the billionaires even confessed that they don't know what to do with all their money. They agreed with me the world was in a crisis and that things would most likely get worse if we didn't do something about it. They were disturbed by what was happening and wanted to help, but they didn't know how. They had everything everyone ever desired but they were trapped behind their electronic gates in a world that was getting increasingly hostile and out of control, where the gap between the rich and poor was growing exponentially – a fault line that could soon destroy the planet.

* * * * *

So these are the extremes: unhappy billionaires in California and happy peasant farmers in Bolivia. The capitalist system is broken – it's simply not working. The traditional political philosophies have failed to come up with the answers. Old labels such as 'left' and 'right' are no longer useful. And we all agree action is needed. Even the world's richest people agree. We are in crisis and a new approach is needed.

Intervention is a complex and difficult subject but to sit and do nothing is a dangerous game. The challenge is always to strike the right balance between intervention and interference, to empower people and enable change, rather than providing them with 'charity' and thinking we have done our moral duty. It is hard, I admit, to walk past someone begging in the street, or refuse a starving man a bowl of soup. But these are acute problems, not chronic issues which require a radical long-term approach. As the saying goes, much better give a man a fishing rod than give him a fish. And the same goes for tackling the homelessness issue. It is not about providing homes or money but building an organisation which enables homeless people to change their own lives, learning how to make their living – learning how to live before they find themselves somewhere to live. On the surface, some ideas make perfect sense, but can also be counter-productive. One innovative idea was converting buses into mobile showers for homeless people in California, but this may make it easier to carry on being homeless. In some cities in the us, homelessness has almost become something normal. You sleep rough, wake up in the morning, get washed, go to work, eat and sleep rough again the next night, just like someone living in suburbia, except that you're homeless and have no possessions. 'What to do?' is a question we all have to ask. There are no easy answers but we need to do something or nothing will change. It all starts with belief and ends with action. We should be helping people make their own decisions and stand on their own feet by providing not a hand-out but a hand-up, as street papers always believed. Everybody has the potential to change but everybody also deserves to be given a chance.

Irupana is an excellent example of radical thinking which has made a huge difference to thousands of people, and continues to inspire countless others. It started up in 1987 with just $4,000, one store, one employee and a second-hand truck, and today it is Bolivia's biggest exporter of quinoa, a 'superfood' becoming increasingly popular in countries all over the world.

Javier died on August 27, 2012, two months before the Homeless World Cup opened in Mexico City. He will be badly missed by everyone who knew him and valued his talents.

The lesson is that Javier got up and did something constructive. And all of us should follow his example – before the wheels come off completely and we run out of road.

* * * * *

When I meet up with Fernando later on that day, he asks another question I am asked every year: 'But why get involved with big business? Are they not the cause of the problem?'

'To achieve our aims, the Homeless World Cup works very closely with corporate partners,' I tell him. 'Sometimes we are criticised for doing so. But I believe collaboration is key to success, not only for us and the hundreds of thousands of people who take part in our programmes but also big business itself.'

I also tell Fernando that I recently went to Seattle, and give him a sound-bite: 'Three-thousand people sleeping in the streets of Seattle is not the American Dream.'

We have created a society where it is easy to fall off the edge. Innovations are emerging all around us but what about values that people can live by? Where will we find inspiration? 'Too many people are excluded who should be actively encouraged to participate in shaping our future,' I say. 'And this divides us and creates two different worlds with different values, living in different conditions, within the same borders.'

We all want to change things. But we won't change the world by dividing ourselves. The world is divided enough and becoming more divided every year, but we won't make things better by building more walls. To create change, we have to join forces.

Large corporations are not necessarily the 'enemies' of progress but can actually be part of the solution. They have the opportunity to build a world in which success is something to be proud of and enjoyed, in a society where no-one is excluded. There is no satisfaction in feasting while others around you are starving, and ultimately that means corporations have to balance their interests and play a responsible role in the communities where they do business – and live. The world has to change, or destroy itself because of its own contradictions.

The key point is action. To build a new society, we need a new mentality and new ways of working together. In many ways, the most successful people in the corporate world have more progressive and constructive ideas about changing the world for the better than most of the conventional political parties.

The Homeless World Cup is a new way of changing the world. It is not a coincidence that many of the people involved with the organisation come from every part of the political spectrum. But everyone shares the same horror of poverty and deprivation. Everybody wants to eradicate homelessness. Everyone is working to include the excluded – including Telmex Foundation and Nike.

* * * * *

Our partnership with Nike has been a great learning experience, not just for us but for Nike itself. During the week, I get a message from my friend Maria Bobenrieth in Amsterdam, saying how much she would like to be with us in Mexico City – she's hardly missed a single tournament since Edinburgh.

Maria was the Global Director of Community Investments at Nike until she joined *Women Win* two years ago, to focus on 'empowering women through sport'. When she first got involved with the Homeless World Cup in 2003, we understood each other right from the start, because we were on the same wavelength when it came to believing in the power of sport to create social change.

According to Maria, the word that best described both our organisations was 'entrepreneurial' and that is what continues to drive the relationship now. She explained:

> We looked at the description of what they were trying to do – eliminate homelessness through football – and we thought that's really crazy, it will probably work! What was really stunning was that Mel never asked us for money. We had a three-hour conversation, and at the end of it, I asked him what he wanted from Nike, expecting him to say he wanted us to write a cheque for two million dollars. But he didn't. He said: 'I'm building a world-class sporting event, and building a world-class brand, and I need you guys to be my partner, and transfer those skills to us – that's what we want.' And I went away and thought that's the first time ever someone has led with that story, and that is the foundation of our partnership.

When Maria went to her first Homeless World Cup, she saw for herself the potential. 'It's compulsive viewing,' she said. 'You're not there for more than two minutes before you stop thinking about homelessness, because what you are watching is just brilliant football – that's why sport is such a great tool for social change.'

One of the key things that Nike has gained from the Homeless World Cup, Maria once said, is that it 'really wakes us up about entrepreneurship and intrapreneurship.' She continued:

> There are lots of intrapreneurs at Nike that don't necessarily want to go off and start up the Homeless World Cup, but they've got great ideas... And this sparked us to thinking about how we might create a platform where employees will be able to hook up with social entrepreneurs, and let their intrapreneurship skills be used for the greater good, because at the end of the day, not only the business but the social challenges are going to require all of us to access the wealth – and the crowd wisdom.

Maria's colleague, Hannah Jones, now CSO & VP of the Innovation Accelerator at Nike, echoed her words when she said: 'We came to realise that this could have long-term impact. It's a way of mobilising and bringing people into an environment of teamwork and commitment.'

Nike's commitment was not without risks, supporting an organisation which rose out of nowhere, with nothing to show for its efforts so far. 'These guys had never done this before,' they said after Graz. 'And this had the potential to be the biggest disaster ever. So we thought: We like that! We like people with crazy ideas!'

In other words, for Nike there is something in the partnership with the Homeless World Cup which goes beyond the simple act of sponsorship or even the personal impact on its own employees, who volunteer their services year after year. There is almost a 'magical' impact – its involvement could encourage innovation and invention in the future, as the relationship continues to evolve.

* * * * *

Unlike the mysterious and sometimes unaccountable financial world, large corporations have to be responsible – to customers, employees, shareholders and regulatory bodies. And part of that means rising to the ethical challenge and playing a constructive role in the communities in which they operate.

The business world today is much more powerful than governments in many regards, and that power has to be channelled in useful directions for positive change. You cannot be successful in a world full of failure. Success – like opportunities – should always be mutual. And that's why we partner with the corporate world, to put an end to homelessness by working together for win-win success.

I am full of admiration for protesters but it's easy to be negative, much harder to be positive and come up with alternatives which actually work.

You've got to start somewhere. But there has to be somewhere to go.

* * * * *

Viktor Kirkov is someone who is going places – and taking lots of other people with him. The CEO and founder of the Team of Hope, our partners in Bulgaria, joins me and Fernando for a chat over coffee, and I'm pleased to hand over to Viktor to talk about working with corporate partners.

As soon as you come into contact with Viktor, you know he means business and knows how to 'market' his project and win major sponsors. But I tell Fernando not to be fooled by the corporate jargon – Viktor is a man on a mission to liberate people from social exclusion, and he wants to take big business with him by delivering concrete results – or 'return on investment.'

Viktor's journey started in 2011, when he visited the Centre for Temporary Accommodation in the church of St Sofia, recruiting excluded young men to play soccer. Viktor quickly discovered the power of soccer, and the scale of the problems that so many young people faced.

Many of the players had grown up in orphanages in Sofia, but only ten per cent of them were actually orphans. The vast majority were simply abandoned by parents who could not afford to look after their children, then abandoned again by the system as soon as they were adults.

Gradually, the Team of Hope built up a nationwide network which now covers nine different cities, with about 100 players taking part two times a week for sessions of about 90 minutes, supervised by volunteer coaches. Viktor also organises ten competitions a year, to select the Bulgarian team for the Homeless World Cup. The project also helps the players with accommodation, jobs and education.

Initially, the focus was on young men who had got into trouble and ended up homeless or living in shelters, after leaving the 'security' of state institutions, with no academic qualifications or basic life skills. The 'lucky' ones may find a place in state-funded accommodation but many of them find themselves forced to survive on the streets.

Today, the project also works with younger people, getting them involved from 12 years old onwards, and Viktor plans to widen the net so that more excluded people can be part of the programme, including people in prison, as well as members of the Romani community – about one million people out of seven million in Bulgaria. Social integration has always been an issue for Romani people, while they also have problems with identity papers, and the selling of child brides as young as 11 years old is also a cause for concern.

Viktor also tells us that he plans to get more older people involved in the project, forming a partnership with an organisation called 'Urban Nomads', which works with homeless people by providing them with temporary houses, job training and psychological counselling. 'Within the next two years, we want to reach 1,000 people a week,' Viktor tells Fernando, who underlines the figures in his notebook as if they have special importance. 'The major problem is how many people get stuck in the poverty cycle,' Viktor continues. 'If they don't have any qualifications, they can't get a job or hold on to a job, and if they lose their identity papers, they can't apply for new ones because they do not have a permanent address, and they can't get a permanent address because they do not have identity papers.' Unfortunately, this classic *Catch* 22 situation results in some young men getting a criminal record, which makes it even harder to get into employment, so Team of Hope helps players get identity papers as well as medical certificates and criminal checks – all required for employment. And it is through employment, Viktor believes, that the project has been most successful.

Viktor also wants to help the social enterprise sector develop in cities all over Bulgaria, forming partnerships with similar organisations in other countries. In Sofia, says Viktor, there are 15 to 20 organisations 'who do not even know they're social enterprises yet.' By sharing resources and working more closely with overseas partners, they could make dramatic progress, says Viktor.

For Viktor, it is all about social entrepreneurs working side by side with corporate partners to achieve mutual aims – not just encouraging business to tick all the CSR (corporate social responsibility) boxes but making people realise that human values count as much as profits, and that there are personal rewards worth more than dollars and cents. 'Social entrepreneurship is a phenomenon which enables everyone involved to get more then they give, and it could also be a successful business model,' says Viktor. 'Focusing on profit is not the only way to succeed in business. It's possible to focus on people in need *and* make a profit. It's also important to engage in civic society because the more active we are, the wider our sphere of influence is and the easier it is to guide our own destiny. And I want civic society to represent the state, not the political elite. We should all support people in need, and get a sense of accomplishment by doing so, because we feel much happier by investing some of our spare time.'

Viktor also has a simple philosophy for social entrepreneurs and their partners. 'When the sponsors see results,' he says, 'they want to become more involved. If they get good publicity because of their support, it's good for business and they also deserve it. We share the good results – the success on the soccer field and the success in the lives of the players. We work hard and we give them good value for money.'

The Team of Hope has had three major sponsors from the start: Telenor (the new name for Globul), EKO fuel stations and Dundee Precious Metals. In addition to financial assistance, some sponsors also provide goods and services, including transportation, food and drink, as well as free smartphones and discounts on fuel. Viktor says there are 'no strings attached' to the sponsors' support, and they understand exactly what the project is trying to do. 'The main aim is to help excluded people,' he explains, 'but if you are professional, the sponsors will always support you.'

'It's an interesting theory,' Fernando says, putting his pen down as if he has finished.

'It's more than a theory,' says Viktor.

* * * * *

In the evening, I meet Patrick Gasser for dinner with Harald – the three of us have been good friends for over a decade. Patrick is the Senior Manager of Corporate Social Responsibility at UEFA, and Harald and I will never forget the support we have had from UEFA since the first Homeless World Cup in Graz. It may not seem now like a huge sum of money – 15,000 euros, rising to 45,000 euros the following year – but the fact that UEFA was willing to back us, before we had proved ourselves, made all the difference.

UEFA also recognised right from the start what the Homeless World Cup was about. 'The success of the Homeless World Cup is built on the enormous power of football in social inclusion,' said Lars-Christer Olsson, then UEFA's Chief Executive. 'The Homeless World Cup has set up a new frame for empowerment of homeless people, and a new image of homeless people in the world.'

This ringing endorsement from one of the world's most influential organisations, backed up by funding, was a great boost when the impact of the Graz event was only just beginning to emerge, but our money problems did not end in Austria. Two years later, just before the tournament in Edinburgh, we were struggling to survive when once again UEFA came to the rescue.

Because of visa problems, New York had been cancelled as the venue for the third Homeless World Cup. It was a major disappointment to us and our partners in the USA, because we lost the opportunity to reach a bigger audience than ever before and highlight the scale of the homelessness problem in the world's richest country.

Jeff Grunberg of *Big News* was the driving force behind the USA bid and the local organising committee had already found a venue in the heart of Manhattan. HBO were keen to be our media partners and plans were well advanced, but we couldn't risk having the players refused entry into the country at the very last minute.

We had a few ideas for alternative venues, then the City of Edinburgh Council, the Scottish Government and the local business community all pulled together to host the event in Edinburgh, at the very last minute. But even though we were delighted to have this support on the ground, the event was still at risk because of shortfalls in funding.

* * * * *

Then one day, Harald calls me at seven o'clock in the morning...

Is he calling from the hospital? No, not another heart attack! What crisis this time?

'Great news, Mel – we've won a prize from UEFA.'

I am shaving, in front of the mirror. It's great to win UEFA's recognition but this news will not change the world. 'You call me at seven o'clock in the morning for that?' I say, thinking that Harald has lost it. 'To tell me we've won an award?'

'No, you don't understand, Mel. It's a million Swiss francs.'

And I cut myself shaving.

When we got the money from UEFA, we knew we could make it. The Edinburgh tournament could go ahead as scheduled, with Nike and UEFA both behind us.

'That money was the food for the baby!' says Harald. 'Otherwise the baby would have starved!'

* * * * *

Years later, in Mexico City, funding is still a big challenge, but UEFA is still right behind us. Patrick is particularly happy to come back to Mexico City – he studied Spanish here in 1982. He also loves the Zocalo's spectacular setting. When the tournament takes place in the heart of the city, it's not just good for atmosphere but also attracts passers-by and makes people much more aware of the issues involved. It's hard to walk past stadiums packed with spectators, with dozens of national flags proudly flying above, without asking what's going on here.

As we talk about old times, we suddenly realise this is the tenth year UEFA has been one of our partners, and ten years since Patrick himself got involved.

Every week, UEFA receives piles of project proposals, but Patrick says the Homeless World Cup 'struck a special chord' despite the fact it had ambitions far beyond the borders of Europe. Our proposal also interested UEFA because it talked about the power of soccer to change people's lives and help address the problem of social exclusion, not just soccer for its own sake. 'That was what made it so special,' says Patrick. 'The thinking was outside the box – to make a contribution to society beyond the game. We also see street football as a great tool to reduce social marginalisation, taking advantage of the cultural enthusiasm associated with football to engage with homeless people.'

Later, Patrick also wrote about the impact of the Homeless World Cup:

> The potential to play for your country at the Homeless World Cup is an experience none of the players will ever forget. But the lasting impact comes from the number and scope of the programmes run by NGOs and other international partners, and activities which take place every day of the year, around the world. It is these programmes that offer the potential for change on a significant scale.

> Regular playing helps homeless people gain more confidence and become fitter. They build trust in other people, including their team-mates, and this deepens the potential for change. Regular attendance at training is also good for outreach – for example, they can get advice on employment, addiction and health, as well as housing, family planning, etc.

The funding from UEFA meant much more than money – it gave us the official credibility we needed to approach other sponsors. In addition, many of our national partners in Europe have an active relationship with members of UEFA. But our relationship also goes further than this – for example, workshops like the one in Sarajevo the week before kick-off in Mexico City, focusing on social responsibility.

Professional soccer is often attacked for the huge sums of money involved and the sometimes astronomical salaries earned by the players, but many teams and individual players give something back to the game. For superstars, it's also true a ball can change the world.

Patrick is also aware that the Homeless World Cup is not only an annual event but a programme that goes on all year, and in Mexico City, he once again appreciates the huge psychological impact of playing for your country in front of so many supporters. As soon as he arrived in the Zocalo this morning, he could hear the applause of the crowds. 'Maybe it was quite a crazy idea,' says Patrick, 'but it's also been highly successful.'

* * * * *

When I meet journalists or students or celebrities or billionaires or corporate executives or anyone else with an interest in what we are trying to do, I always ask what *they* can do – because I think that every single individual *can* change the world. Some people have much more money or power than others, but everyone has something to contribute, no matter how small, whether it's a few hours or just a few cents.

For example, Carlos Slim and the Telmex Foundation have been great supporters of the Homeless World Cup, but what they have contributed goes far beyond money. And for businesses with relatively modest resources, it is also about more than money.

* * * * *

Alex Chan may not be the world's richest man but he's played a key role in supporting the work of our partners in Hong Kong, whose team – called The

Dawn – made their début in the tournament in Edinburgh in 2005, thanks to Alex and his business friends in Hong Kong.

Seven years later, I meet up with Alex in Mexico City. He wants to present me with a copy of a book about the players who have played for Hong Kong in the Homeless World Cup, because I wrote the foreword. And as we pose for photos, Alex starts to talk about the possibility of Hong Kong becoming the first city in Asia to host the event.

'Why not?' I ask. It would be a spectacular setting.

Alex first got involved in 2005 after reading a story about a local social worker called Ng Wai-Tung who was trying to organise a team to represent Hong Kong in the Homeless World Cup. And that was the beginning of Alex's love affair with the event, and my friendship with Alex.

Because of his passion for football and because he was intrigued by the idea of the Homeless World Cup, Alex phoned Wai-Tung to ask how he could help.

Alex explains: 'Wai-Tung was very well known amongst homeless people in Hong Kong because of the work he has done through the years, but he didn't have connections in the business world and was finding it hard to raise the sponsorship money he needed for the team to fly to Scotland. So I got in touch with two of my good friends in business and they immediately agreed to back the cause. And once he had the funding, Wai-Tung could focus on selecting the team.'

In 2006, Wofoo Social Enterprises joined forces with the Society of Community Organisations (SOCO) to organise the local Homeless World Cup campaign, looking after team selection and training as well as the travel arrangements. Since then, the organisation in Hong Kong has grown every year, including social workers and a publisher.

Says Alex: 'We are all united either by our passion for football or the drive to help less privileged people, or both. Every year, we run a special tournament to raise funds to sponsor the team for the Homeless World Cup and this has grown to 20 teams this year. Each team pays HK$15,000 to take part in the tournament, and we also run a full-day event to select the players for the Homeless World Cup, and enrol them in a comprehensive rehabilitation programme.'

Local sports and business organisations have also been major supporters: 'We have formed a partnership with leading Hong Kong soccer club Kitchee SC, which helps us with coaching, and the Keswick Foundation funds the Hong Kong Street Soccer League.'

Another local company which lends its support is PARKnSHOP, the largest supermarket chain in Hong Kong, which arranges three to four days of on-the-job training for players. The Tung Wah Group of Hospitals, a charity which runs schools, hospitals and other community services, sends trainees to film games and interview players.

Persuading local businesses to get involved has been one of Alex's greatest achievements, but what is the secret?

> First of all, we show them that the Homeless World Cup has real social impact – over 90 per cent of the players who represent Hong Kong in the Homeless World Cup really do change their lives after the tournament and are no longer homeless. Taking part in the fund-raising tournament has also proven very popular with sponsors because it benefits their staff.

In Alex's view, the social impact and the fact that local businesses get so involved is a win-win situation for players and sponsors, making connections between corporations, charities and foundations, social workers and volunteers, whose commitment makes the movement more sustainable.

Alex and I pose for our photographer, Anthony Epes, who is planning an exhibition of portraits from the Homeless World Cup when he gets back to London. Anthony wants to show the players 'transformed by their environment' exactly as Alex describes.

As the camera captures the moment, and Alex smiles his winning smile and formally presents me with a copy of his book, I wonder if the tournament will one day go to Hong Kong as Alex has dreamed. And then I think, it's not if the tournament goes there but when...

* * * * *

This evening, a group of us go to the Museo Soumaya, the ultra-modern palace of the arts built by Carlos Slim in memory of his wife Soumaya Domit, who died in 1999. The museum houses a world-class collection, including works by Michelangelo, Diego Rivera, Van Gogh and Salvador Dali.

Tonight, the Homeless World Cup will be hosted by the world's richest man, introducing potential new sponsors. Carlos Slim and his family join us and tell me how much they look forward to seeing the Finals on Sunday. I never know what's going to happen as the tournament reaches its climax. I never know how I will feel when it comes to an end, and as I look across at Harald as he chats with Arturo, in the shadow of Rodin's *The Thinker*, I realise how far we've come since Finals day in Graz, when we wondered if that was the end of the Homeless World Cup or the start of an incredible journey to where we are now – and wherever we're going tomorrow.

174

9

The Human Factor

Q: Why do so many people get involved with the Homeless World Cup?
A: There is more to life than money...

SATURDAY, 13 OCTOBER 2012: As I stroll around the Zocalo, I bump into Australian referee Hary Milas, one of the many volunteers who has been changed by his experience at the Homeless World Cup and goes out of his way to attend every year, no matter where the tournament is held.

For Hary, something happens every year which he'll never forget, including Paris in 2011, when a young man from Phnom Penh thought his world was about to collapse, as the 'Man In Black' approached him at the end of a game, with a look on his face that spelled trouble...

Near the end of the game, the young Cambodian player was feeling so drained he could hardly put one foot in front of the other. The game had been tough and the other team easily won – they were simply much faster and stronger. Then as soon as the whistle was blown for the end of the game, Hary walked towards him, looking him straight in the eye, as if he was going to give him a lecture. There had been a few muscular challenges during the game, and the young man from Cambodia had committed a couple of fouls.

Before he said anything, Hary knelt down at the side of the pitch, and the young Cambodian knelt down in front of him, fearing the worst. Maybe he had lost his cool and cursed a decision? Or gone in too hard for a challenge?

It was a difficult moment for the young man who'd travelled to Paris a few days before, as he looked up at Hary. But for Hary, this was one of the moments he lives for – and a world away from being a regular ref in Australia.

Soccer is not always a beautiful game...

* * * * *

Several years ago, Hary was refereeing a game between two junior teams in his home town of Melbourne, when one of the parents approached him.

Even games between very young kids can arouse lots of passion, not only for the kids themselves but also their parents. But this particular parent was even more angry than usual, and Hary still has all the scars to prove it.

The angry parent stormed up to Hary 'because he didn't like a decision' and without any warning attempted to stab him with the point of his umbrella. Hary held his hand up to protect himself but the umbrella pierced his hand so badly that it took him several years to recover full use of his fingers.

Then the parent got even more angry and launched himself into another much wilder attack. 'He stabbed me in the back,' says Hary, 'several times.'

The blade passed through his body and into his shoulder, missing his spine by two millimetres, and narrowly missing his heart and his lungs. 'He could have severed an artery. He could have killed me.'

When he woke up in hospital after the stabbing, did Hary feel like quitting? What did his wife Anita think? 'She tells me that the Homeless World Cup is my purpose, my calling,' says Hary. 'As referees, you get this angst – week in, week out – from spectators and players, because there's always somebody who hates the Man in Black. But at the Homeless World Cup, everybody just wants to hug you and show you respect. It's totally addictive. I count every day leading up to the Homeless World Cup, and when I get here I just walk around hearing these incredible stories and meeting incredible people.'

* * * * *

Several years after the stabbing, when the young Cambodian player was kneeling in front of him, fearing the worst, Hary's life had changed out of all recognition. 'As soon as he knelt down,' says Hary, 'I gestured to him to stand up. He had played so fairly and with such great respect for the game, but everybody thought he was in trouble – including the young man himself.'

Via an interpreter, Hary thanked the young man for inspiring him and everyone around him. And the worry that he was in trouble soon melted away, as they smiled at each other in silence. 'There weren't too many dry eyes round the pitch after that,' says Hary, 'including my own.'

* * * * *

Hary first got involved in the Homeless World Cup when the tournament took place in Melbourne in 2008. 'I was honoured to be part of it – without a doubt the pinnacle of my career.'

One of Hary's friends had read about the Homeless World Cup in *The Big Issue Australia* and said that it would be a good idea to volunteer. After doing some basic research, Hary put a notice on his referee's website and within two days got 35 responses. Then he and several others signed up as officials and soon after, the tournament opened in Melbourne. 'They referees are like my second family,' says Hary, 'and my experience from Day One was amazing. We turned up on the Sunday and were briefed by Iain McGill, the referee in charge of international officials. I also met Kim Milton Nielsen from Denmark, a legend among referees.'

Today, the 'family' of referees has grown to several dozen, with new officials added every year – like Mexican referee Antonio Gutierrez, who was so desperate to be part of it, he sold his car to get there the next year in Poland.

* * * * *

Hary will never forget refereeing his first game in Melbourne – Poland versus Russia. 'At the end of the game, one of the Polish players approached me and in his broken English simply said, "Thank you." Then his manager told me that the player wished to thank me for treating him like a real human being. You're a man in uniform, he told me, and back home everyone in uniform would treat him very badly. No respect. They would tell him to get off the streets and make himself invisible. That is why he said thank you!'

That was the moment Hary fell in love with the Homeless World Cup and he still gets emotional telling the story: 'That was a powerful message for me on my very first day, and that still continues today. It changed me as a person, just the same as it changes the lives of the players.'

Melbourne was particularly special for Hary because his home town rose to the occasion in such spectacular style, with huge crowds in the heart of the city and games 'live' on national TV. Hary also thinks Australia's passion for sport and traditional 'love of the underdog' made a big difference in people's reaction. 'Melbourne is still buzzing,' says Hary. 'Nothing like that ever happened before. I was humbled.'

* * * * *

According to Hary, the Homeless World Cup is simply an idea that works. It also seems to have a special 'magic' and has given him some very precious memories – as well as some very proud moments. In 2011, for example, Hary was chosen to referee the Final in Paris, and he freely admits he was nervous: 'I had a few butterflies, if I am honest. It was a big game for the players and I was really proud to be the official.'

For Hary, the power of the Homeless World Cup has a big impact on everyone involved, including volunteers, spectators and the media as well as the players. 'And when I referee a game back home and somebody gives me a piece of their mind, or I have a bad day at the office, I remember what it means to be part of the Homeless World Cup.'

The common goal, says Hary, is to 'share each other's pain' at the same time as enjoying the soccer. In Hary's view, the concept of the team is another key factor. 'You see teams get together on the same side of the pitch, and they stand arm in arm, as one team. Even though they come from countries which are often sporting rivals, they have a common background and somehow they manage to gel.' Hary always gets emotional at the opening ceremony, and even though some soccer fans may not believe refs are human, he usually sheds a few tears.

* * * * *

The referees play a key role in the Homeless World Cup, and the challenge they face is unique. They have to strike a balance between upholding the rules of the game at the same time as also maintaining the spirit of the tournament – building confidence and self-respect, and motivating players. 'Soccer is a contact sport,' says Hary. 'The ref's job is to prevent anarchy but you have to be careful not to be too tough.'

Hary's 'softer' side emerged when he devised his signature gift for the players – presenting special whistles to recognise the 'many acts of sportsmanship, perseverance and good will' which Hary has witnessed: 'The whistle is a sign of my respect for the players.'

Hary usually makes a short speech to the player before he presents it. 'It's sometimes hard to single out one individual player,' says Hary, 'but it doesn't always have to be the best – just someone who tries hard or does something sporting.'

Every year, one special player stands out – like India's goalie in Paris, who let in goal after goal but kept on going right to the end of the game, with a smile on her face. In another women's game, between the USA and Canada, one of the players broke through near the end and suddenly found herself 'one on one' with the goalie, with seconds to go in the match and the score zero-zero. As she rounded the goalie, the players accidentally collided, and the goalie collapsed. The player only had to tap the ball into the net and the win was assured. But even though she hadn't committed a foul and Hary had not blown his whistle, she knocked the ball away and picked up her opponent, rather than taking advantage to kick the ball into the unguarded net. 'She got the whistle!' says Hary.

* * * * *

Another player Hary will always remember is a member of the USA team in Melbourne. Hary refereed one of his games at the start of the week and the player started following Hary, to observe how he refereed matches. When Hary noticed he had a new 'fan,' he talked to him and learned about how he had ended up homeless, estranged from his family and friends. 'He told me that when he returned to the States, he wanted to become a referee, and two years later, he had qualified, and was back with his family.' The experience of being a referee changed his whole life. He told Hary:

> You go out as the referee and for that 90 minutes, you are the one in control. You may have had a problem in the past with drugs or alcohol, or homelessness, but now you are the person people look to for decisions, even though it's often an impossible decision.

Hary gets emotional recalling the story. 'It's awesome,' he says. 'You start a little something and it changes the world.'

Emotional moments like this can sneak up on you all of a sudden. And they happen to most of the people involved in the Homeless World Cup, when the human drama simply overwhelms you like a tidal wave that sweeps you off your feet – as you realise the scale of the problems the players confront every day and the courage they have deep inside. 'That is the power of the Homeless World Cup,' says Hary. 'It changes people and it has also changed me.'

* * * * *

The Homeless World Cup would never have happened if it hadn't been for all the people who believe that the empowerment of individuals is key to addressing the homelessness issue and changing the world with a ball.

These individuals, from every part of the political spectrum, are committed to helping homeless people and building sustainable organisations to support them. They are passionate people who are driven by different motivations – sometimes political, sometimes religious – but have a similar desire to tackle homelessness. What unites them is their common objective and their willingness to sit down and talk until they reach an agreement, and translate their words into action. And they are able to do so because they take 'politics' out of the homelessness issue.

Every year, volunteers from all over the world come to join us, to act as referees or help the sports or media teams, or welcome VIP guests.

Some volunteers are coaches or managers who come from a social work background or the world of soccer and the media. Others are simply committed to changing the world and come to the annual event prepared to do anything – from laying the pitch to taking photographs or interviewing players for stories to go on the website.

Local volunteers act as guides and translators for all of the teams, and become friends with the players and the managers – plus doing countless other jobs like making sure the players have plenty of water or sunblock.

The people employed by the organisation could have taken other more 'rewarding' paths in life, and they show unbelievable patience, supporting people who have often been damaged by the experience of homelessness. They also 'bang the table' when they need to.

The volunteers and other staff are full of life and energy, and many of them work throughout the year, fund-raising or simply spreading the word. Many of them make a big sacrifice in order to help, but they love what they do and are deeply affected by their experience – working closely together with colleagues and players – and that is why so many of them return year after year, like veteran referee Iain McGill.

* * * * *

Whistle blower Iain doesn't like to be known as the 'head' referee, saying he is just another member of the team, but he has been the referee that everyone has turned to for advice since 2005, when he made his début at the Edinburgh Homeless World Cup. Another volunteer, Kim Milton Nielsen, refereed the Final of the UEFA Champions League in 2004, but Iain has an equal claim to fame – he refereed the Final of the Homeless World Cup in Cape Town in 2006.

Just a few weeks after he had gained his official refereeing certificate in 2005, I got in touch with Iain to ask if he would help. The Edinburgh event was being put together on a shoestring at the very last minute, and we couldn't afford to pay any officials to referee games.

Iain was not only the official we needed but someone with experience of homelessness issues who had also helped with other disadvantaged people in countries all over the world, including Mozambique, Malawi, Zimbabwe, Brazil and Albania. For all of these reasons, he seemed the right man for the job, and he 'volunteered' three of his friends, also recent refereeing graduates. There was one complication, however. Two weeks before the tournament, Iain and his business partner Harmony Schofield had set up an employment agency, specialising in social care, and now he was proposing to take a week off. It was a lot to ask, but the business continues to thrive, and Iain continues to give up his time every year – and another adventure as head referee.

*****

Iain also loves to travel, and as soon as the tournament ended in Mexico City, he took a flight to Haiti. In Port-au-Prince, he saw the devastation all around him – tens of thousands of homes destroyed, 1.5 million homeless, 86 per cent of the people living in slums, and half the population with no running water. The city resembled a war zone and when Iain arrived at his hotel, he found out that he was one of only three tourists in Haiti that week.

The next day, Iain took a taxi to Cité Soleil, where our national partner, Foundation L'Athletique D'Haiti, was set up almost 20 years ago, in one of the poorest and most dangerous places in Haiti. 'You sure you want to be here?' the driver asked Iain, as they pulled up outside the address. 'Before I go, you wave to me, to tell me that you are OK!'

When Iain met Boby Duval and his team, he was moved by the warmth of their welcome, and spent the day finding out more about what the Foundation was doing, and the problems they faced after recent disasters. The details were enough to break anyone's heart, but Iain didn't know that less than two weeks later, another disaster would strike, when Hurricane Sandy was the next to arrive, leaving dozens more dead in its wake.

*****

'Edinburgh was soccer with a smile,' Iain tells me in Mexico City. 'And every year, that smile lights up the city where the tournament is hosted. It was soccer as it should be, free to watch and fun for players and spectators.' Edinburgh also deserves lots of credit for hosting the event at such short notice, we agree. And it was Edinburgh where Iain caught the bug.

The next year, Iain and his fellow Scot Niall Waters-Fuller were joined by two Austrian colleagues in Cape Town, plus several local referees including Abdul Ssekabira and Jabulane Nkosinathi Mahono, better known as 'Shoes', who both try to come every year. And every year, new referees are recruited, to become the latest members of the 'Crazy Gang'.

Abdul is a lecturer and also a professional referee in the South African Premier League, and he is always moved by the experience of being an official at the Homeless World Cup: 'The behaviour of the players touches me and puts poverty into perspective. The camaraderie between them is fantastic. And as referees, we can also be part of this change – part of the family.'

Kim Milton Nielsen refereed in Copenhagen in 2007, followed by Melbourne and Paris, and he was also part of the family: 'The Homeless World Cup generates much happiness,' he said. 'The spirit of the players also makes it very different. No matter if they win or lose, they still enjoy the game. Sometimes professional football can be too serious – and without happiness.'

The referees may be unpaid volunteers but they also have to be as professional as any pro – in some ways, even more so. In future years, says Iain, the referees may become a permanent team, but no matter what happens, the 'Crazy Gang' will always be a key part of the annual event.

* * * * *

Later on, I catch up with another volunteer, Chandrima Chatterjee, who typifies the spirit of the Homeless World Cup in terms of personal commitment and unshakeable belief in the power of soccer to change people's lives. She is only one of many hundreds of people who have volunteered over the years, paying to travel to the opposite side of the world, just so they can make a contribution – make a difference in somebody's life.

Chandrima signed up for the Homeless World Cup in Milan in 2009, after watching *Kicking It*, the documentary film about the tournament in Cape Town, narrated by the actor Colin Farrell. 'That movie literally transformed my view of the world,' says Chandrima. 'It led me down a path to sports for social change and sports for public health education. And straight away, I wanted to see it in action, to be a part of this incredible tradition which brings together people from all over the world, in a spirit of hope and peace.'

That first experience fired up Chandrima and sent her on a journey that continues today. 'Milan was magical,' she tells me, 'so full of hope and joy. I made instant friends with everyone I met there. My first 'job' was helping Team Finland, spending ten to 15 hours a day with the players, walking all around the city, sharing stories, eating meals together, having adventures which will last me a lifetime.'

* * * * *

Over the last few years, talking to players and coaches, Chandrima has also learned a lot about what it is like to be homeless in Finland. Like most other countries in Europe, Finland's homelessness problem is linked to other chronic social challenges such as substance abuse, mental health problems and unemployment. A relatively wealthy country, Finland has also been a pioneer in measuring – and reducing – homelessness. At the end of the 1980s, there were almost 20,000 homeless people in Finland. This fell to about 8,000 people by 2010, but an innovative national programme was set up to eliminate long-term homelessness in Finland by 2015.

A number of agencies help in this national effort, including the Finnish Homeless Academy, which became a second family for Chandrima. 'Milan was a life-changing week for them all,' says Chandrima. 'And since then, I have heard of lots of marriages and children, jobs and homes.'

The next year in Rio was another great experience for Chandrima, working with other volunteers such as Grecia 'Gigi' Garcia, who is also in Mexico City this year. When I talked with Chandrima in Rio, I encouraged her to join Street Soccer USA and work with Lawrence Cann, whom she later described as 'one of the best mentors in the world of sports for social change – he really changed my life.'

Chandrima is still in close contact with several players and coaches from Finland, including Ari Hulden (better known as Huli), a former player who went on to become a leading coach. Before he got involved with the Homeless Academy, Huli spent time at sea as a cook and came back to dry land to work as a roadie. Eventually, his appetite for alcohol and drugs took over Huli's life, and he ended up in rehab.

Huli was always a soccer nut, and it was soccer that saved him. When he first got out of rehab, he was 'discovered' by Maukka from the Finnish Football Federation, who was trying to organise a Finland team to travel to South Africa for the Homeless World Cup in 2006 – and Huli went to Cape Town as a player. Back in Finland, his great love of soccer took over his life. He wanted to help other people use soccer to stay clean and sober and set up a team called The Stray Dogs who still play today. Huli also tries to help his players as much as he can on a personal level, with emergency housing and counselling – the kind of help that he once needed when he was down. 'He's the heart of Street Soccer Finland,' says Chandrima.

Another player Chandrima will never forget is Patrick Kulmala, who represented Finland at the Homeless World Cup in Rio and went back home inspired to change his life.

Unlike many other players, Patrick had a 'normal childhood' – going to school, playing hockey in winter and soccer in summer. In his teenage years, however, he started taking drugs and getting into alcohol. 'When I was 20,' he says, 'I realised I had major problems with substance abuse but I still was not ready to quit. As a result I spent much of my youth in prisons, hospitals and institutions.'

In September 2006, Patrick's drug abuse led to serious medical complications, resulting in the amputation of his left arm. Desperate to get clean, the young man sought help. 'This was a very sad time in my life,' he explains. 'I tried many methods to get clean. I moved from area to area, country to country and through various rehab programmes. It was then that I discovered the Finnish Homeless Academy.'

For Patrick, playing in Rio was an eye-opening experience: 'I met a lot of people from across the globe, and realised I've nothing to complain about, especially when I compare my situation with players from places like Uganda and Haiti. At the Homeless World Cup, I was an athlete and part of a team. I scored five goals and took away a lot of self-esteem.'

After Rio, Patrick stayed away from drugs, was reunited with his family and friends, and started working for the Finnish Homeless Academy, as part of the support team the next year in Paris. 'My life has changed completely,' he said at the time. 'Now I have the opportunity to help other players enjoy the same experience.'

Chandrima is an excellent example of how volunteers get involved with the Homeless World Cup in a very deep personal way. Later, she became the Communications Director for Street Soccer USA and the programme director for the Philadelphia chapter of Street Soccer USA – spreading the word about the power of soccer and providing a platform for players to speak their own minds.

*****

Meeting Hary earlier also reminds me of Melbourne. One of the key figures in 2008 was George Halkias, the driving force behind Team Australia, better known as the Street Socceroos, who unfortunately have not been able to make it to Mexico City – along with India and Spain, and several African countries, all of them equally missed.

Team Australia was started by George and a number of colleagues at *Big Issue Australia*, which runs the Community Street Soccer Programme and organises weekly training sessions in 18 towns and cities all over Australia. Sponsored by the Australian Government, Street Soccer 'promotes social inclusion and personal change' as well as the importance of commitment and team spirit. The players meet in 'a safe, non-threatening environment' which encourages them to get fit and make friends, and access services to deal with issues such as homelessness, substance abuse, family breakdown and mental illness. Many of the people who engage with the programme have given up on counselling and other basic services, but Street Soccer 'puts the person at the centre of the solution and provides them with the support and tools they need to make positive changes to their lives.'

Australians are renowned for their competitive spirit and their passion for sport, but George also sees the bigger picture: 'I sometimes coach players in prisons – people who feel like they "lose" every day. But after a while, they value their participation rather than the victories they might achieve on the field. And these are the skills they need to change their outlook. Football skills don't help you when you're released. The challenges will still be there. What counts is how you deal with them.'

George himself confesses that he hates to lose any game but channels this energy into his work as a coach. 'Sport brings out people's competitive instincts,' he says, 'but every player must be realistic. We all like to win but it's also important to learn how to cope with losing. Some homeless people get too used to losing all the time. And what is so good about the Homeless World Cup is that the players always get a chance to win the next game, take defeat and learn from it. You have to find the positives. And there are always positives.'

Some teams take the soccer more seriously than others, and experienced coaches like George understand this: 'You have to strike a balance and respect other teams. You don't want to demoralise the lesser teams too early. We've all got different abilities – you might be a good player or a good person. You might hold the trophy aloft at the end of the game, but have you learned from the experience? You might finish last but you might also learn more than anyone else.'

George trained as a psychologist and after graduating worked with homeless people in an area of Melbourne where he 'learned much more in two years' than his formal education, helping people deal with problems like substance abuse, as well as helping victims of crime. In 2004, he got involved in *Big Issue Australia*, and heard about something that was scheduled for New York the following year – an international street soccer tournament called the Homeless World Cup.

Soccer is a long way from the Number One sport in Australia but George and Martin Hughes, then editor of *Big Issue Australia,* still managed to persuade enough vendors to come along and take part in a kickabout, using the carrot of free magazines. As it turned out, Edinburgh hosted the tournament that year when New York was cancelled. 'It started slowly but it didn't take long to find players, or for them to see the benefits of regular sessions – a sense of purpose and a sense of belonging. Some of the players would follow us back to the office when the sessions were over. They might have been drinking the night before playing but after a good game of soccer, they would sleep a lot better.'

George also says that, apart from the obvious health benefits, regular games are 'something positive in a sometimes bleak outlook – a constant in a life that is often chaotic. For those who are experiencing social isolation, it's a way of building self esteem and confidence.'

Soon the team became known as the Street Socceroos, to echo the name of the national soccer team. Playing regular games in a housing estate, George and his colleagues started getting feedback from city officials, who had noticed the impact the sessions appeared to be having. 'Playing seemed to change the vibe,' he explains, 'and people also came along to watch. There was a community atmosphere.'

In 2005, the Street Socceroos headed for Scotland, thanks to funding from a number of people, including an Australian steel magnate who sent a cheque for several thousand dollars 'no questions asked' after seeing a TV documentary about the team's need for a sponsor. The journey to Edinburgh wasn't entirely smooth sailing, however. The week before kick-off, three suicide bombers killed dozens of people in London, and the UK authorities suddenly tightened restrictions, requiring visas for all of the players – but not George and the rest of the support team. Then just before leaving, the team lost its goalie – a young man who decided to turn himself in to the police because he was an illegal immigrant. Three years later, he was one of the stars for Australia, but in 2005, the team had to find a last-minute replacement.

After flying to Canberra to sort out the visas, George and the team flew to Scotland, not sure how the players would cope with the journey or being in a new country. One player also needed regular doses of methadone throughout the trip, but George was relieved that when everyone got over jet lag, the mood was more excitement and euphoria than nervousness and fear of the unknown. 'The opening day was amazing,' says George,'with all the colour and the chanting and the energy of all the other teams. We were overwhelmed by the support from other players and the atmosphere in Princes Street Gardens. Some of the players were shaking with excitement, and I think that also rubbed off on the crowd.'

George will never forget the quarter final game with Scotland, when local captain Gary Lipscombe scored the winner in the very last second. 'We won a few games,' says George, 'but when we played Scotland, the atmosphere was totally electric, and the football was fantastic. We wanted to win but we got on with Scotland so well, bonding with them during the week, that we were happy to see them go through to the next round.'

* * * * *

Inspired by this experience, George then applied to be host of the Homeless World Cup, backed by the Victorian government. 'We had a few challenges,' George explains, 'but in the end we thought the benefits could be enormous for the organisation as well as the individuals involved.'

The first goal was to get a group of sponsors, and this received a boost when I met a group of Australians at the World Economic Forum in Davos, including representatives of Goldman Sachs and BHP Steel, who quickly signed up to the project. Meanwhile, George and Steven Persson, the General Manager of *Big Issue Australia*, were also expanding the street soccer programme, not just in Victoria but throughout Australia, eyeing 30 different sites for regular sessions. As the project gathered momentum and the media helped raise their profile, people started knocking on George's door asking to help.

It was clear Melbourne had what it took to be host. The city had a strategy for staging very large international events, plus a great infrastructure. And Melbourne put on a great show in 2008, attracting crowds of over 100,000 spectators and winning the hearts and the minds of the people at the same time as transforming the image of homeless people once and for all, in Melbourne and beyond.

George was widely quoted in the media before the event, and got his ideas across with great power: 'We're dealing with a group that have so many issues that you wonder whether one thing you say or one decision that you make might put them over the edge. The players will receive so much positive affirmation and that's something that they've never received in life. For the first time they're going to feel good about themselves. They can look back and say, *I can do it again*.'

I have a lot of precious memories from Melbourne, including a meeting just before the event with the Australian Prime Minister, John Howard, who understood exactly what the Homeless World Cup was about, and came up with government funding. Once our formal 'business' was completed, the PM got on to his favourite subject and delayed his next appointment so we had more time to talk about the power of sport – a typical Australian who also happened to be the Prime Minister.

With the funding in place, George threw himself into the programme and established the 30 sites as he had planned, locating them in some of the most disadvantaged places in Australia.

The event itself in Melbourne was the biggest so far, with 'live' TV broadcasts and a huge media presence. Free local radio adverts and billboards also helped to get the message across. George and his committee did a great job, organising everything from food and accommodation to psychological support and lots of activities to keep players busy – learning from previous tournaments that players can get very restless between games if they have nothing to do. Melbourne also attracted an amazing number of volunteers – over 1,000 people.

I realised how much the Homeless World Cup had affected the people of Melbourne when I caught a taxi to return to the stadium one afternoon. Stopping at a traffic light, the taxi driver pointed at the stadium and asked me if I'd heard of this fantastic event called the Homeless World Cup. 'You should check it out, mate!' he told me, and I promised to take his advice.

*****

When the billboards came down and the overseas players had gone to the airport, George thought he would get a little time to himself to reflect, but his job wasn't finished. He shed a few tears as he drove home and opened the door, then the phone rang as soon as he entered the hall. It was terrible news – the partner of one of the Australian players had committed suicide. 'I was ready to clock off and sleep,' said George later, 'but the player needed all the support he could get.'

George knows that the tournament can transform people's lives but he is also realistic when it comes to the challenges some still face after it's over: 'The players can have a great experience during the tournament but they can also go back to some very tough times.' Knowing this continues to motivate George in his work for the programme, expanding its activities and working on the streets. He also recognises that there has to be a balance between playing soccer and social inclusion: 'Some players couldn't kick a ball to save themselves. But when they represent their country, and take responsibility, it works.'

George may have a serious objective in mind but he also wants the players to have fun – win lose or draw. 'Australia was the best 43rd team in Cape Town,' he jokes. 'All those losses, all those tough times brought people together. It has a family feel to it – a bond that will last for the rest of their lives.'

When players lose, they can feel quite dejected and deflated, and even start to argue and blame other players, so sometimes, it's important to put all of this in perspective, says George. In Cape Town, for example, the Australian players learned a lesson they will never forget when they visited one of the townships. They'd been badly beaten in a couple of matches, but as soon as they arrived in the township, they realised this didn't matter at all. 'The kids were so happy when we gave them some sweets and some footballs,' says George. 'The players began to appreciate just how much they had in Australia in terms of support – things like welfare and shelters.'

For George, the Homeless World Cup is not just about playing soccer but also making new friends. 'We always aim for the Fairplay Award,' George explains. 'That is our priority and we have won it now two times already!'

* * * * *

One of the most sensitive issues that had to be dealt with in Melbourne was the runaways – 15 players from Zimbabwe, Afghanistan, Rwanda and Liberia who were encouraged by a group of human rights activists to seek political asylum during the tournament. I have always believed that nothing is solved by transferring your problem from a poor country to a rich country, but at the same time it is easy to understand why homeless people are tempted to flee, especially when they have come from a war zone. More than anything, however, this kind of behaviour could threaten the future of the Homeless World Cup, so after this incident, we had to change the rules to make sure it would not be repeated, excluding countries where there was a conflict going on. It was a difficult and highly complex issue, but the Victoria state government was very sympathetic. The players were entitled to apply for asylum and everybody recognised that the Homeless World Cup was no different to the other major sporting events which are staged in Australia.

George summarised it neatly when he said: 'I haven't had much contact with the players (the asylum seekers) since then but I've heard mixed reports. Even in a land of opportunity like Australia, there are still challenges for everyone. It ain't Utopia.'

* * * * *

The managers and coaches who come to the Homeless World Cup every year are a very diverse group of people, but they share a great passion for soccer as well as a desire to work with homeless people, using the power

of soccer. And one of the most colourful and passionate characters is
Sergio Rotman, who has led Team Argentina to every event since Gothenburg in 2004.

Sergio first got involved in homelessness issues in 1998 when he met
Patricia Merkin, who had worked for *The Big Issue* in London and wanted
to do something similar in Buenos Aries. 'I was really impressed with the
concept,' says Sergio, 'and we launched *Hecho en Buenos Aires (Made in
Buenos Aires)* in June 2000.'

'Buenos Aries may look like Europe,' said Patricia at the time, 'but out
there on the streets it might as well be Africa – there are literally millions of
people who are vulnerably accommodated in slums, run-down hotels and
squats, with 30 per cent unemployment in parts of the city.'

Sergio could also see that homelessness was not just about sleeping rough
but living in low-standard housing. In Argentina, there are still about 18,000
people sleeping rough (among them, many street children), about 11,000 in
illegally occupied houses (squats), 180,000 in shanty towns, 70,000 in illegal settlements and 60,000 in homeless shelters and small hotels.

After attending the INSP Conference in 2001, Sergio first heard about
the idea of an international tournament for street-paper vendors. 'I love soccer and I thought it would be another incredible project,' he says. For the
next two years, however, Sergio and his colleagues at *Hecho* focused on
launching two new projects for homeless people – the Culture Centre and
the Health Bus. 'We couldn't afford to go to Graz in 2003,' Sergio recalls,
'but we promised our vendors we would take part in the tournament the
following year. In March 2004, we launched a soccer workshop for a group
of 50 players, with the dream of representing Argentina at the Homeless
World Cup in Gothenburg.'

Three years later, Sergio founded an organisation called Hecho Club
Social to look after soccer-based projects. 'We decided to extend participation to the rest of the homeless community, in addition to street-paper
vendors,' Sergio tells me. 'So cardboard collectors, people living in shanty
towns and later on, immigrants, refugees, drug and alcohol addicts, former prisoners and also people with HIV/AIDS took part in our activities. We
also extended the project to other NGOs working with homeless people and
created the Soccer Urban League for Social Inclusion, organising soccer sessions three times a week, as well as monthly tournaments for organisations
who work with vulnerable and homeless people.'

The philosophy is simple – to create an opportunity for everyone to get
involved with sport and be part of a group where respect for other people

is the law. The players also have the opportunity to get advice from social staff (psychologists and social workers, etc.) who help them reintegrate into society and organise workshops in health care, employment, education and housing, as well as gender issues and citizenship.

After working with the players through the year, Hecho Club Social selects the teams to play for Argentina, including men and women who deserve 'a chance for a new way of life.' Its chief goals are to 'increase people's self esteem, generate a sense of belonging, strengthen ties and recover a positive outlook on life.'

Since 2008, Hecho Club Social has also reached out to homeless people in public places to talk about reintegrating into society, as well as their rights, complementing these activities with regular workshops. There are also special programmes for women and young people at risk. Today, it is also developing leagues in other cities and provincial towns.

Sergio describes the dramatic impact on participants: 'People enjoy playing soccer and encourage their friends to join in. They understand that our goals are to help change people's lives, completing their studies or finding a job, being reunited with their families, finding their own place to live and finally becoming positive leaders for change.'

Sergio loves soccer but what does he say to the players when they leave Argentina for the Homeless World Cup? 'Everybody knows that being selected for the national team is a recognition of their personal efforts, and this provides an extra motivation,' he tells me. 'Our teams are made up of the best people rather than just the best players. Of course, we also try to win every game, and we train every week to become better players. But we also want to enjoy the event, meet people from different countries, as well as Argentinians living abroad. Such experiences have a greater impact than winning a match or a trophy, especially for people who are living in such vulnerable conditions.'

Sergio has also helped to export the Hecho Club Social model to neighbouring country Peru – creating a clone of the organisation in Lima. And Peru has since joined the Homeless World Cup family. 'I have been going to Peru two or three times a year since 2006,' he explains. 'I was working with vulnerable people so I thought it would be interesting to run a similar soccer project to help youths from gangs. I joined up with a group of local professionals from different disciplines to launch the programme there, passing on our knowledge and experience, as well as legal and financial assistance.' The programme started running in the capital city of Lima in 2011, focusing on youth at risk and later extending to women. And the next year Peru played in Mexico City.

Sergio remembers many magical moments in the Homeless World Cup through the years, including Copenhagen, when his players made friends with a group of homeless people living in the square beside the venue. The Danish guys showed the team how to collect cans and bottles and cash them in for money at the supermarkets, just as many of them did in Argentina. On their last day in Denmark, they collected and sold lots of bottles, so they would have some money when they flew to Buenos Aries the following day. But two hours before departure, Hugo, the team's oldest player, disappeared – he'd decided to give his new Danish friends all of his money.

Sergio sums up his personal feelings:

> The Homeless World Cup is utopian. It has harnessed the magic of soccer, and also has the power to motivate people to transform their lives. The vision was to turn excluded people into soccer stars, not just motivating players but also changing public attitudes to homelessness. But the real power of the Homeless World Cup is the international network. It may have started off as a crazy idea, but now with over 60 countries taking part every year, the Homeless World Cup is a strong social force.

* * * * *

Brazil boss Pupo Fernandes is another veteran of the Homeless World Cup who has helped build a nationwide organisation, now active in 16 cities all over the country. Based in Sao Paulo, Futebol Social (Organização Civil de Ação Social or Civil Organisation for Social Action) provides sports and social training for players at a regional level, and organises tournaments across Brazil. It focuses on men and women aged 16 to 20 years old who are in 'precarious housing conditions,' homeless or socially disadvantaged, and encourages them to find permanent employment to help them out of poverty.

As well as playing soccer and training, participants are also expected to take part in other activities to aid their re-integration into society, including workshops on education, relationships and social awareness.

Pupo and his team are always popular whenever they play at the Homeless World Cup, and even though they sometimes struggle to raise enough money for airfares, their programme continues to grow every year, expanding into more and more states every year.

The Brazil team has not only won the tournament twice but produced a string of players who later went professional, including our Global Ambassador, Michelle da Silva, and Pablo Anderson, who played at the Paris event and now plays for a leading team in Rio.

Not every player makes it to the big time, but Pupo is equally proud of the others who go on to get jobs in soccer or other sports, working as coaches. 'Our main concern,' Pupo explains, 'is not just their development as players but as people. It's great to see some of the players succeed in professional teams, but our primary aim is to turn out good citizens. In Brazil, once you are 16 years old, you are already too old to make it in professional soccer. Most major clubs are looking out for much younger players, but we want to produce the next generation of community leaders.'

Our Global Ambassador Michelle da Silva is an excellent role model for other players, but Pupo also explains that players still have many choices to make if they want to stay off the streets. Soccer also gives them many other opportunities – for example, they may study physical education and go on to teach it at school. That is a major achievement which is just as important as becoming a national star, and a lesson that Pupo continues to teach every year.

Brazil has always been the glamour team in international football and produced some of the game's biggest stars, but Pupo also thinks Brazil is changing – and that attitudes to soccer are also beginning to change. 'People used to play in every corner of Brazil, including the beaches in Rio, but we are starting to lose this,' he says. 'Everybody still dreams of becoming a professional player, but instead of learning their skills on the street or the beach, young people are now taught in school about strategy, tactics and so on. It is much less informal, and much more mechanical, so the challenge now is how to take the street skills to school.'

* * * * *

The Homeless World Cup in Brazil was staged in one of the world's most spectacular cities. What more could we wish for? Some tournaments are special because they were firsts, or because of the people involved. Sometimes, it's the iconic setting that sticks in the mind – like Copacabana. But every tournament is special for the players because they only have one opportunity to play.

Sometimes, you don't even realise how good the tournament was until after it's finished, because you are so deeply involved in the action. And for Alessandro Dell'Orto, Milan in 2009 was a year he will never forget because he was in charge of the local organising committee, and hardly had a moment to think about anything else for a year. 'There were lots of problems at the time but later on I realised how much the players enjoyed it – for them, it was just like a holiday camp! And that is what matters,' he tells me, when we meet in the media tent. 'You believe in the dream,' Alessandro continues. 'But sometimes it was tough.'

I know exactly how he feels – because like Alessandro in his home town, Milan, I had a similar experience in Edinburgh four years before.

Like Alessandro, I also remember how the players responded and mixed with each other throughout the event in Milan. And I also remember the celebrity visits – including Formula One world champion Lewis Hamilton and Marco Materazzi, the Italian defender who won a winner's medal in the FIFA World Cup in 2006. Celebrities are used to being idolised by fans but when Hamilton and Materazzi met at the Homeless World Cup in Milan, I will never forget how they treated each other – like any other fan who asks their sporting hero for an autograph. And when they watched the soccer from the VIP stand, the 'superstars' were not the celebrities but homeless players showing their skills on the field.

Alessandro had quite a few sleepless nights in 2009, but there were also many magical moments he'll never forget: 'My own special moment was when we had the FIFA World Cup sitting there alongside the Homeless World Cup, and the players were touching it and taking pictures. That was a dream moment.'

Alessandro also had to be diplomatic when dealing with different political interests, and even got help from the army, which helped with food and accommodation. 'Only in Italy could this ever happen!' he says.

At the pre-event press conference, a right-wing politician was part of the panel. Later, Alessandro got a letter from a left-wing organisation, saying they did not want to help because they didn't want to be associated with 'the military and neo-fascists.'

The priority for Alessandro was to make sure the tournament kicked off as planned and made everyone welcome. The political arguments go on forever, but it is homelessness which matters most – and homeless people coming to Milan to play soccer. 'Homelessness is getting worse in Italy, because of the continuing economic crisis,' he tells me in Mexico City. 'Lots of people, me included, have lost a lot of work or even lost their jobs, and some have also become homeless, too, over the last two years. There have been a lot of suicides.'

On a more positive note, Alessandro tells me that the economic crisis has not made much difference to media attitudes to homelessness. Italians in general feel solidarity with homeless people, and the church works very closely with the homeless, including recovery programmes. 'If there is a problem, people tend to look first to the church for solutions,' Alessandro explains. 'Perhaps there will always be poverty but we have to work hard to transform people's lives. We all have to fight every day.'

* * * * *

So what attracted Alessandro to the Homeless World Cup? 'I am an architect and first got involved as a sponsor,' he tells me. 'Today, we are expanding the project across Italy, joining up with other cities and communities. It's very tough – we all have other jobs. There are no full-time workers, but we want the players to play every week.'

Italians have a huge appetite for soccer but this makes little difference to Asd Dogma Onlus, the non-profit organisation established in Milan by Alessandro and his colleagues to promote sports and physical education through football. 'People in Italy don't think of sport in terms of using it to improve people's lives,' Alessandro explains. 'They think of it in terms of professional sport. The first question people ask after the Homeless World Cup is, *Did you win? Did you win?* But even though we've won the trophy twice, what's most important is for players to enjoy the experience. They are trying to improve their lives, whether they win or not. When they play football, they communicate with each other. They are not alone.'

Image is also important, he adds: 'I would also like people to understand better what homeless people are like, and see that they are also human beings who do not only need help but continue to grow and develop.'

His experience with homeless people has changed Alessandro in multiple ways. 'I am not a dreamer,' he tells me later on that week. 'At first, I had to be a dreamer, but now I have to be a builder.'

* * * * *

The Philippines have been a great supporter of the Homeless World Cup, partly thanks to Bill and Debbi Shaw, who founded the Manila street paper, *The Jeepney*, five years ago, and introduced the idea of the Homeless World Cup to soccer-crazy Filipinos. This year, Bill and Debbi have made it to Mexico City for a taste of the action, and I know that they can't stay away from the tournament – or from their beloved team, the Philippines.

Bill and Debbi first went to the Philippines in 2002, to do voluntary work. Like many people who fall in love with a country they visit, they intended to stay for a year and stayed there for almost a decade. Their daughter Haley also spent a year there, working at an orphanage, and 'will forever have some shrapnel in her buttock' after being caught up in a shooting.

In 2007, Bill and Debbi returned for a visit – and stayed for another four years. And during this period, they started thinking of ways they could 'directly impact the lives of impoverished Filipinos'.

I first met Bill and Debbi in Poland that summer at a street paper conference. They were contemplating setting up a paper in Manila, and when I told them all about the next Homeless World Cup in Melbourne, they jumped at the idea right away. They hadn't yet published a single edition, but within a year, they sent a team to Melbourne, and have been big supporters of the tournament every year since. Bill and Debbi now live back in Michigan, but a big part of their hearts is in the Philippines – and always will be.

*****

Bill and Debbi have thousands of stories to tell about the people in the Philippines, including the story of Eddie Alivio – one of the stars of this year's Homeless World Cup, just a few months after living in an orphanage in Cebu.

Soccer is Eddie's great love, but he knows that his studies will always come first. His mother died young, leaving Eddie and his 13 siblings to fend for themselves. The family lived on the streets near the pier, using a push cart to unload boats arriving in the harbour, and as a shelter at night. And when he was 11 years old, Eddie was sent to an orphanage because the family could no longer support him.

Seven years later, his family is proud of him and what he has accomplished. Before he flew here, Eddie dreamed of seeing the shiny glass towers in Mexico City, and now he has done it. He's loving every moment but he's keen to return to the Philippines to finish his studies, and one day give something back to the people who helped him.

During the week, I watch the Philippines beat Cambodia eight goals to five, and Eddie is once again one of the stars. The same day, they also lose eight goals to six in a game against Wales, but win or lose they always show the same fighting spirit, and never lose the smile on their faces.

*****

The leader of our programme in South Africa, Clifford Martinus (Cliffy) has spent over 20 years working in youth and community movements and founded the Oasis soccer club 12 years ago, using the power of soccer to get young people off the streets and turn their lives around. The South Africa team coached by Cliffy has been involved right from the start, and every year we try to catch up, between games. 'Before the first event in 2003, we spent a lot of time on tours within South Africa, but since then we have had the opportunity to go to many countries. I have always talked about the power of football. Now we travel the world,' Cliffy tells Fernando in the media tent.

Fernando asks about the homeless people in Cape Town. Cliffy answers: 'A few years ago, the numbers were falling, but they're rising again – there are so many people living in the streets.'

Over the last 13 years, Oasis has spread from the centre of Cape Town to other areas in Western Cape. It tries not to compete with NGOs in urban areas. In many cities, the centres are places for tourists and 'problems' like homeless people are pushed to the outskirts. 'But we should be solving problems,' Cliffy says, 'not just moving them around from one place to another.'

Hearing Cliffy talk about South Africa reminds me of the time that the Danish team visited one of the townships in Cape Town, during the Homeless World Cup in 2006. The Danish players thought they were 'the poorest of the poor' but as soon as they got to the township, they realised this wasn't true, and ended up giving the kids they met whatever of value they had at the time – a couple of miniature footballs, some candies and coins. The experience changed the young players from Denmark. They realised that they were not as badly off as they had once imagined. And the local kids realised 'white guys can be homeless, too.' 'Even in South Africa, in Cape Town, it's hard to get people to understand what we mean by homelessness,' says Cliffy. 'Are all the people in the townships homeless?'

The Oasis players usually come from a background of violence or drugs. Some of those who live on the streets or in squatter camps are generally looked after by the NGOs. But asylum seekers are not selected for the team – according to Cliffy, if they were allowed to choose asylum seekers, South Africa would win the Homeless World Cup every year.

Cliffy also talks about projecting the right kind of image. One year, the players spiked their hair up, but Cliffy thought this made them look 'typical homeless' when the real challenge was to move on. 'Why does football have such a magical impact?' Fernando asks Cliffy. 'I grew up playing soccer in the streets,' says Cliffy. 'But I never imagined it would change so many lives. These guys also played in the streets, just like me, but for them it has an even greater impact.'

Soccer is also a sport which is easy to set up and good fun to watch. 'All you need is two bricks in the ground,' as Cliffy puts it. Back in South Africa, Cliffy hopes to get support to set up 11-a-side games, and play in the townships, getting local people involved as supporters. 'It's about a lot more than the players,' says Cliffy. 'We also want to get the whole community involved.'

Cliffy also talks about the concept of *ubuntu* – the idea that people must care for each other. 'I see this develop in some of the players, this emotional thing,' he explains. 'When the team sits down to talk about difficult issues, tears are shed, but people in the crowd can see how much it means to them, and show their support.'

We often talk about exclusion – how people can fall off the edge in rich countries, mostly due to drugs and alcohol. But in Africa, where poverty is the main issue, there is a strong sense of community, and people in the West should try to learn from this – this sense of sharing and caring. Cliffy says it's also like singing together, before playing soccer together, and trying to match the achievements of famous star players.

Cape Town will always have a place in my heart, and Cliffy quotes another manager who said to him that even though the Mexico event was fantastic, Cape Town was the best event for warmth and sense of unity. I remember Richard Ishmail and suggest that maybe it was something to do with the struggles the people had been through before then, and the influence of people like Nelson Mandela, that made Cape Town such an iconic event, despite problems under the surface. 'But is South Africa still struggling to cope with transition?' Fernando asks Cliffy. 'Is it still as violent? Is it making any progress?' 'We are making strides forward,' says Cliffy, 'but the gangs are still a problem, and some kids even video the violence on their cell-phones as if it's a movie. It's crazy sometimes. And there's a lot of impatience about the lack of services from government – for example, infrastructure, housing, sanitation.'

Fernando shuts his giant leather notebook and Cliffy and I sit alone in the media tent for a couple of minutes, enjoying a moment of peace in the middle of what will be one of the busiest days of the week, when the teams play in groups for the next round of games, paired with teams of similar ability.

Cliffy talks about his plans for the future and something he calls 20:20: 'If all goes well in Western Cape, we'll get 20 teams, 20 players in each team, or 400 people involved every week. From these teams will emerge the future leaders, and the players we'll select for the Homeless World Cup.'

Cliffy and I toast each other with bottles of water (it's hot today and some of the players will feel it) and promise to meet later on in the week. Both of us are well aware that this may be impossible because we will both be so busy from morning till night. But we know that the next time we meet we will pick up the threads of the same conversation again, as if it was just a few moments ago...

* * * * *

Later on that evening, Fernando appears in the lobby. When he asked me why so many people get so involved with the Homeless World Cup, it got me thinking of 1,000 different people through the years, but I don't have enough time to tell every story. And then I get a lucky break – Mick Pender of Ireland arrives in the lobby and I introduce him to Fernando. 'If anyone can help you, it is Mick,' I tell Fernando, as I leave them together to talk. 'He will tell you all about the Homeless World Cup.'

* * * * *

'I've danced for it and boxed for it. I'd walk nude through Dublin if it raised us some money.'

The Ireland coach Mick Pender is a Homeless World Cup veteran and one of its greatest supporters – he has been at every tournament since Graz in 2003. Every year is another adventure for Mick and his players, and you could also say that Mick was truly 'thrown in at the deep end' from the very beginning.

As an employee of the Football Association of Ireland (FAI) in Dublin, the popular coach got a phone call just two or three weeks before Graz, inviting him to go along and meet some players training for a new competition called the Homeless World Cup. 'I didn't have a clue what the Homeless World Cup was about' Mick explains, 'but I thought I would give it a try.'

Still very much in the dark about what to expect, Mick went along and met the other coaches at the session, including Stephen Kenny, now the manager of Irish team Dundalk. He also met Sean Kavanagh, the editor of Ireland's *Big Issue*, which was trying to organise the Irish team heading for Graz. 'I thought it was a wind-up,' Mick said later. 'At any moment, someone would jump out and say *You've Been Framed*.'

After Sean explained what the Homeless World Cup was about, the next shock for Mick was the schedule – there were only three weeks to prepare. No money. And Mick was the only coach going to Graz. 'But how will we get there?' Mick asked himself. 'And how will we pay for the tickets?'

Mick had no previous experience with homeless people but now he was in charge of eight men representing Ireland at a tournament dreamed up a few months before, still just a crazy idea. And three weeks later, Mick was at the airport in Dublin, wondering if any of the players would turn up on time for the flight – or even turn up at all. The fund-raiser organised by *The Big Issue* would cover their basic expenses, and Mick had selected the team, but he still didn't know what he'd let himself in for.

To make the players feel more like a team, everyone got special haircuts, and as the new-look Mick sat in the airport, he thought he looked more like the boss of a criminal gang, not a team selected to play for their country.

When they finally made it to Graz, Mick thought his world had collapsed – he and the rest of the teams would be sleeping in dormitories, ten to a room, on blow-up mattresses. It wasn't exactly the Hilton Hotel, so instead of going training, the players decided to go to a bar...

Through the years, a lot of homeless players have had problems with addiction, but Mick was not a social worker or a psychologist – he was 'just a soccer coach' who took every day as it came. In Graz that year, he didn't think he had a right to tell the players, 'Don't have a drink!' For some of the players, it could be like detox, and he knew that they still had some money to spend. He also knew the players were more street-wise than him and knew how to keep out of trouble. But every time Mick heard the police sirens screaming in Graz, he imagined the lads were the cause.

The 'training session' didn't help the players in their first game against the 'Old Enemy,' England – they were well and truly hammered. 'The goalie was crying,' says Mick, 'and accusing the rest of the team of not trying.'

Then suddenly, their fortunes turned around – they had spent all their money and started to win a few games. 'Suddenly, they understood what it was about,' says Mick, 'and focused much more on the football.'

In Mick's opinion, it's important for the players to have things to do in the evening and keep busy in between games, as well as get exposed to different cultures. 'I don't want players flying half way round the world, just to hang out doing nothing,' says Mick. 'They could do that at home!'

Another key activity is regular training, not just so the players are ready for games but to make sure they return to Ireland fitter than they went away, and better prepared for whatever the future may bring. 'Today, we are more knowledgeable,' Mick says with the benefit of hindsight. 'We very quickly learned from our mistakes. We have much stricter rules about performance and selection now. There's always someone waiting to replace you, if you fall out of line. Back in those days, we were only beginning to learn, but without Graz, we would never have achieved so much over the years.'

The flight home was another challenge, stuck in the airport in London because of industrial action, without any money. And things were not helped when one of the players announced he would 'blow up the plane' – overheard by nearby policemen, armed with machine guns.

Spotting one of Ireland's favourite singers, Johnny Logan, in departure, the players decided to 'tap him' for money, to pay for some beers, but as soon as they spoke to him, Logan ran off.

Coming back to Dublin that year was not the ticker-tape welcome that the players deserved – four of them were forced to sleep on benches in the airport because they had touched down too late to get beds for the night. 'It was a journey into the unknown,' says Mick. 'Not everything was perfect. But it was a fantastic experience in a wonderful venue, and a real eye-opener for me and the players.'

* * * * *

After Graz, Mick and the rest of the management team got together to share their experience and work out plans for the next time – if there was indeed to be a next time. 'We were more serious and also more professional in later years,' Mick explains now. 'It was a steep learning curve for everyone.'

For Mick, the playing surfaces are symbols of the changes through the years. In Graz, the games were played on concrete, on the street, but now they are cushioned and perfectly flat. 'The difference is like moving from a building site to Wembley,' says Mick. 'In Graz, the Homeless World Cup was totally new for the players, as well as for me. But at least when we got there, I knew that it wasn't a wind-up!'

The turning point for Mick was the debrief with Sean and the others, the week after Graz, when they discussed the good and bad of the experience, including the players returning to Dublin without having somewhere to sleep. 'We told each other that would never happen again,' says Mick. And since then, they have lived up to that promise. The first street soccer league was set up in Dublin immediately after, with games played every Saturday, and the Irish Street Leagues have since spread to locations all over the country, sending teams to the Homeless World Cup every year – at this year's trial, 450 players competed for places.

Nine years later, Mick is still involved, and every year he still does his best to ensure that the players enjoy themselves – and learn as much as possible during the week. 'When the team flew out to Sweden,' he explains, 'we told the players this would be a proper international tournament and they were going out there to represent Ireland.'

The week before, the team had spent the weekend in a top-class hotel, to get to know each other better and do some serious training. Irish society has changed a lot since then, but Mick remembers one of the most moving things during that weekend, when one of the players came up to him at dinner one evening and asked if he could say a few words to the rest of the team. The player then stood up in front of everyone and announced he was gay, and was met by a thunderous round of applause. Since then, Ireland has voted in favour of new laws permitting gay marriage, but in those days, to 'come out' in public was highly unusual – as well as courageous. 'He said he just felt comfortable,' says Mick, who knows that environment makes a huge difference to so many players.

The next surprise was when the players arrived at the airport in Dublin, and were handed their suits, shirts and ties. A few weeks before, the professional team had been photographed flying to Euro 2004 in their flashy new designer suits, and one of Mick's friends offered to create official outfits for his team, so they looked the part when they arrived, complete with proper training gear and national colours.

* * * * *

Before every Homeless World Cup, Mick always says to his players: 'I will treat you as an international player, with the same respect as any other international player. As an international, you will want for nothing when we go away. But don't forget you're also representing yourself and your family as well as your country. You don't have to win every game, but when the tournament is over and you look in the mirror, make sure you tell yourself you've done the best you can.'

Mick recognises that most of the players have difficult backgrounds – including former prisoners and people who are struggling with addiction. 'They're living day to day,' says Mick, 'so when they come along for the football, we want to offer them something extraordinary, including a decent hotel room. If we promise something, we have to deliver.' Sometimes, Mick has had to use his credit card to pay for expenses, but that is insignificant compared to all the sacrifices so many people have made through the years, whether players or coaches. 'Go away as a team and return as a team' is the mantra that Mick now repeats every year.

The next big turning point was Scotland in 2005, in the shadow of Edinburgh Castle. Mick thought the Ireland team were good enough to win the trophy that year, beating the eventual winners Italy during the group stage then narrowly losing to the Italians in the quarter-final. During the second game, one of the Ireland players went up for a header with one of his Italian opponents, and their heads collided. 'There was blood everywhere,' says Mick. When the referee sent off the Ireland player, Mick was not happy, but all that was forgotten when the players were presented with FAI caps and given permission to play in the national colours.

In Cape Town the next year, the team got involved in a project with sports broadcaster Tracy Piggott, the daughter of the famous English jockey Lester Piggott. Tracy was making a documentary for RTÉ about the Kenya team, and her charity *Playing for Life* also sponsored the African players.

The Ireland team had mixed results in Cape Town, but everything was put in perspective for Mick and the players by meeting with the Kenya team – the Ireland players gave them 'pocket money' during the event, then travelled to Nairobi the following week to coach local kids at an orphanage funded by *Playing for Life*.

Back in Ireland, work continued as the Leagues spread all over the country, including games in prisons. 'I've been involved for years,' says Mick. 'And while I don't profess to know how much it costs to put a lad through prison, ask these lads here and they'll tell you they are much better off playing football. I've seen guys getting degrees; guys reunited with their families; I've seen guys get jobs and go back to education. Of course some have fallen by the wayside, but all you can do is hope that what you're giving them will help them recharge their batteries and lead to a better life.'

'We started the Street Soccer League to offer homeless, unemployed and marginalised young people a chance to change their lives using sport as the catalyst,' Sean Kavanagh said two years later in Chile. 'Right across Ireland we have seen the changes participants have made in their lives through their involvement in the Leagues. Being given the chance to represent Ireland in the Homeless World Cup develops a new sense of self-worth and is often the first step back from the peripheries of life into mainstream living. Lads start to realise their own worth, and often their lives change accordingly. But it's about much more than just a game of soccer. It is about re-building and empowering people to overcome adversity.'

Mick also wants to help players fulfil their potential, as well as get employment and somewhere to live. The organisation has had many successes, but Mick points out that sometimes, there are tragedies mixed with the triumphs. One player who came back from one of the tournaments seemed to be on the right track when he and his girlfriend moved into a flat, but one day when she came home, he was sitting there dead, in his armchair, with a suicide note by his side, wearing his full Ireland kit. He had also left a poem for Mick to read out at his funeral. 'Sometimes, there's a very thin line between going one way and going another,' says Mick.

Even for Mick, the experience of going to the Homeless World Cup can be bitter-sweet, sometimes. 'The players exist in a bubble,' he says. 'When they come back, they want to be part of the world again, but it can be a bit of a comedown for some of the players – as well as the staff. When you find yourself in places like Chile, and you look up and there are the Andes, it's like a dream come true. But when you come home, you return to your everyday problems.'

Mick also recognises he is lucky – not every player comes back to a new home or job, like himself. Many players get jobs or enrol at university, re-engage with their community or keep up their connection with soccer by coaching. But some players need more support. 'If I won the lottery, I'd chuck in my job and go full-time,' says Mick, 'because if one guy breaks the cycle, it's worth it.'

10

What Do Homeless People Look Like?

Q: Most of the players do not look like homeless people.
A: What do homeless people look like?

SUNDAY, 14 OCTOBER 2012: Fiona Crawford, who is busy taking photographs while I'm talking to Fernando and a journalist from Poland (who will host the next Homeless World Cup in the city of Poznan), smiles as she listens to this brief exchange. She has heard the same question before many times, and like me, she is still waiting for an answer.

Fernando scribbles something in his giant leather notebook and I'm starting to wonder how many words so far this week. He must be writing an epic. Soon he will know more about the tournament than anyone else in the world.

Five minutes later, as I walk past the media tent, wearing a brilliant-green Mexico shirt, I realise I look like many other people ready to cheer on their team. And by wearing the national colours, we all look the same as the players. So do I look as if I am homeless? Do the fans look as if they are homeless? Do the players look homeless?

* * * * *

Today I will change my shirt several times in the course of the day, wearing the colours of as many countries as possible to show that I support them all and honour every player taking part. It's something I've started to do every year, and as I go 'around the world in 80 shirts', I remind myself how great a challenge we face in the fight to eliminate homelessness in countries all over the world – including the USA and Canada, Norway, Japan and Australia, which we think of as being the richest until we scratch under the surface.

At some point in the course of the day, I will pull on my red-and-white Switzerland shirt. Our partner in Switzerland, Surprise Strassensport (based in Basel) has taken part in every Homeless World Cup since the start. Most people's image of Switzerland is of a prosperous, peace-loving country in the middle of Europe where rich folks go to open secret bank accounts, but under the surface it also has deep social problems. The players are either street-paper vendors, long-term unemployed or homeless. They may have mental health or alcohol or drug addiction problems, and some of them may also be asylum seekers – just like many other teams from countries in the West. Homelessness does not respect any national borders. It can happen to anyone, anywhere at any time. It can happen to me and to you.

* * * * *

Next, I wear my Ghana shirt to honour the players who have not been able to make it. Some countries could not come because they could not raise the money, or because they had other priorities this year, but it's sad when they can't come, no matter the reason.

I also think of countless other players who for millions of reasons will never be able to come – not because they are not good enough at soccer or have no other talents to share (like a shoulder to cry on, a smile or a word of advice to a team-mate) but because homeless people would fill this square many times over.

I also think of Loredan Bulgariu, stabbed to death in Romania three months ago, soon after being chosen for his country. He isn't the first homeless person to have his life taken away from him almost before it began. So later I will wear my Romania shirt, in memory of all those homeless people who are victims of violence each year – to remember the countless millions of 'statistics' that are never reported and the people who will never be able to come to the Homeless World Cup.

* * * * *

As I wander around in the Zocalo, another reporter from England (we have registered several hundred from countries all over the world) asks how different countries deal with homelessness issues, and this gets me thinking of new ways to tell the same story. 'The Homeless World Cup has a different impact on individuals in different countries, and seeks to achieve different goals,' I tell the reporter as we sit watching one of the games, early on in the morning, before it gets too hot to sit in the sun. 'In most developed countries, it is all about inclusion, and in other countries, all about employment, education and community building.'

'But how do you measure the impact on players?' the reporter asks next, and I quote him the headline statistics.

The numbers are impressive, but the impact goes much further than what we are witnessing right at this moment, as we sit watching one of the games. 'These ten days are a great celebration of what we are doing but the work goes on 365 every year. And our impact can also be measured in terms of the number of successful social enterprises run by our national partners, some of which started as soccer-based projects and gradually grew into something much bigger.'

I then explain how we coordinate the international network and try to help our partners, from Afghanistan to Zimbabwe, not only by giving them something to aim for by attending the annual event but also by assisting them with funding, especially when they are just setting out on their journey. We also try to make sure every dollar is spent on effective and relevant programmes, and we are helped in this effort by various organisations including Global Giving, which has audited some of our programmes.

We also stress the importance of leadership in every country, ensuring all the programmes are run by highly capable and motivated people with local knowledge and local interests, as well as a global perspective. 'So, how do you choose all your partners? And how much do you get involved with their everyday work?'

First, we identify a national partner and support it however we can. As time goes by, the partners become more independent, raising their own local funds. The strongest partners also get a chance to be hosts of the Homeless World Cup, by demonstrating they can attract enough sponsors and provide the infrastructure needed for such a big venture, and this in turn can be a huge boost to their national status. For example, after Melbourne in 2008, our Australia partner won extra funding worth two million dollars a year from the Australian government, plus significant corporate funding. As a result, Team Australia is developing programmes in 30 locations all over the country, without a single cent from the Homeless World Cup.

Every country focuses on different objectives and uses different approaches to reach out to players. Some countries also need more help than others – for example, Zimbabwe. This year, they'll be missed again, but one day I'm sure they'll return.

At the opposite end of the spectrum, Street Soccer USA and Street Soccer Mexico are two of our biggest successes, with nationwide networks and sponsors who enable them to operate as independent, self-sustaining organisations.

* * * * *

Today, as the tournament reaches its climax, sitting in the stands with the other supporters, I find myself smiling like everyone else. Soccer is a universal language and the players instinctively know how the other teams feel – they know where they come from and share the same hopes, dreams and fears. And for 15 minutes while they are playing, the pain is forgotten. The future can wait. I am simply enjoying the soccer in peace. There are always important decisions to make, but sometimes I just like to sit there admiring the skills of the players, and kick every ball in my mind – just for 15 minutes, we're united as players and fans.

* * * * *

One of the first games I manage to see on Day Nine is Argentina versus Denmark, when the Danes win five to four in a nail-biting penalty shoot-out. The Argentina players are all disappointed but it is not the end of the world, and the two teams embrace at the end as if both teams have won.

Sergio, the Argentina manager, comes up to greet me. By coincidence, one of my first memories of Sergio was several years ago, in Denmark. The tournament was all going well until Sergio arrived in Copenhagen with several players missing – having lost them in Paris. We found out later that instead of remaining in transit and boarding their plane, the players somehow managed to exit the airport and disappeared into the city.

When I met Sergio and asked him what had happened, he assured me that the players would be perfectly fine. 'They are street wise,' said Sergio, shrugging his shoulders. 'They know how to look after themselves.' But they are homeless guys who've never been abroad before or flown before, I told him. 'Don't worry!' said Sergio, smiling. And three days afterwards, they finally made it – we had managed to locate them in the middle of the city and sent them new tickets to fly up from Paris.

Sergio and his teams are not so concerned about winning. They may have a passion for soccer, but this is a social event – an opportunity for individual players to grow and develop their life skills.

Despite the fact he looks so laid back, Sergio is totally committed to his work. Sometimes, I wonder how he manages to operate in Argentina, but his passion for soccer and his passion for empowering the homeless players always shines through.

Today, Argentina have lost – but the score doesn't matter. What matters is what happens whey they fly back tomorrow, and what they have learned in the course of the week.

*****

Next, I catch up with Peru – the team which is modelled on Sergio's project. As I sit and watch the players displaying their skills on the pitch, I learn about the three young men from Lima – Carlos Alvarado, Denis Mendoza and Anthony Ticse – whose lives have been transformed this week in Mexico City.

The three young men share similar stories and come from the same city streets. Denis (25) has spent most of his life till now mixed up in drugs and criminal gangs. He became a father at the age of 17 but has never been close to his son. 'I acted like a child, not a father,' he says. But after witnessing a friend killed in a street fight, he decided it was time he changed his life.

Goalkeeper Carlos Alvarado (23) reached the same conclusion. After leaving home, he also found himself involved in drugs and gangs. 'I almost ruined my life,' he says, looking off into the distance. 'I knew this world was not for me,' says Anthony Ticse (19), the youngest of the group. 'My friends used to tell me to go with them to walk the streets, pressuring me to leave home,' he recalls, describing how he had to leave school early and find a job to support his whole family. But despite these early challenges, he always listened to his parents and avoided the world of the gangs. He chose soccer instead.

In 2012, the three men got involved with Hecho Club Social Peru. And because they showed so much commitment, attending all the games as well as educational classes and talks, they made it to the final squad for Mexico City.

Despite the language barrier, they've mixed with many other players during the week. 'It's important to make friends with people from countries all over the world,' says Peru coach Eduardo Izaga. 'That is how they realise they are not alone.'

Today, all three young men have stable jobs and no longer live on the streets. Denis has another child and promises he will not make the same mistakes that took him away from his first son. 'This time is different – I've grown and now I realise that I have many duties to fulfil,' he says.

The three men say that soccer is their passion, and want to coach the children in their neighbourhood in Lima. Through Hecho Club Social Peru, they've found the motivation to transform their lives – and also found a new family.

*****

Next, I catch up with Indonesia – one of the most colourful and popular teams at the Homeless World Cup. This year, the players are sporting Mohicans – their hair is dyed and cut into a bright-red stripe you see 100 yards away.

The team have played their hearts out since the start of the week and have reached the semi-finals, but despite all their courage, they lose out to Mexico nine goals to six in a thriller, then later on are edged out by Brazil in the play-off for third in the rankings. Back home in Indonesia, the fans will be sad the adventure is over but they can all be proud of what they have achieved this year, not just as soccer stars but wonderful ambassadors.

Yesterday, one of the Indonesian players, Bongsu Hasibuan, dedicated his 'goal of the tournament' (an overhead bicycle kick), to a friend and former team mate who had passed away at home in Indonesia early that morning. Wearing black armbands to remember their friend, team Indonesia beat the Czech Republic in a superb display of entertaining soccer, and Bongsu's spectacular goal was not just a memorial but also a spectacular celebration of life.

Until this year, Bongsu was homeless for over 15 years, and next year, his ambition is to coach the team in Poland. He says it is a blessing to have turned his life around, so he can help others do the same. 'Most of the time it feels like a dream,' he says, after the game.

Five players in the current Indonesian team are HIV positive, mostly as a result of intravenous drug use. One player, Arif Apriadi, is a former heroin addict who decided to reduce his methadone intake during the lead-up to the Homeless World Cup, as part of his attempt to stop completely. This decision not only demonstrates his personal strength but also shows how much it means to him – and many other people – to play in the Homeless World Cup. 'He's the real winner,' says management team member Feddy Arhemsyah. 'Arif plays really well but more importantly he really wants to change his life, too.'

Arif and many others in the soccer programmes organised by Rumah Cemara receive support from treatment centres located throughout Indonesia. Recently, Rumah Cemara expanded its programme by launching what it calls 'the League of Change', a tournament that brings together teams from the treatment centres and other disadvantaged people in areas all over Indonesia. The opportunity to play for your country is a strong motivator, but like Arif, it is always the players themselves who make the decision to transform their lives – that victory is theirs and theirs alone.

Rumah Cemara envisages an Indonesia which does not discriminate against people with HIV/AIDS and the victims of drugs, seeking to reduce the harm of drug addiction and engage the general public. They may still have a mountain to climb, but judging by the way they throw their hearts into soccer, these players will achieve their goals and also inspire other people to follow.

* * * * *

People in Asia have been big supporters of the Homeless World Cup since the start, with Japan the first country to represent Asia, in Gothenburg in 2004 – when they won the Fair Play Trophy and the hearts of the Swedish supporters. The Japan team is managed by the Big Issue Japan Foundation, a not-for-profit organisation which runs programmes focused on soccer as well as contemporary dance, music, walking and writing, so homeless people can 'regain their self-confidence and reconnect with society.'

Homeless people in Japan face the same basic challenges as homeless people in most other 'rich' societies, but recent years have seen a massive increase in their numbers. Homelessness used to be almost unknown in Japan, but after the 'Lost Decade,' everything changed.. The idea of a 'job for life' is now a distant memory, unemployment has soared and homelessness has devastated many peoples' lives – rising from an estimated 5,000 people in Tokyo in 1998 to five times that number in 2001, with other major cities like Osaka facing even bigger problems.

At the beginning of the 1990s, homeless people were regarded as a nuisance who 'spoiled' the environment, and were barred from applying for welfare. Homelessness was also a cultural issue, and single men were also badly treated since employers favoured married men with families to support and tended to discriminate against older people – according to one major survey, the average age of homeless people in Japan is 56 years old, with those from 50 to 64 years old accounting for about two-thirds of the total.

The media and government have not traditionally been sympathetic to the homelessness issue – one publication even described homeless people as 'a sight which violated public good' as 'cardboard villages' appeared in the land of the Shogun, and homeless people were evicted from their temporary shelters by a government which claimed people 'chose to be homeless'. According to anti-poverty activist Mitsuo Nakamura, 'most of the homeless are systematically eliminated from society.'

* * * * *

Japan has always been a great supporter of the tournament, but they were almost forced to cancel their appearance in 2011, in the wake of the Tsunami which not only claimed thousands of lives but also made a lot of people homeless – putting extra pressure on our partner, *Big Issue Japan*.

In Paris, the Japan team suffered several heavy losses on the field but the players refused to give up – they had seen much more suffering back in Japan. Some of the players based in Tokyo had volunteered to help out in the worst affected areas, including leading player Akikazu Ishizuka, who organised soccer games near Fukushima for people who had lost their homes because of the disaster, to keep up morale. 'I don't have a job, but I still want to help,' he said, reflecting the attitude shown by so many people involved with the Homeless World Cup, whenever catastrophe strikes.

That same year, in Paris, the Japanese captain, Yoshihiro Matsuda, described how he had struggled to regain his identity, after both his parents died of cancer and he lost his job at a construction site in Kobe – ending up in Tokyo, homeless and freezing in the middle of winter.

Yoshihiro's sister had filed a missing person report, and his personal records were later deleted, because she assumed he was dead. But thanks to *Big Issue Japan*, Yoshihiro managed to recover, signing up as one of the street paper vendors and later taking part in preparations for the Homeless World Cup.

When Yoshihiro was selected as the keeper for Paris, he needed a passport to travel to France, and had to get in touch with his sister to re-establish his identity – the first time in 11 years they'd spoken to each other. Yoshihiro was nervous at first but his sister was delighted to find him again.

Yoshihiro then got a job and found somewhere to live – he needed an official home address to get a passport, and seven months later, just ten days before the team travelled to France, he got all the papers he needed, and was also appointed the captain.

In the first two games, the team lost 12-0 to Argentina and 18-2 to Greece, and two of the players were so disappointed, they said that they wanted to quit. But Yoshihiro told them: 'If you run away now, you'll be making the same mistake you have made all your life.' He knew that he had also run away from his problems, and understood exactly how his team mates were feeling. But now was the time to face up to their problems.

Yoshihiro's pep talk worked its magic and even though the team lost their next game to Spain (5-2), they ran themselves into the ground, and Yoshihiro burst into tears as he bathed in the warmth of his team mates. He had come a long way from the freezing streets of Tokyo in winter, when people had shunned or ignored him. Now he was a hero, representing his country and inspiring his team mates.

As I sit watching Japan in the centre of Mexico City, I hope that this year's players also go back to their homeland with the energy needed not just to change their own lives but also change public perceptions, so other homeless people also get the opportunity to shine.

*****

South Korea shares many similar problems to its neighbour Japan – not just its public attitudes to homelessness but the shock to the system to realise that such a successful industrial power has homeless people to start with.

That was why *Big Issue Korea* was founded in 2008, when a group of young people who had seen the magazine in other countries launched their first online version. The following year, a not-for-profit organisation called 'Street Angels', which had been supporting homeless people in Seoul since 1997, joined forces with *Big Issue Korea* to publish a new magazine – not just to create jobs for the vendors but to raise awareness of homelessness in South Korea.

Later on, the new social enterprise started a street soccer programme, to help get homeless people off the street – not only because it was good for their physical and social health but to prove to the general public that homeless people can play soccer like everyone else. And in Rio de Janeiro in 2009, South Korea made its début in the Homeless World Cup.

Today the team – made up of street paper vendors and people from Seoul's homeless shelters – play two games. In their first match, I see Finland beat them by six goals to one. In their next match, they're beaten by Sweden. But even though they lose both games, the South Koreans came here not only to win games of soccer but also to win recognition and public respect.

One day, South Korea wants to host the annual tournament, and I'm confident one day it will – even though Indonesia, Hong Kong and several others are also lined up in the queue.

*****

Later on, I catch up with the Bosnia team, and watch them play Portugal, losing by seven to four. As I sit back and enjoy the game, one of our reporters – Ben Carpenter – is writing a story in the media tent, fighting back the tears as he tries to express how he feels. Later, his story goes up on our website, and I understand why Ben became so emotional, writing the story: 'This story is not about football. It's about a new friendship between a young boy and a nation. Steve is 11 years old and has had a life-changing experience at the Homeless World Cup in Mexico City this week.'

Steve had fallen in love with the Bosnia team (and the way they played football) when he saw them on TV a few years before, and remembered their badge and their national kit. One day in the Zocalo, he was watching a game in the stands when Alan, the Bosnia captain, sat down beside him, and the two started talking – friends for life already. Yesterday, Steve and his father presented some gifts to the Bosnia team, and the players immediately burst into tears. Steve was even wearing a blue-and-white shirt like the Bosnia kit, so he could feel part of the team, and joined the team out on the pitch at the end of their match.

The Bosnia street soccer programme has only been running for 15 months but has already made a big difference in the lives of many people, organising tournaments for young men aged 16 to just over 30 who are refugees or orphans from the war who have been homeless all their lives.

On Finals day, the Bosnia team wanted to show Steve how much they valued his support and how much they loved him. After the game, Steve was presented with a Bosnian kit and a commemorative flag – one of only three in the world. Now officially the team's Mexican mascot, he joined them when they collected their medals and was raised shoulder high by his new team-mates – to roars from the crowd. The story concluded:

> Steve can't fight back his tears any more: 'He's such a good person! How can someone who is such a good man be out on the streets? He has no home! It makes me want to help them all and I *will* help them.'

Steve's father vows to help him keep his promise and exchanges contact details with Bosnia manager Kenan, who says he'll host the family when they visit the country.

Ben is close to tears and says he he is struggling to finish the story. I understand exactly how he feels. There are so many moving stories every year, and sometimes we all find ourselves lost for words when we try to describe them.

* * * * *

It's Finals Day in Mexico City, 2012, and everything is coming to a climax – you can sense it in the atmosphere. The crowds are streaming in from every direction, pouring out of the Metro and into the stands, waving hundreds of colourful banners and flags. Thousands more excited fans are gathering in front of the giant electronic screens set up outside the main stadium, cheering every goal and every spectacular save, every neat sidestep and every tough tackle. Mexico are into both the men's and women's Finals, and the fans are fired up for the action to come, but they've also been infected by the Homeless World Cup fever and support every team, every player and every display of good soccer. They've forgotten the players are homeless, and for just a few moments, the players themselves have forgotten they're homeless.

My next stop is the players' tent to meet my old friends Jacek Czapliński of Poland and Arkady Tyurin of Russia, who have both been to every event since 2003, and for just a few minutes, we forget about Mexico City and the noise all around us. We are sharing a magical moment together, like three old friends aboard an ocean liner on a journey to an unknown destination. 'Here we are again,' we silently say to each other, as we gaze at the crowds. 'We have created something truly revolutionary, and it's not just the soccer or even the people involved that have made it succeed, but the spirit behind it. It is more than a tournament, more than an organisation. It is a movement that is gathering momentum every year.'

Somehow we communicate, despite the fact that Jacek hardly speaks any English and Arkady speaks like a poet, and I start to speak pigeon English, as if my whole vocabulary has suddenly reduced to a few dozen words.

We had a funny feeling at the start that it could become something like this but we couldn't imagine the scale of it all, and the impact it's had through the years. Now, here we are surrounded by thousands of people who've come to see some homeless people play a game of football. A lot has changed but we just see each other as we were 10,000 years ago, preparing for the first event, with hope in our hearts that it would come to this. Today we know something amazing has happened because of the seed that we planted together in Graz.

Our musings continue for several minutes in my pigeon English and Arkady's poetic translation of what he thinks Jacek is trying to say, and we smile at each other because we do not need to speak to each other in words all the time. We know each other so well we are finishing each other's sentences now, even though it's almost beyond understanding what's happened since Graz.

Then, suddenly, the Polish players also get involved, and we're reminded why we're here and what matters to these guys, and the challenges faced when they go back to Poland tomorrow. Poland will be hosting the tournament next year in the city of Poznan, but for these players, this is the time to decide what their personal future will be. After Mexico City, the most difficult part of the journey begins. Will they find work and somewhere to live? Will they go back to school? Will they make up with their family and loved ones?

I talk to a few of the players and ask them how they feel about the tournament and Mexico City – the usual things I ask the players year after year.

But I remind myself that even though I go to every tournament, for these young men, this is their moment to shine.

We talk about their hopes for the future and what they will do back in Poland, and we talk about how they have played in the course of the week. Any personal highlights? Your favourite teams?

On the surface, none of this seems very deep. But every single player is fighting for life, as we speak. They tell me they're determined to transform their lives, and how they have been able to do this because of the power of soccer – and they tell me that a ball can change the world. And I say I agree.

I am always amazed by the players and how much they get what the Homeless World Cup is about. It's as if no-one needs to explain to them what they are doing, and when they start repeating it – the idea that a ball can change the world – and when they start saying that they are determined to change, I know it will happen. And I don't need to say any more to these people. They write their own speeches much better than I could.

Jacek knows exactly how the players feel because he was homeless a few years ago, just like them. He is totally focused on helping the players, and every year he dreams that they will win, and every year he learns again that winning is not what the Homeless World Cup is about.

I hear the sound of cheering in the stadium, just a short distance away. It's time for the Finals...

* * * * *

As I walk towards the stadium, already overflowing, and I see the fleet of bullet-proof vehicles parked at the side of the square, I think about how much it means to Carlos Slim and his family to be here today, and all the other people who have backed us through the years. Without them, the tournament would not have happened, but every year I wonder if this is the last time the Homeless World Cup will be held.

As I navigate through crowds of smiling people at the entrance, I realise the city is in love with the Homeless World Cup. The eyes of the nation will be on the Finals today, watching 'live' on TV, and Mexico's First Lady, Margarita Zavala, is waiting for me up in the stands.

Margarita is a tireless campaigner for child and family development in Mexico, as well as promoting educational programmes, and has served as a federal deputy in the Mexican Congress, but for me, the simple fact that she is here today supporting us is even more important than her politics or status – and she clearly enjoys watching soccer and knows what we are trying to achieve.

As I walk up the steps, passing several armed bodyguards blocking the entrance, I see Carlos Slim with my wife Rona and Margarita, talking as if they have been friends for years. I apologise for being late and welcome Margarita to the tournament, noticing how Carlos Slim, still wearing his signature baseball cap, has been the perfect gentleman by introducing Rona, before I arrived. Today, we are the Homeless World Cup family, and we sit together watching as the Finals begin.

First up is the Women's Final, Mexico versus Brazil, and the soccer now takes centre stage.

* * * * *

People often ask what Carlos Slim is like. After all, he's one of the world's richest men. But Carlos Slim is also like a lot of other people who are trying to change things – in his case, through the Telmex Foundation, which focuses on youth, justice, health, education and sport.

The first time I met Carlos Slim, I was invited by the Telmex Foundation to speak at a conference for young people. At first, I thought the audience would be a few hundred but when I turned up, it was thousands.

Since then, I have spent a lot of time with Carlos Slim's son-in-law, Arturo Elias Ayub, and Joe Aboumrad of the Telmex Foundation, and what always strikes me is how much they're committed to Street Soccer Mexico and the Homeless World Cup. They 'got it' straight away – and quickly decided that Mexico City would one day be host.

When the tournament finally started, Carlos Slim and his family enjoyed it as much as the rest of the crowd, and shared the highs and lows of the Mexico teams.

As I sit there, I am not thinking 'this is the world's richest man' but someone who's watching the soccer like everyone else, kicking every ball and making every tackle. When the Finals kick off, it is not about homelessness, not about business or wealth or celebrity. It is all about soccer and the passion of sport. Without Carlos Slim, this would never have happened, but now he is just one of thousands of fans in the crowd.

Later that evening, Carlos Slim took all the Mexico players for dinner. They treated him like any other person in Mexico City, and he treated them all with respect. They did not talk about his billions but the soccer and what happened during the week – the wins and the losses, the heartaches and triumphs.

* * * * *

Above my desk, I have a favourite photograph which tells the whole story of Mexico City and the Homeless World Cup. And in the picture, Carlos Slim and Margarita Zavala are sharing a moment with Ana Aguirre, the injured star of the Mexican team.

While play continues, Ana forgets all about life in Ciudad Juárez – the drugs, the unemployment and the young men showing off their guns, as if they are trophies. But when the tournament is over, Ana wants to go back to work with people like herself who love playing soccer and need to escape from the violence around them.

Nearly half of the Mexico team also come from Ciudad Juárez, where more than 10,000 people have been killed since 2006. Another player, Alvaro Antonio Orellana, recently lost six good friends in a shooting. And the men and women wearing the Mexican colours are not just playing for themselves and for their country – they are playing for the thousands of others who play every week, nationwide, and have similar stories to tell.

Two years ago, Ana had a narrow escape when gunmen opened fire on students in the middle of a party, killing 18 young people. Ana had planned to be there with her friends but decided to study instead, and she still finds it hard to believe she survived – she had gone to school with some of the dead and their killers.

And now she is sitting in the VIP stand with the country's First Lady, posing for a photo with the world's richest man.

You could say that the photo shows the world's richest man and the President's wife with one of the world's poorest women. But what the picture says to me is that this is the Homeless World Cup. This is why we started. This is what it's about. These three people would not be standing together if it hadn't been for the Homeless World Cup. By changing the environment, we've made them united – thanks to the power of soccer.

* * * * *

Sometimes people ask me why I don't go up to billionaires like Carlos Slim, Bill Gates and Warren Buffet and demand that they give us some money to fund what we do. But if we go around banging our fists on the door, we will never succeed. It is more than their money we need. We need them to join us and be part of the movement.

But we have to start somewhere.

And the Homeless World Cup has created a space where we meet. It's created a space where we all share a moment, like Carlos Slim, Margarita

Zavala and Ana Aguirre. It's a ball that has brought us together, and proves that we can change the world.

* * * * *

It started with a young man being stabbed to death in Romania and ends with fireworks in the centre of Mexico City.

We started with nothing a decade ago and we still can't afford to hold next year's event unless something miraculous happens. But as I watch the players dancing the conga and singing their hearts out, in languages I've never even heard before, and the fireworks explode overhead, I realise what we've achieved.

We've created a global event like no other event on the planet. We started with a simple idea which everyone told us was crazy, and somehow we have made the dream come true. A million homeless people have been part of our movement, and most of them have managed to transform their lives – many of them here in the plaza tonight with their teams. In the midst of the chaos and the media madness, it's easy to forget what we've achieved – and how everything starts with a ball.

A ball can change the world. It's sometimes as simple as that. I should be celebrating, dancing and singing like everyone else. But the work must go on. Just over the horizon, there are millions of people still homeless and desperately poor. Just a few hundred metres away, there are people in Mexico City still homeless and desperately poor. The next 500 players will come from those millions, and thousands of others will take part in one of our national programmes. But tonight we cannot see them, through the smoke hanging over the square. Tonight they're still invisible.

Another firework explodes in the night sky above us, and a single flare tumbles to earth. It makes me think the Homeless World Cup is a very small light in the darkness. And it makes me ask, how can we make that light bigger? How can we light up more faces like these homeless players and light up the darkness for those millions and millions of others who cannot be here?

I feel such contradictory emotions. At the same time, I am very, very happy and also as sad as can be. To have made so much progress and still have all these challenges ahead. I could cry but I wouldn't know why.

11

The Story Continues...

SATURDAY, 9 JULY 2016: After Mexico City, the Homeless World Cup moved on to Poznan in Poland (2013) then Santiago, capital of Chile (2014), and Amsterdam (the Netherlands) in 2015. And this year, it will be in George Square in the centre of Glasgow – Scotland's biggest city and one of the most football-crazy cities on the planet.

Just before the tournament kicks off in Glasgow, I talk to David Duke about our very different personal journeys to George Square and Glasgow today. David's come a long way since he was a player in Gothenburg 12 years ago, and so has the Homeless World Cup since Mexico City.

For David, the tournament coming to Glasgow is also a time to remember when he became homeless and lived in a hostel a very short distance away that was so bad it shut down a long time ago. But he picked himself up, played in Sweden and came back to Scotland, and picked himself up yet again from the depths of despair to become an example to others and found Street Soccer Scotland. He also reminds me that he couldn't make it to Mexico City four years ago, due to a shortage of funds. It is easier this year – just one hour away from his new home in Edinburgh. A lifetime away from the hostel in Glasgow.

*****

Since 2012, the Homeless World Cup has continued to grow and attract more supporters. In Poznan the following year it was hard to repeat the spectacular setting and get the same huge crowds squeezing into the stands, but I'll never forget at the start of the week when the players were invited to the local soccer stadium, home of leading Polish team Lech Poznan, to share their big moment with thousands of fans, 'live' on national TV.

For Jacek Czapliński, the tournament coming to Poznan was special and the opening ceremony moved him to tears. Before he got involved with the Homeless World Cup, he was a therapist in Poznan, counselling addicts and addressing their homelessness issues. And now his dream was coming true and hundreds of players were in his home city, the stars of the show.

Jacek also knows what it is like to be homeless with nothing to live for. Many years ago, he was an addict, and after one attempt at suicide, he realised with horror that 'he could not live or kill himself' because he'd sunk so low. But for 25 years he's avoided drink and drugs and for most of that time he's been helping people going through the same kind of horror he once knew himself, trying to prepare them for employment and regular home life again.

Jacek also has a very interesting perspective, believing 'if you lose all your money, you really lose nothing; if you lose your friends, you lose much; but if you lose your nerve, you lose it all.' Work gives courage, he says, and it helps restore faith in the meaning of life.

Right from the beginning, Jacek also recognised the value of the Homeless World Cup: 'Homeless people need bread, but they also need games.' After every tournament, he also keeps in touch with former players, checking their progress, believing that returning to a life without drugs is the best way to measure individual success.

Long ago, like many people, Jacek also wished to be a soccer star, and it is moving to watch as the captains of all the teams march onto Lech Poznan's field with their flags in the air, to the cheers of the crowd. This was the beautiful game at its best, and the players – and Jacek – felt seven feet tall.

* * * * *

Every year, the host country brings into focus the scale of their own local homelessness issues, thanks to the arrival of the Homeless World Cup. Official statistics will never be perfect, and the number of homeless people in Poland varies between 30,000 and 500,000, depending on which figures you believe and how homelessness is defined. But whether it means sleeping in the streets or being addicted to vodka or drugs, a victim of domestic violence or simply social exclusion, the problem for some can be fatal – especially during the winter when hundreds of people can die of the cold.

The Polish government has asked the general public to dial 112 in the winter as soon as they see someone outside in danger of freezing to death, but for many years the focus has been on providing emergency services rather than addressing the roots of the problem. A lack of social housing, poverty and unemployment puts a lot of pressure on local authorities, but some of them even deny that there is any homelessness problem.

In many towns and cities, there are dormitories for homeless people but they struggle to cope with demand. Many people spend the night at tram stops in the centre of Warsaw or live in run-down houses on the edge of the city or huts in abandoned allotments where stray dogs run wild. Social workers try to help and bring them soup and offer them somewhere to sleep, but many people choose to stay in terrible conditions rather than move to a hostel, making a few cents from selling scrap metal and hunting for something to eat in the bins.

This is the reality of homelessness in Poland and countries all over the world. And this is the challenge for Jacek and thousands of others as they try to help the half a million people who are struggling to survive in modern Poland.

* * * * *

While I was in Poland, I had the opportunity to meet lots of players, including South Korea's Chang Yong, a young man who learned how to live for the first time through soccer.

After a difficult time as a teenager, Chang Yong became depressed and struggled with drug and alcohol problems, even contemplating suicide several times. Although he went to rehab, he always seemed to end up in the same situation – unemployed, depressed and lonely.

During his last stay in rehab, *Big Issue Korea* approached him and three months later, he was chosen to captain the team at the next Homeless World Cup in Poznan, and 'found hope again'.

'Someone once told me the first times are always the best,' said Chang Yong. 'And everything was new for me in Poland – my first time in Europe, the first time I had met so many people, the first time representing my country, and the first time I'd ever felt proud of myself.'

Today, Chang Yong lives in a two-room apartment which he got through *Big Issue Korea*. His family are happy to see him stay sober and clean for so long. He has even quit smoking and started playing soccer once a week – and been offered a job at *Big Issue Korea*. But Chang Yong has even greater ambitions. 'I want to make the world a better place,' he said, after returning from Poland.

* * * * *

As the tournament kicked off in Poznań, I could see how emotional Jacek was feeling, as if the years of struggle now seemed worth it. Fighting back the tears, he later described it: 'I never used to think I was a patriot. But being on the pitch with the white eagle on our shirts made me feel part of something much bigger, as if we belonged to our country again.'

Another major plus in Poznan was the fact that the players all boarded together in nearby university accommodation halls, which meant it was more like a village. One night, I went there to talk with the players, and one of them suddenly burst into song – Bob Marley's wonderful *One Love*. As he strummed his guitar and the rest of the players joined in, it was one of those magical moments you never forget for the rest of your life. I still feel shivers running down my spine when I think of those players united in song, one voice adding to another until the whole building was filled with their singing.

Throughout the week, the atmosphere was similar, and the stadiums built looking over the lake provided a picturesque and peaceful setting very different from other host cities.

Brazil were crowned men's champions, beating Mexico after a penalty shoot-out, with the player of the tournament, Brazilian Darlon Martins, keeping his cool for the winner. Because they were struggling to raise enough money for tickets, Brazil arrived in Poznan with only four players, but we saw from the start they were clearly a talented team, and the crowd were delighted to see them emerge as the winners.

Before they flew to Poznan, the Brazil team held national trials, but they only chose players who already had passports – they didn't want to raise the hopes of too many players, only to let them down later because they could not afford passports for everyone. So out of 16 players, men and women, they chose two players from Sao Paulo and two players from the *favelas* in Rio.

It's a long way from Rio to Poznan, but that was far from every player's mind as the tournament came to its climax. The Final was a tight game and both teams were able to show off their skills, with Brazil going into a three goals to one lead at the end of the first half and Mexico fighting back, making it three-three with seconds to go – only to lose in the shoot-out. For Mexico, this was the third time in three years that their men's team had lost in the Final, but Daniel Copto and his coaching staff did all in their power to make sure that everyone focused on the positive aspects of playing and went back to Mexico proud of their record, while the Mexico women's team won for the second year running, beating Chile four goals to one in the Final – gaining revenge for a loss in the group stage a few days before.

As the President of Poland handed over the trophies, I was watching the sky getting darker and darker as storm clouds gathered overhead, threatening rain. In Rio three years earlier, we even had to do the presentations indoors when a tropical storm burst immediately after the Final, but this time the rain held for just long enough for the players to pick up their medals – which is always a highlight for me.

Then just as I prepared to make my closing speech, the heavens exploded, and everyone immediately raced to find cover. I had just picked up the microphone, ready to speak, and felt as if this somehow triggered the storm, as I watched the crowds vanish in front of my eyes, addressing the now empty seats. I can't remember my exact words but I smiled to myself when a few people joked that my speech caused the exodus – 'nothing personal intended'.

*****

Santiago (2014) was another amazing event, with the stadium set up in front of the National Congress, which military dictator General Pinochet had closed down in September, 1973. We usually have stands on four sides, embracing the players and the roar of the crowd, but the local organisers decided to open the view to the Congress, as if the building symbolised how fragile is democracy. Perhaps they also wanted to send out a message expressing their feelings on homelessness issues.

Chile is a highly politicised country, and demonstrations fill the streets of Santiago every week. On one march held during the tournament, a totally naked man danced for the crowd, demanding equal rights for everyone across the sexual spectrum, and bank workers went on strike, blocking the streets, blowing whistles and waving red flags.

It seemed, at times, that everyone was seeking to participate and make sure their voices were heard, in a world where the voices of too many people are silenced.

Despite this political backdrop, the Homeless World Cup quickly captured the imagination of soccer-mad people in Chile as a sporting event – not a tournament which helped to change the lives of homeless people but an international soccer cup which they desperately wanted the host country, Chile, to win. As soon as the tournament started, I could feel this intensity growing. In the cafés in the centre of the city, crowds of people were watching the games on TV, as if it was the most important sports event that anyone had ever seen in Chile. Walking down the street one day, I saw a taxi driver parked at the side of the road, listening intently to the radio, broadcasting one of the Chile games 'live' from the stadium just a few hundred metres away, with a small crowd of passers-by starting to gather around him, to hear if their heroes would win.

Back at the stadium, I had my usual conversations with the media, and one reporter commented that local fans seemed more concerned about Chile winning than the fact that the players were homeless. 'That's good news,' I told him. 'That's exactly what we set out to achieve in the first place.' The fans may have been desperate for Chile to win, but suddenly their view had changed because we'd changed reality by placing homeless people in a shiny, new environment – not feared or mocked or hated but respected and even admired, like any other soccer stars. Like fellow human beings.

Before their semi final versus Brazil, I saw the Chile women's team preparing for the game, outside the stadium. This wasn't even their official warm-up – this was the warm-up before they went onto the field. But as I looked around, I saw the fans beginning to gather and watch them in action, just stretching their bodies and starting to focus their minds on the challenge ahead. And more fans began to surround them, until there was hardly enough room to move.

In the stadium a few minutes later, as the players stood still for their national anthems, a dog ran out onto the field, sniffing round near the players and happily wagging its tail, as the music began and the cameras started to roll. I had noticed these stray dogs before, being given scraps of food and bowls of water by people in neighbourhood cafés, to help them survive in the terrible heat. In most other countries, the dogs would be treated like vermin. But here they were treated like family pets – even as the players and officials prepared for the game.

Luis, the Mr Fixit who had probably built the whole stadium all on his own, the night before the tournament opened, approached the dog as it curled up in the back of the net for a snooze, and gently picked it up and patted it, and carried it away to the side of the field, as if it was nothing unusual. The national anthems had not been disturbed. All the players had stood to attention without even looking, as if the dog was part of the event. Then the match began. Chile won four goals to one with another impressive display. And Luis adopted the dog.

*****

In the men's Final, Chile beat Bosnia & Herzegovina by five goals to two, and the women from Chile beat Mexico four goals to three in a match which saw players on both sides sent off for two minutes, with Chile captain Denise Silva firing in the winner, igniting the screams of the local supporters.

When the whistle blew to signal the end of the Finals, the stadium erupted, and Chile's 'Golden Boy' Ismael Mariqueo did something which surprised us all by publicly proposing to his girlfriend, sparking even more cheers from the already jubilant crowd.

As the tournament ended in chaos, with the trophies displayed for the cameras before we could officially present them to the winners, I couldn't help smiling. The fans may be in danger because they were trying to climb over fences to get themselves close to the action, but that just reflected their passion and national pride in their teams. Good for them. They have won. Homeless players have won. Not just Chile but all homeless people are national heroes.

* * * * *

The soccer is always exciting but human drama makes the Homeless World Cup unforgettable, year after year.

During the event in Santiago, one of the highlights for me was a special meet-the-players media session, when journalists were able to hear for themselves the remarkable stories of some of the players. The media are always requested to respect players' privacy during the week, so they don't intrude on sometimes very vulnerable people. Our media volunteers work very closely with coaches to make sure the players are happy to talk, and publish player stories on our website, but it's always a sensitive issue. We want to celebrate success and tell the world these players are a brilliant example to others, but we also have to make sure they are comfortable telling their stories – which may be inspiring to others but can also be painful for the players themselves to revisit.

* * * * *

A number of players came forward in Chile to share their experience with our reporters, like the captain of Greece, Alexandro Aggelis, who got involved with criminal gangs in the capital Athens and then got addicted to drugs, aged just 13. 'But today,' Alejandro declared, 'I am 857 days clean!'

The Homeless World Cup also brought him closer to his family again, and during the tournament they were following his progress on the Internet and cheering him on. But he also knew the Homeless World Cup was not the end of his journey, and said that one day he would also like to have a family of his own.

* * * * *

Thanks to soccer, Romanian captain Stefan Octavian Pavel was also able to reject a life of street crime and addiction. After his parents divorced, he started getting into drugs, 'to escape from the troubles at home.' But he quickly developed a 'full-time addiction' while still only 15 years old, and his brothers and sister soon joined him. To pay for drugs, they started selling anything of value from their family home, but before long, there was nothing left to sell, so they all became dealers to fund their addiction.

Six months later, Stefan was arrested and sentenced to five years in prison, where he carried on using and became more and more anti-social, still only interested in drugs. This was the low point and he finally realised he needed help, and enrolled in a programme which helped him get off drugs and won him an early release.

After prison, he discovered *Fotbal de Strada* – the Homeless World Cup Partner in Romania. Stefan was selected for the Homeless World Cup and has since become a social worker, based in the same rehab centre which helped him before Santiago.

* * * * *

Like several Cambodian players before him, Theng Langeng was one of the stars of the Homeless World Cup. The smallest player in the tournament in Chile won the hearts of opponents as well as spectators. And after a game against England, the English captain Scott Fitzgerald picked up his diminutive opponent and paraded in front of the crowd – another great example of the international brotherhood of soccer.

Langeng is the eldest of three children and his family was too poor to send him to school. He could have followed in his mother's footsteps – sifting through garbage to find stuff to sell on the street – if the Cambodian Children's Fund had not intervened and enrolled him in school. Later, they encouraged him to join Homeless Football Cambodia Australia, our partner in Cambodia, and Langeng was selected for the team which went to Chile. 'I was so excited and so happy to get the opportunity to play here in Chile,' said Langeng. 'I will always remember the support from the crowds and the friends I now have all over the world.'

After returning to Cambodia, Langeng started coaching the Under-14 team, and vowed to return to the Homeless World Cup as a coach, 'so the next generation of players will get the opportunity to change their lives, too.'

* * * * *

Ireland goalkeeper James Traynor is still shocked he was given the chance to represent his country at the Homeless World Cup, but there were times when he could hardly imagine the future at all.

When you meet James, it is hard to imagine that he was not so long ago a very troubled addict who had also been to jail. His mother died when James was only five, and after years of being bullied, he dropped out of school, ran away from home and ended up living in squats. After a violent incident, James was given a seven-year sentence in prison. Walking through those prison gates the first time was scary, but James went on to learn from his mistakes.

After his release, James went to live with his grandfather and tried to settle down to 'normal' life. He got a job, but inside he was suffering and started using drugs again. 'I could do my job and meet my responsibilities, but I was a train wreck,' he later told Jennifer May, writing in Ireland's *Big Issue*.

When his grandfather died, James became homeless again and started taking heroin, but got a break when he was accepted by Coolmine Therapeutic Community in Dublin. 'I cried when I was told I'd been accepted,' said James. 'I broke down like a baby, but I learned about addiction, and the wheel of addiction, and how to look out for danger spots, behaviours that lead you to repeat addiction.'

James felt sub-human and was 'sick of feeling sick'. He also knew that something had to change, then rediscovered soccer when he kicked his first football in years – and was chosen from hundreds of hopefuls to play for his country in Chile. 'I began to feel part of something and believe in myself,' he said. 'Representing your country, wearing that jersey, seeing that Irish flag, it's such a great honour.'

Back home in Dublin, James gives talks in prison to share his experience, and also plans to do a counselling course, 'to turn those negatives into something positive'. He also hopes to coach the next group of players to Homeless World Cup glory. 'I've been clean for a year and a half,' said James. 'I'm 39 years old but I believe that you are never too old to keep learning and go back to school. I would like to work in psychotherapy after all it's done for me.'

* * * * *

A drug user since she was just 17, Sweden's Camilla Lindén has been sober for more than a year – thanks to her team mates and the coaches at Gatans Lag, our partner in Sweden. 'In Chile and Sweden, I have a team of wonderful people. They are my family,' she said.

Camilla had tried to give up drugs before, but was in and out of rehab. 'When you give up drugs, you are all alone. All your friends do drugs, and it is too easy to start taking them again,' she said. 'But with football, I have focus and purpose. I belong to something. Soccer has been like a best friend to me.'

Drugs are not Camilla's only challenge in life: 'I have multiple sclerosis, which means I get dizzy and have problems with keeping my balance – I thought I would never be picked for the team.' But the Gatans Lag coaches saw Camilla's potential. 'If you never miss a single training session and commit to do your best, you'll go to Chile,' they told her, and Camilla did not let them down.

Camilla's fondest memory of Chile was not a thrilling victory but losing to India: 'When we lost, we felt really low. But the Indian girls were so happy. They don't have very good opportunities in their own country, so I'm happy for them.'

Back in Sweden, Camilla said: 'No one can ever take this experience away from me. I did my best. I failed before because I had no goals. But now I feel good about myself and my future.'

* * * * *

Three years ago, the Scotland captain Toby McKillop was lying in a stranger's house, surrounded by half-conscious users, and went upstairs to hang himself – and end it all for good. After fighting drug addiction over two decades, he was homeless and desperate. 'The last few years were absolute hell,' he said. He'd lost everything – home, partner, daughter and parents. Now all he had to lose was life itself.

The only thing that stopped him was the thought of leaving young daughter Molly without any father. He knew he'd hit rock bottom. It was time to get help.

After an initial four-week detox at a rehabilitation centre in Glasgow, Toby did a six-month residential course to concentrate on coping and his negative behaviour, but one month after finishing the programme, he overdosed and says that he was lucky to survive. He went back into rehab and started training with Street Soccer Scotland. 'They helped me stay focused, get fit and feel good about myself. I was committed to be part of something positive. I wanted to make it to Chile.'

While he was training for Chile, Toby slowly regained the trust of his ex-partner Lindsay and his proudest moment was when Molly came to stay with him in Glasgow a few weeks before Santiago. 'The Homeless World Cup has completely changed my life. It's hard to explain it. Something changes inside. The way you see yourself. You're positive. Everything is now a possibility. You know what's important. And everything I do now is for Molly.'

Back in Scotland, Toby spoke in public about his experience, and started volunteering at the rehab centre. 'Molly says I should write my life story,' says Toby, 'but thanks to the Homeless World Cup, I'm only half-way through my life, and still have a lot more living to do.'

* * * * *

'Angela, a ray of light from Sacramento, California shines brightly in the Santiago sun as part of the USA women's team in Santiago. But Angie has not always been in such a golden state,' wrote two of our reporters (Sian Downes and Katharina Rueberg) in Chile.

Angie battled drug addiction for 17 years. For four more 'extreme' years, she went into hiding and shut herself off from the world. 'I didn't think I was allowed to exist,' she explained. 'I lost everything – family, job, home and self-worth. I was looking for unconditional love in all the wrong places.'

Everything changed in 2012 when Angie stepped out of recovery onto the soccer field. 'Soccer is like my serenity now, but above all, it has brought my family back to me,' Angie explained. Soccer has also allowed her to trust other women again after bad experiences with female friends during her dark days, and playing soccer even helped her deal with post-traumatic stress while she went clean.

Street soccer has not only taken Angie to new places emotionally but also geographically, including Santiago, and she hopes that it will take her even further. 'The Homeless World Cup has empowered me to be my true positive self.'

* * * * *

Mónika is only 28 years old but her eyes tell the story of someone's who's seen more than most through the years. 'I had no family growing up,' she told Chandrima Chatterjee during the Chile event, through her interpreter and mentor Roland Zajkó. 'And my advice to others growing up without a family is: eventually people are going to help you, but you will also have to make choices on which path to follow, so choose the right person, and don't waste the moment.'

Monika added: 'Someday you'll have a family, and have the chance to build a better life – the family you never had.'

Soccer has not only given Monika her new 'family' in Santiago but has also been a stepping stone to college, thanks to the Oltalom Sport Association, who have supported the Hungarian Homeless World Cup team for years.

Mónika turned down a job for the opportunity to come to Santiago, helping her team finish fourth in the women's event, but back in Hungary she plans to be a social worker or work in health care. Above all, she wants to continue living her life the same way she plays soccer – with plenty of heart and a strong sense of purpose.

* * * * *

Soft-spoken Indonesian Akhmad was a recovering addict when he was talent-spotted by the national coach and selected for the national team at the Homeless World Cup.

For Indonesians, communication can be a challenge – the people speak over 300 different dialects. To deal with this, Akhmad made a big effort to learn the other dialects used by his team mates, and also made a lot of friends from other countries, using soccer as the universal language.

*****

Denmark goalkeeper Peter from Aarhus has a confident presence both on and off the field. But his road to the Homeless World Cup has been far from easy, and it took him more than one try to be picked for Team Denmark.

When he was only ten years old, Peter started on the road to becoming an addict. At first, it was just recreational drugs, but later he progressed to using heroin, and eventually found himself homeless and then sent to jail, where he continued to use drugs and came close to death on several occasions.

For the next few years his struggle with addiction continued, interspersed with periods of trying to go clean. Peter found the process very difficult and often relapsed. 'I had no confidence or motivation,' he said. 'Drugs completely took away any emotion.'

Then one day, his determination beat the attraction of drugs, and Peter now has a new home in Copenhagen. Adjusting to home life is not always easy for people like Peter. 'The first day I moved in, I felt nothing but pressure,' he said. 'It was so intense to live between four walls; it was like being back in prison.'

Peter is now studying for a Master's degree in music, and hopes that one day he can share his experience with other people in similar places in life, and 'inspire them to make a change through music and football, as I have.'

He sums up what the Danish programme, OMBOLD, has brought him in three simple words: 'Now I belong.'

*****

At just 18 years old, Mensah McDonald Ezekel is a star in the making. The Ghanaian winger and dedicated Arsenal fan had a long trip to Chile but his journey began long ago. 'I am here to make my family proud,' said Mensah. 'We are very poor back home, but coming here is not just for me – it's also for the people of Ghana.'

Mensah 'eats, sleeps and drinks football' and during the tournament appealed to Arsene Wenger: 'If you're reading this, I'm ready!' But until he gets the call from the Arsenal boss, he'll chase his other dream – to go to university and get a degree in computer science.

*****

Shane Bullock (originally from Maine, now San Francisco), lost his father to drugs when he was only two years old. Then 14 years later, his mother was murdered, and very soon afterwards, Shane became homeless.

Shane found out about Street Soccer USA while staying in a shelter for the homeless. At first, he didn't think that simply kicking a ball around would make any difference, but he gave it a chance – and now it is changing his life. The programme taught him the importance of mindfulness and leadership, and helped him become more confident and open to life. 'I didn't even know that programmes like this existed, let alone the global impact they are having,' he said. 'At first, I thought that it was just guys from my shelter playing soccer once a week – and now I'm here in Chile!'

* * * * *

The list of heroes grows as the stories pour into the media centre...

Norway's Anne Cathrine Johansen never thought soccer would help her defeat drug addiction, but five months after training with Frelsesarmeen, she found herself in Chile, looking forward to a clean and brighter future.

Sitting in the lobby after breakfast is a world away from Martin Limonchi's previous life on the streets, and now he's playing for Peru at the Homeless World Cup in Chile. Since discovering street soccer, Martin believes he has changed and now wants to inspire other people: 'Like many of the players here, I felt I had no purpose in life. Before, I didn't want to learn new things. I didn't want to find a job. Every day, I would wake up with no motivation, but ONG (an educational organisation set up to empower deprived children and adults) and street soccer changed that, and being here in Chile is the best experience of my life – meeting people from countries all over the world.'

Nicknamed Qoo, the 29-year-old keeper from Hong Kong has been playing street soccer for years. After serving time in prison for drug offences, the Hong Kong Children and Youth Service gave him the chance to start a new life, and less than 11 months since his release, he's now back in society, transforming his life with the power of sport. When he was chosen to play for Hong Kong in the Homeless World Cup, Qoo was keen to do well for his country. But after meeting other teams from all around the world, he now knows there is much more to soccer than winning.

Wendy Brouwer from the Netherlands loves scoring goals – but her goals off the field are even more impressive. Street soccer has changed Wendy's life and helped her to complete a training programme for employment – and find a new home with her boyfriend. Before the players left for Chile, her local soccer team Cambuur gave them a send-off in their stadium – something Wendy will never forget.

'I was in a dark, dark place,' said Wales' Kathryne Breen, describing life before she discovered street soccer. After her mother died, Kathryne had nowhere to go and felt let down by the authorities. She ended up sleeping in bus shelters, then Street Football Wales came along, and she found herself in Chile. 'These girls are like the family I lost' she said. Back home in Wales, she now lives with her partner and works in McDonald's, where she was recently promoted. 'My dream is to continue to develop at work, and one day I would love to help with Street Football Wales, and help others like me.'

Demir Kuburić always loved soccer, but he never thought that one day he would represent his country at an international tournament. His childhood friend took part in a previous Homeless World Cup, and inspired him to follow his 'positive path'. Soccer gave Demir a structure in life and 'the team is like a family'. When he returned to Slovenia, Demir was aiming to work with computers.

War has had a huge effect on Bosnia & Herzegovina, and Alen Hodžić's story is typical. When he was only three years old, his family had to flee their home town Zvornik, and his father was killed, leaving his mother to look after him and his brother and sister in a refugee centre. But it was here that Alen later discovered his passion for soccer when he met a former player from the Homeless World Cup in 2012. Chile is a different world entirely for Alen: 'In my country, many people are closed off from one another. Here, the culture is much more relaxed.' Soccer has changed Alen's life and now he is studying Turkish – and hoping to become a professor.

Scotland's Ryan Murray was one of the tournament's most popular players, and local children queued to have their photo taken with him. But life has not always been so picture-perfect for Ryan, who became homeless after he spent time in jail. Ryan credits Street Soccer Scotland with helping him back on his feet by improving his confidence and connecting him to other people in a safe environment – and the result has been transformative. Ryan now has a job and a young daughter, and wants to make her proud of his achievements. 'Life is always changing and you have to embrace it. To be here in Santiago is surreal,' he said. Ryan also hopes to mentor Scotland's squad in Amsterdam, so they will be able to 'embrace the excitement' like him.

For Peru's Allan Rojas, scoring goals in soccer is a symbol of everything he's ever worked for. 'The Homeless World Cup made me want to be a better person,' he said. In the past, Allan had no motivation to get work or study. But when he discovered his passion for soccer and felt the support of his team mates and coaches, he totally transformed his outlook, and now he wants to share his 'amazing experience' in Santiago and help other people.

* * * * *

Monday, 27 October 2014: It's the morning after. Santiago, capital of Chile. Another great tournament comes to an end in another iconic location, and I don't expect anyone else to emerge for a couple of hours yet. It's exhausting and exhilarating working for the Homeless World Cup, dealing with the media, the managers and coaches, and the players, and the local organising committee. Everybody wants it to be perfect every year, and everybody knows that is impossible. And when it is over, you feel as if you're waking from a non-stop dream you thought would last forever. It's hard to adjust to the real world again, and the rhythm of ordinary life.

The Homeless World Cup is emotional for everyone involved – morning to night, from beginning to end. And it's players who touch you the most. Their stories seem to follow you. You can't get them out of your mind. They have come from a difficult place and will go back today or tomorrow to what you are hoping will be somewhere better. Will they get a job? Go back to school? Stay sober? Make up with their families? Get somewhere to live and call home?

I don't know what will happen to all of the players, but I know we have created opportunities for everyone. And I know that the people of Chile will never forget them – the spectators and the taxi drivers, glued to their radios, carried away by the action.

All these thoughts are swimming around in my mind as I leave my hotel in the morning to go for a jog through the streets of this beautiful city, overlooked by the majestic snow-capped mountains of the Andes.

As I run into the square beside the stadium, I notice Luis is still busy, as always – picking up the piles of plastic bottles and other miscellaneous litter left behind from yesterday's Finals. We wave at each other, exchanging a silent good morning, the same as every other day during the week, as if we are the only ones awake at this time in the morning – apart from the dogs who are sniffing around at the garbage.

As I run through the surrounding streets, I think ahead to Amsterdam. It's not even 24 hours since the tournament ended, but already it's on my agenda.

First though, I navigate the streets of Santiago, and like every morning this week, there are homeless people sleeping in the doorways of shops, on the sidewalks, on benches and underneath trees, with yesterday's newspapers wrapped round their bodies.

More stray dogs every time I turn a corner. More people in doorways, on benches and underneath trees. The dogs go up to some of the sleepers and nudge them, as if they are begging. The city is gradually coming to life again. And yesterday's challenges now reappear as today's, like the sun every morning rising over the Andes.

* * * * *

After Santiago, in the shadow of the world's highest mountains, we moved down to sea level next when the tournament was staged in the Museumplein, the city centre park in Amsterdam where some of the world's greatest art treasures – housed in the Van Gogh Museum and the Rijksmuseum 100 metres away – were witnesses to one of the world's greatest sporting events.

I have been visiting the Netherlands for many years and built a close relationship with several key supporters of the Homeless World Cup, including Arne de Groote, the founder and director of our national partner, the Life Goals Foundation (Stichting Life Goals).

The Netherlands have taken part in every event since 2003, but nowadays the set-up is much more extensive and focused on soccer, with a solid infrastructure to support the wider needs of the players.

While he was still working for the Dutch Football Association in 2007, Arne was so inspired by what he saw in Copenhagen at the Homeless World Cup that he decided to set up the Life Goals Foundation to build on the excellent work of the street paper network who had managed the Dutch team until then, despite their very limited resources.

Today, Life Goals organises weekly games in 36 locations nationwide and once a year stages the Dutch Street Cup in the middle of Amsterdam's famous Dam Square. And when the Homeless World Cup was held in the city, with Life Goals working closely with its national partners, the Dutch Football Association (FA) and Dutch Salvation Army, the programme attracted more interest than ever before.

* * * * *

During the last few years, I've worked very closely with Arne, and our dreams became reality when the King of the Netherlands opened the Amsterdam Homeless World Cup, soon joined on the pitch by Irish actor Colin Farrell.

I often describe the Homeless World Cup as a movement, but as Colin stood shoulder to shoulder with the players from Ireland for the national anthem, I wondered what about a blockbuster Hollywood movie? Was Colin rehearsing his role for the movie by immersing himself in the atmosphere, kicking the ball around like one of the players?

During the Cape Town event, directors Susan Koch and Jeff Werner made a brilliant documentary called *Kicking It!* which attracted a lot of attention

– helped by Colin doing the narration, adding an emotional dimension to the story which very few people could manage. 'Football is a poem that beats in the heart of those who play it,' the story began. 'It has every emotion – hope, fear, love, strength, generosity – every emotion that we feel as people.'

Colin was also so inspired by the project that he teamed up with Blue-print Productions to develop the script for a movie about the Homeless World Cup, following the adventures of the Irish team in Paris, starring Colin himself with a screenplay by Frank Cottrell-Boyce.

For a few years, the project has gathered momentum, and when the movie is released, millions of people will share the excitement and joy of the Homeless World Cup, and realise how homelessness affects so many millions of people all over the world.

As the whistle blew for Game One of the tournament, I looked across at Arne and knew exactly how he must be feeling. Like most of the people I work with in countries all over the world, Arne is completely committed to what he is doing. And like most of them, the story of how he arrived here is a personal journey which started many years ago before the idea of the Homeless World Cup had been born...

* * * * *

Millions of children around the world do the same thing every day, throwing down their coats and sweaters to make goals for impromptu games of soccer. And Arne de Groote was no different, at eight years of age, as he and his brother kicked a ball around with some of their neighbours – most of them adults much bigger than them.

What made it different for the boys was that their neighbours were mentally and physically disabled people living in supported housing managed by their father, who was so impressed to see how much the people in his care loved playing soccer that he got them involved with their local team, doing odd jobs and going to games. 'That was the first time I experienced the power of soccer,' says Arne.

The Dutch FA has since established special leagues for disabled people, and has also managed international programmes for several decades, sending coaches overseas to pass on their soccer skills and also assist social projects. It has also played a major role in Arne's life and now supports Life Goals Foundation, set up by Arne and Judith de Keijzer in 2011.

Arne's involvement with soccer was 'on ice' for a number of years, when as a teenager he had to choose between his love of soccer and the Netherlands' second most popular sport, speed skating – and he opted for skating.

One of Arne's friends went on to win an Olympic Gold Medal, but about a decade later, having had some success as a skater and gaining a degree in economics, Arne decided to hang up his skates. Then, encouraged by one of his neighbours, he applied for a job at the Dutch FA in 2005, and two years later found himself watching the Homeless World Cup in Copenhagen – an experience which changed his life forever.

According to Arne, a number of related factors led to the founding of Life Goals. In 2006, the Dutch government decided to do something to address the homelessness problem, working with the Salvation Army (5,000 employees and 35,000 clients) and other interested partners. The ambition was to get all homeless people off the streets and into hostels, and ultimately homes and employment, transforming people's lives and changing social attitudes – there used to be an emphasis on shelters but this was very basic accommodation which did not address long-term issues. The government recognised it needed help and backed its plans with massive investments, providing funds to organisations including the Salvation Army to set up new hostels. The Salvation Army also saw an opportunity to work with the Dutch FA, already helping with the socially excluded in overseas countries and supervising 33,000 games every week, involving 1.3 million people.

At this time, Arne saw a lot of people sleeping in the tunnel near the station in his home town of Utrecht, and was already starting to think about what he could do about homelessness in Holland as a whole – at that time estimated to affect about 72,000 people. Working at the Dutch FA also inspired him, but seeing the Homeless World Cup for himself was an eye-opener for Arne – 'a great example of best practice and the power of soccer'. And the idea was already brewing inside his head. 'We initially organised games in eight cities,' says Arne, and Life Goals is now active in 35 cities and towns nationwide, organising soccer-based activities three or four times a week, including games and access to advisors. 'The soccer is where it all starts,' explains Arne, 'but it's about much more than soccer. It's all about developing real social programmes and getting specialists to help, with soccer the route to engagement. The main objective is to get excluded people integrated into their communities again, and into work and into their own homes.'

Life Goals also work with prisoners, sending coaches to prisons to organise games, then building on that when the prisoners come out. Lots of people come forward to train to be coaches, says Arne, but they have to do much more than teach people how to play soccer – they have to connect with the people they coach. They also have to learn to develop their own social networks, linking up with other like-minded people and organisa-tions. 'Coaching is a big responsibility. You have to build bridges – you have to be able to network at local and national level,' says Arne.

Arne has also learned how to connect with different organisations including his former employer and the Salvation Army, as well as local and national government bodies, to keep Life Goals going and grow in the future.

* * * * *

As he stood in the Museumplein, a few weeks before kick-off, Arne knew the Netherlands would make it a tournament people would never forget – by welcoming the world to Amsterdam. He hoped the event would attract crowds of tourists and locals, as well as massive media interest, so people would learn more about what homeless people can achieve, becoming soccer stars and changing their lives in the process. He hoped it would also attract some new corporate sponsors, so Life Goals could build a new network of well-structured organisations to deliver social programmes across the whole country. 'We need the power and the energy of everyone involved,' he said before the tournament opened, 'but funding is also essential. We started small but now we are upping our game.'

But above all, he'll never forget that the players will always come first. It is their event – their chance to shine. 'We want to do everything possible to make sure they all have the week of their lives,' Arne told me. 'We want it to be great for the players.'

As I stood with Arne, gazing out across the tree-lined park, and imag-ined what the stadiums would look like when Amsterdam burst into life for the Homeless World Cup, I could feel the excitement already. I also realised that Arne would not be with me now in the centre of this beautiful city if he and his brother had not played those games with their neighbours, and discovered the power of soccer as very young children.

* * * * *

I know like many other of our national partners, Arne is looking ahead to the future and making his plans. He wants to build a multi-city network which is strong enough to manage itself. Taking full advantage of the media spotlight and the power of soccer, the network in the Netherlands will trans-form the lives of thousands of people, setting an example which more and more countries will follow.

As I discuss these ideas with Arne, I can see he has worked it all out in his mind, and I know it will happen exactly as planned, with some help from the people who share Life Goals' vision, and want to make a difference to the lives of homeless people in the Netherlands and far beyond.

* * * * *

The journey from that beach-side bar in Cape Town to Rio, Paris, Amsterdam and this year to George Square in Glasgow has been an amazing adventure – and the journey continues, with the next generation of leaders coming up with fresh ideas all the time and providing the energy needed to accelerate progress worldwide.

No matter how much we've achieved through the years, there is always another new challenge ahead. The problem of homelessness has not been solved. And as long as one person is homeless, it is a tragedy for him or her as well as the community at large. There are millions of people with nowhere to go tonight – and nothing to look forward to tomorrow. There are countless other millions who will suddenly find themselves homeless one day, just like millions of people before them – like me and like you. And that's why we'll continue to do all in our power to change things.

* * * * *

In July 2016, I am standing in George Square in Glasgow, with David Duke the CEO of Street Soccer Scotland, looking forward to the 14th Homeless World Cup. For David, it's a bitter-sweet experience. He's achieved so much since he was homeless in Glasgow just over a decade ago, but the memories still haunt him. Maybe in the crowd or somewhere else in the streets of the city, there will be a face from the past, a reminder of where he has come from – or a warning of what could so easily happen to anyone down on his luck. He sees the Scotland players, men and women, in their shiny new tracksuits, and realises what it means to every single one of them, and how they are trying to transform their lives – with a ball. It worked for him, but will it work for this year's generation of players?

Fourteen years ago, as David stared up at the ceiling, unable to sleep, in the soul-destroying hostel in Broad Street, he could never have dreamed of this moment.

And neither could I.

But even though it may have been a crazy idea, we believed from the start that a ball really can change the world. And as the 14th Homeless World Cup kicks off in Glasgow, I know a ball *will* change the world.

Appendix

HOMELESS WORLD CUP VENUES

2003, Graz, Austria
2004 Gothenburg, Sweden
2005 Edinburgh, Scotland
2006 Cape Town, South Africa
2007 Copenhagen, Denmark
2008 Melbourne, Australia
2009 Milan, Italy
2010 Rio de Janeiro, Brazil
2011 Paris, France
2012 Mexico City, Mexico
2013 Poznan, Poland
2014 Santiago, Chile
2015 Amsterdam, Netherlands
2016 Glasgow, Scotland
2017 Oslo, Norway

Luath Press Limited

committed to publishing well written books worth reading

LUATH PRESS takes its name from Robert Burns, whose little collie
Luath (*Gael.*, swift or nimble) tripped up Jean Armour at a wedding
and gave him the chance to speak to the woman who was to be his wife
and the abiding love of his life. Burns called one of the 'Twa Dogs'
Luath after Cuchullin's hunting dog in Ossian's *Fingal*.
Luath Press was established in 1981 in the heart of
Burns country, and is now based a few steps up
the road from Burns' first lodgings on
Edinburgh's Royal Mile. Luath offers you
distinctive writing with a hint of
unexpected pleasures.
Most bookshops in the UK, the US, Canada,
Australia, New Zealand and parts of Europe,
either carry our books in stock or can order them
for you. To order direct from us, please send a £sterling
cheque, postal order, international money order or your
credit card details (number, address of cardholder and
expiry date) to us at the address below. Please add post
and packing as follows: UK – £1.00 per delivery address;
overseas surface mail – £2.50 per delivery address; overseas airmail –
£3.50 for the first book to each delivery address, plus £1.00 for each
additional book by airmail to the same address. If your order is a gift,
we will happily enclose your card or message at no extra charge.

Luath Press Limited
543/2 Castlehill
The Royal Mile
Edinburgh EH1 2ND
Scotland
Telephone: +44 (0)131 225 4326 (24 hours)
email: sales@luath. co.uk
Website: www. luath.co.uk

1	2	3	4	5	6	7	8	9	10
11	12	13	14	15	16	17	18	19	20
21	22	23	24	25	26	27	28	29	30
31	32	33	34	35	36	37	38	39	40
41	42	43	44	45	46	47	48	49	50
51	52	53	54	55	56	57	58	59	60
61	62	63	64	65	66	67	68	69	70
71	72	73	74	75	76	77	78	79	80
81	82	83	84	85	86	87	88	89	90
91	92	93	94	95	96	97	98	99	100
101	102	103	104	105	106	107	108	109	110
111	112	113	114	115	116	117	118	119	120
121	122	123	124	125	126	127	128	129	130
131	132	133	134	135	136	137	138	139	140
141	142	143	144	145	146	147	148	149	150
151	152	153	154	155	156	157	158	159	160
161	162	163	164	165	166	167	168	169	170
171	172	173	174	175	176	177	178	179	180
181	182	183	184	185	186	187	188	189	190
191	192	193	194	195	196	197	198	199	200
201	202	203	204	205	206	207	208	209	210
211	212	213	214	215	216	217	218	219	220
221	222	223	224	225	226	227	228	229	230
231	232	233	234	235	236	237	238	239	240
241	242	243	244	245	246	247	248	249	250
251	252	253	254	255	256	257	258	259	260
261	262	263	264	265	266	267	268	269	270
271	272	273	274	275	276	277	278	279	280
281	282	283	284	285	286	287	288	289	290
291	292	293	294	295	296	297	298	299	300
301	302	303	304	305	306	307	308	309	310
311	312	313	314	315	316	317	318	319	320
321	322	323	324	325	326	327	328	329	330
331	332	333	334	335	336	337	338	339	340
341	342	343	344	345	346	347	348	349	350
351	352	353	354	355	356	357	358	359	360
361	362	363	364	365	366	367	368	369	370
371	372	373	374	375	376	377	378	379	380
381	382	383	384	385	386	387	388	389	390
391	392	393	394	395	396	397	398	399	400